INDIA *and the*
FUTURE *of* ASIA

INDIA *and*

the FUTURE

of ASIA

by Patwant Singh

New York

1 9 6 6

Alfred · A · Knopf

To the memory of my parents

I would like you to think of this major
adventure of India that is taking place
today. Criticize it whenever there is any
failure, whenever there is any falling off,
whenever there is weakness. Criticism
will be an incentive to better work.
But try to understand and appreciate
that something magnificent and colossal
is happening in INDIA.

Jawaharlal Nehru

Preface

Asia today occupies a position in the dead center of the international stage. Its turbulent politics epitomize its desperate need for time in which to overcome the legacies of its wayward history. The two nations that will determine the outcome are India and China. The one is dedicated to the rule of law and democratic practices; the other is closed, brooding, aggressive, obsessed with its own purposes and contemptuous of the means and methods used to attain them.

No matter how great the involvement of world powers in the politics of Asia, in the final event Asian nations will determine their own destiny. The smaller among them will learn to trust and rally around the bigger, which are powerful in their own right yet not given to subverting the rights of others. Some such enduring pattern based on sober statesmanship will eventually emerge—as it has in Europe—to give stability to this troubled continent. But in the period of time between now and then there will be many ambuscades.

India's pivotal role in Asia holds great promise. Too often comment on India, however, is provided by those who, though genuinely concerned with her and her problems, are not perceptive enough to appreciate how actions of old civilizations in new situations are as much sensitized by sentiment, custom, and the weight of history as by inexperience and the inability to rise quickly to new challenges. The aim of this book is neither to praise India to the skies nor to scorn and damn her, but rather to present facts in as objective and critical a manner as possible so that those who do not know India—or know her but are dubious about her doings—will realize that India is an open society with nothing to hide, that though mistakes are possible, as in all societies, they are subject to scrutiny, discussion, debate, and criticism. An articulate public opinion can check the willful ways of those in authority, and in India such a public opinion exists. It is the great hope for India's future—and for the future of Asia.

Apart, of course, from my own views, what I have written in this book represents the thinking of many men of knowledge and experience in India who are either actively engaged in the affairs of state or influence its actions in a number of ways. While they are troubled by the failures, they are already working to apply the lessons of the past to the problems of the future. For obvious reasons many of them wish not to be named, but my gratitude to them for their help is immense.

I also want to acknowledge my debt to N. A. Palkhivala, Ashish Bose, K. D. Malaviya, M. R. Masani, Frank Moraes, E. M. S. Namboodiripad, David Hopper, Katherine Kuder, Gen. K. M. Cariappa, and K. P. S. Menon for being so generous with their time and so kind and helpful with their suggestions.

I cannot thank my research assistant enough (she wishes, alas, to remain anonymous) for being so infinitely patient with me and for unraveling with such superb aplomb the skein of facts, figures, information, and interpretations. Without her this book would not have been written. As for typing and advice with the text, the work of my secretary, Rosemary Harris, is in itself a saga of endurance. I am also deeply indebted to Ann Ryan for so heroically undertaking, on a hot sultry afternoon, the chore of making copies of the first three chapters of this book. And lastly I thank K. B. Kumar for helping with the difficult task of drawing the maps that accompany this book.

Patwant Singh

New Delhi
April, 1966

Contents

MAPS

INDIA *and the*
FUTURE *of* ASIA

1
Picture in the Mid-Sixties

The crowds kept swelling. In hundreds and thousands they came, converging on Delhi's Palam Airport and on Janpath, the broad tree-lined avenue eight miles away. They were thickest around No. 10, but they were everywhere, along the entire route. A solid, somber mass, dazed, disbelieving, deeply moved by the dramatic unexpectedness of the tragedy.

It was January 11, 1966. The previous night, in Tashkent, India's Prime Minister Lal Bahadur Shastri had died suddenly at a moment of great personal triumph. A sorrowful climax to his persevering and dedicated statesmanship through which he had hoped to create amity between his country and Pakistan. Within hours of his signing of the peace agreement with Pakistan's President Ayub a heart attack had ended Shastri's life.

Now his body was being brought home. And the people had come from near and far to pay mournful homage to the gentle little man. And perhaps to get near enough to throw a handful of rose petals on him.

Then the focus shifted to a quiet road off New Delhi's busy Parliament Street. The men who flocked during the next twelve days to No. 7 Jantar Mantar, headquarters of India's largest political party, the All India Congress Committee, were of a different stamp. These were men of political power: chief ministers of the Indian Union's sixteen states, Members of Parliament and state legislatures, presidents and secretaries of Provincial Congress committees, party workers, lobbyists, and such.

Their parleying, politicking, browbeating, bullying, and horse-trading in the days following Shastri's death was the turgid and tantalizing sequel to that sad event. Its outcome, the election of the late Jawaharlal Nehru's daughter Indira Gandhi as the Prime Minister of India and leader in Parliament of the party in power, was a triumph for Indian democracy. Just as the turnout of the millions who came to pay a last tribute to Shastri was a vindication of the Indians' infinite capacity to give, without compulsion and with great spontaneity, devotion to a national leader.

Those two weeks in January, between Shastri's death and Indira Gandhi's election, placed in perspective the possibilities and the paradoxes, the triumphs and the tragedies, the hopes and the hopelessness of India in the mid sixties.

The capacity of the people to give a great deal without being made to do so at bayonet point is the great possibility in India today. The paradox is that despite this extraordinary, this willing and voluntary faith placed in them, the leaders have not been able to channel the vast energies of this human material by inspiring leadership.

The triumph of democratic practices at a time when dictatorships and *coups d'état* are a way of life, gives India cause for pride. The tragedy can well be that a leadership, indifferent to the miseries some of its policies are causing the people, might yet precipitate adventurist action.

While there is hope in the fact that in nineteen years of independence great steps have been taken toward an economic and industrial breakthrough, a sense of hopelessness persists from having had to watch murky and meaningless measures get in the way.

In India today there is a crisis of leadership. Of small men unable to rise to the big challenges facing them as leaders of the world's largest democracy. Of politicians politicking at the expense of national stability. Of those in positions of pre-eminence weakly submitting to the capricious demands of power-hungry men jockeying for high offices in the Federal Government and in the states. All this is mirrored in the directionless drift of the people, in the near-paralysis sapping the vitality of India's economic, political, and social institutions.

What shines brightly through, on the other hand, is the fact that the rule of law prevails in India. That people and political parties can protest. That democratic institutions have survived many vicissitudes. And that during the first ten to twelve years of independence a great deal was achieved.

But dark and demanding challenges face India's new leadership. Principally, a floundering economy, regional rifts, an utterly irrational linguistic intolerance, rising prices, and—casting a long shadow over all—a menacing, aggressive, and expansionist neighbor, China.

When the British left India, Indians inherited a backward economy, appalling poverty, and the discouraging, wasting, exacting aftereffects of alien rule. However, there is disturbing evidence of the fact that although it ended nineteen years ago, Indians still tend to attribute to the legacy of British rule many of the things for which they have only themselves to blame.

Obviously, the scars of years of colonial domination cannot be removed overnight. Neither can they, in all justification, be used to smoke-screen obvious shortcomings of a people. Though British rule sapped the moral fiber of the people, it was nevertheless the same rule that made it possible for Gandhi to emerge on the national scene to project a unique political concept which galvanized millions and won them independence. The British could be ruthless in defense of what was theirs by right of conquest, of which the Jallianwala massacre was only one example, but they did give the country a common law. They exploited its natural resources, its mineral wealth, its manpower, but they also left behind a small but select elite of Indian civil servants, soldiers, administrators, engineers, scientists, jurists, educationists, and professional men who held the country together through a period of violent transition and who were able to set it on a course which by and large has proved to be a sound one.

What India did not learn from the British was that it is one thing to inherit power, quite another thing to exercise power. Where India's neighbors are concerned, this failure to exercise power encouraged China to annex India's territory in Aksai Chin and treat with contempt the MacMahon Line, and finally to mount an offensive which humiliated this country beyond measure, made a mockery of its policies and platitudes, mercilessly exposed its weaknesses, and shook the confidence of the country in its capabilities.

What India can take pride in, on the other hand, is the fact that while Pakistan treated its minorities savagely, India respected the secular spirit of its Constitution. While across the border the state used its power against men, women, and children of minority communities, in India men of the Muslim faith held high office. From the vice-president of India to cabinet ministers, state governors, ambassadors, civil servants, industrialists, and merchants, they carried on their vocations with dignity and respect, denied to minorities in Pakistan. This dedication to, as well as practice of, the secular ideal is India's great achievement, second only to the fact that it has earned the distinction of being the largest practicing democracy in the world.

But what, then, causes the regional pressures, pulls, and animosities? What are the factors responsible for the slowdown of the economy to such an alarming extent, for the state of despair and defeat? What makes bureaucracy—a vast complex which with alarming speed has become an all-pervading presence— add to the crisis by clogging up with rules, regulations, and procedures those very channels through which inspired directives are expected to flow? Why has India's image abroad as an emergent and dynamic new force on the Southeast Asian scene been destroyed? What kind of role have different men and institutions played in all this? From what personal weaknesses and strengths do these dilemmas result? Is their resolution possible without recourse to violent alternatives, and within the framework of India's Constitution? Or is a crisis of much larger dimensions in the offing?

Any evaluation of the Indian experiment must relentlessly probe for answers to these questions, and to find an answer to them one must first know something of the social and political history of this complex land.

2
History's Legacy

The legacy that India inherited was not of British making alone. Against the two hundred years of British presence there were five thousand years of a multiplicity of other rules and rulers, invasions and influences. The result is that there always have been—sometimes dormant, but ever present—deep-seated resentments between the regional and linguistic groups. Conflicts and cleavages stand out prominently in the history of India, and it would be well to see how those of the past, and of today, are influencing current events.

If the nomadic Aryans who came into India through Persia fourteen hundred years before Christ were eventually able to set up kingdoms in the Gangetic plains, it was because the original inhabitants were a fragmented people. They fought and resisted the intruders, but not collectively. Their unconcern for the country's tragedies was an understandable attitude, since no nation, and thus no national feeling, existed then. India was a medley of kingdoms and clans and tribal societies with pockets of settled civilizations, such as Mohenjo-daro, dating back to before 3000 B.C. Its character as a unified nation was to develop only centuries later, and that, ironically, under the British.

Although the Aryans were absorbed and assimilated, as India was apt to do with those who came her way, they brought with them, into a land already riven with complexities of languages and customs, their own disciplines and dialects. One of the results was the introduction of yet another major element into the linguistic fabric of India: the Aryan language. It evolved eventually into classical Sanskrit and became a powerful force in the north as a counterpoise to the language of the Dravidian south. But this linguistic division was only a part of what Indian history had to contend with.

Its mosaic is laid out in an intricate pattern of parallel cultures rising and falling within its borders, and invasions, inroads, and impositions from across its borders. After the early and later Vedic periods (about 1200–800 B.C.), and the periods of the Brahmanas and the Sutras, which were a consequence of the Aryan conquests in India, came Mahavira, the founder of Jainism, and Siddhartha Gautama, the founder of Buddhism. Then through Cyrus and Darius, kings of Persia, came the influence of Zoroaster, a religious reformer of Persia. With the overthrow of the Persian empire by Alexander, and his crossing of the Hindu Kush ranges into the plains of India in 327–326 B.C., the Greek element too was inlaid in the mosaic.

Even three hundred years prior to Alexander, India was witnessing within its borders the emergence of the powerful empire of Magadha, the most significant years of which were those of its Maurya dynasty, from 322 to 185 B.C. This dynasty's span of effective power included Chandragupta Maurya and King Ashoka, whose conversion to Buddhism, publication of his famous edicts, and dispatch of Buddhist missionaries to Southeast Asia, Egypt, West Asia, and Macedon are high points of this country's history. Thus, while varying influences were being brought into India at the point of the sword, India herself was beginning to influence others through ideas and precepts. What is important to note, however, is that each new period, while it no doubt enriched the cultural content of the land, caused further proliferation of religions, languages, creeds, and customs.

The regional and linguistic schisms so markedly evident today go as far back as the dawn of Indian history. They did not lessen but increased with the passage of time.

The attempt here is not to record history in a chronological order, but to show how far back in history the present-day regional pulls and tensions go.

The overthrow of the Sunga and Kanva dynasties in 28 B.C. by the Andhras (a name applied to the Dravidian-speaking Telugus of the Deccan today) was significant because it showed that, parallel to the power play in the Indus and Indo-Gangetic plains, forces existed in the south of India which were equally militant and assertive in defense of their ways of life. Inroads into the Deccan from the north began around the seventh century A.D., though Asoka had sent a Buddhist mission to the Rashtrikas (later called the Maharashtrikas or Maharathas) and Andhras as early as 256 B.C.

The Andhras (invariably referred to as Satavahana kings) extended their dominion during the waning years of the Maurya empire. The Satavahana rule over large parts of the Deccan lasted for nearly four and a half centuries (225 B.C. to A.D. 225), and their kingdom spread from Orissa to Ujjain, including Amaravati in the Guntur district, parts of Hyderabad extending up to Nasik. Concurrently with the rule of the Andhras in the Deccan, the Tamil culture flourished further south. The Tamil and Malayalam states of the Cholas, Pandyas, and Cheras, were in power around the fourth century B.C. The seat of the Chola dynasty was in what is now Tanjore district; south of that was the Pandya dynasty around Madura, Tinnevelly, and South Travancore, while the present coastal areas of Kerala were the seat of the Chera dynasty.

Their maritime strength and control of the fertile Kaveri rice-growing granary must have provided Tamil empires with a powerful economic base which in turn enabled them to prevent incursions into the Deccan and to develop their own political, social, and cultural institutions.

If anything, the pattern of Indian history from the beginning

of the Christian era to the first Islamic invasion of India by
Mahmud of Ghazni (Afghanistan) in A.D. 997 is even more
complex than ancient Indian history. The Indo-Parthian rulers
of the Punjab were defeated by a Kushan chieftain, Kadphises I,
whose successor, Kadphises II consolidated his position across
the Indus. His successor, Kanishka I, established the Saka era
around A.D. 78. The breakup of the Kushan empire in A.D. 220
marked the beginning of a hundred years of disorder lasting till
the dawn of the Gupta era—considered one of the golden periods
of Indian history. It opened with the coronation of Chandragupta
in A.D. 330. Although at its zenith the Gupta empire had less
territory than that of the Mauryas, its rule extended over the
Ganges valley from Prayag (modern Allahabad) to Pataliputra
and Ujjain. The Guptas also defeated the kings in eastern Deccan, Orissa, and Assam, though without permanently annexing
their kingdoms.

Selig Harrison, in his book *India: The Most Dangerous
Decades,* reads these periods of Indian history thus:

> . . . conquered feudatory units ordinarily remained intact within
> an empire, often under their own kings, retaining their autono-
> mous identity for all their payment of homage and tribute. When
> the empire dissolved they reverted back to their old independent
> status as a matter of course. Thus, in the case of North India, the
> growth of separate regional identities in Gujarat, Bengal, and
> Assam persisted despite the recurrent subordination of these
> regions to the dominant Ganges heart-land. Their geographical
> proximity exposed them to the ambitions of each Gangetic empire
> as it arose. Yet because they were, in a sense, so near and yet so
> far—geographically self-contained and each separately strong—they
> were able to reassert independence when imperial authority dis-
> integrated.[1]

What of other "regional identities"? And the imprint they left
in the mosaic of Indian history? Since their assertiveness in the

[1] Selig Harrison: *India: The Most Dangerous Decades* (Princeton, New
Jersey: Princeton University Press; 1960), p. 19.

rough and tumble of political life in India today results directly from a deep-seated consciousness of their role in history, it would be well to examine the more outstanding.

The rise of the Palas in East India in the middle of the eighth century (A.D. 750–1050) marked the emergence of Bengal as a definite regional entity. The rule of the Pala kings extended from Bengal, Orissa, Bihar, as far north as present-day Allahabad, which was conquered from the Pratihara kingdom of Kanauj. These conquests, as well as three centuries (A.D. 750–1050) of rule, left their mark on the Bengalee mind. According to one observer, though, "Bengalee regional consciousness today gains its immediate inspiration from Bengalee initiative in the Independence movement and, to an even greater extent, from the vitality of a Bengalee literary achivement distinctive in its humanist emphasis and notable both in quality and quantity among Indian regional literatures. . . . But historical memories of the Palas and their 11th century Sena successors are alive at the back of Bengalee minds."

Western India, crisscrossed with its own shifting patterns of emerging and receding forces, saw the Solanki dynasty of Gujarat rise to power in A.D. 961. Its period of eminence lasted till A.D. 1297, a span of over three hundred years during which the kingdoms of Gujarat not only ruled over Kathiawar, Cutch, Maharashtra's North Konkan coast, Malwa, and Western Rajasthan, but also laid the foundations for its own distinct language, culture, literature, and customs. If the Marathas, in view of their subsequent exploits, felt centuries later that they had an indisputable case for a separate state in independent India, the Gujaratis were no less vociferous in demanding one for themselves. Each people felt its case was firmly anchored in history. All that, however, was still to come.

In faraway Afghanistan, events were taking place which would influence Indian history more decisively than anything else had done before. A former Turkish slave, Sabuktigin, had founded a kingdom at Ghazni in Afghanistan. He and his central Asian horsemen, lured by India's wealth, now set their eyes eastward and in A.D. 986 entered the plains of India. Their coming marked the advent of Islam in India on a large scale, an event which was to leave its lasting impress on this country.

Sabuktigin inflicted a crushing defeat on a confederacy of Rajput princes arrayed against him. Peshawar was annexed. But it was left to his son, Mahmud of Ghazni, who succeeded him in A.D. 997, to ransack kingdoms, loot temple treasures, detroy idols, and put to the sword those he conquered. Between 997 and the time of his death in 1030, Mahmud's annual expeditions into India took him through Rajasthan and the southern coast of Kathiawar, where he sacked the sacred temple of Somnath, to Bulandshahr, and Mathura.

Though Mahmud returned to Ghazni after each invasion, sporadic colonizing of India by Mohammedans had begun. When a century and a half after Mahmud's death, the Afghans of Ghor, destroyed Ghazni, its people took refuge in Lahore.

It was Muhammed of Ghor's turn now to continue the raids on India, an enterprise he tackled with even greater vigor than his predecessor. From 1175 to his death in 1206 he overran the country from Kurukshetra to Benares, to Bihar, and up to Bengal. As far as North India was concerned, the dawn of A.D. 1200 saw Hindu supremacy largely at an end, with the exception of Malwa, parts of Gujarat and Rajputana.

The span of Muslim influence in India is a long one. Though the Arabs first came to Sind in A.D. 711 and two years later annexed it as a Mohammedan province, it was an isolated foray, a limited and contained operation. The Islamic rule of India really started in A.D. 986, and after a tremendous sweep of nearly nine hundred years ended with Bahadur Shah's deposition by the British in 1858. In actual fact, the Mogul Empire, one of the greatest, had already begun its decline a hundred and fifty years earlier, after the death of Emperor Aurangzeb in 1707. Under his rule India came closest to being governed by one central authority. At the peak of his power he held sway from the

Northwest Frontier to Cape Comorin, from Gujarat to Bengal, Bihar, and Assam, and as far as Chittagong. True, there were many rents in the fabric. India was torn by continuous battles and intrigues, and pockets of independent rule existed. Mogul rule could not be equated with the consolidation of India under the British, but never before had so large a territory come under the suzerainty of one power. Mohammedan customs, culture, creeds, and languages had now become an integral part of the land.

Before recording the final chapters of Indian history, two intriguing and quite penetrating comments on the causes of collapse of Hindu rule at the hands of Muslims, and on the later disintegration of Muslim rule, are worth recording. They are by non-Indians, but sometimes a more objective view can be given by those not too subjectively involved themselves.

The overthrow of the rich and martial kingdoms of Hindustan with such surprising ease is at first sight an astonishing fact. It was certainly not due to lack of valour on the part of the Rajput race. Its causes are to be found in the defects of the social organisation of the Hindus. Owing to this, fighting was left to a single caste, the Kshatriyas; the vast majority of the population was untrained in arms and indifferent to the fate of their country. National feeling did not exist, and even the martial clans had little sense of patriotism. In the face of common danger, it is true, they combined for a time, but otherwise they frittered away their strength in endless internecine quarrels. The Hindus, as al-Biruni says, were too proud and self-centered to recognise the existence of outside nations, much less to learn from them. . . . The hardy Muslim invaders from the north were, man for man, bigger, stronger and better mounted than their opponents, who, for all their valour, were handicapped by a hot and enervating climate, and by a diet which was mainly vegetarian. The Muhammedan religion was a fighting creed; the exterminating of the infidel and the destruction of idols were sacred duties; he who died in performing them was a Ghazi and went straight to the joys of Paradise. The essence of Islam is brotherhood. All Muslims, of whatever race or social position, are equal in the sight of God. Merit was the only test of ability and a slave could rise to the throne of Delhi. In this it contrasted strongly with the endless divisions of caste-ridden Hinduism. . . .[2]

And now for the reasons which in time, caused the disintegration of Muslim rule in India.

The causes of the down-fall of the Moghul Empire in its own turn are many and complex. The first was that the Moghuls were essentially foreigners, and had no roots in the soil. They were aliens both by race and religion from the vast majority of their subjects. The far-sighted attempt of Akbar, the only one of his line with a vision transcending the necessities of the moment, to unite the peoples of India under a truly national government, found no sympathy with his successors. The religious policy of Aurangzeb, which resulted in the alienation of the Rajputs, deprived the Empire of its strongest supporters, and provoked widespread risings amongst the Hindus from the Punjab to the Deccan, while his attempts to check the lax morality and general corruption of the age ended in failure. . . . Of the economic causes at work—the corruption of the officials, the extravagance of the nobility, the waste of money on costly and useless buildings, and the oppression of the peasantry, which was driving large sections of the country out of cultivation—mention has been made.[3]

Two more powerful movements of protest emerged during Muslim rule, before all three went down under British arms. Both, when they started out, were of a regional nature but later spilled over through dazzling military campaigns into territories which spread far beyond their own. The Sikh religion, founded by Guru Nanak (A.D. 1469–1539), subsequently became a militant movement in revolt against Muslim rule. In the Deccan the birth of Sivaji in A.D. 1627 marked the beginning of Maratha ascendancy, which reached its high water mark under the Bhonsles and Peshwas. The Marathas held sway over almost the entire Deccan, as far as Bengal in the east, and up to Delhi and

[2] H. G. Rawlinson: *India, A Short Cultural History* (London: The Cresset Press; 1954), pp. 211–12.
[3] Ibid., pp. 355–6.

Lahore in the north, in addition to large parts of Central India, Gujarat, and as far as Tanjore in the south. Marathi literature and religious practices dated much further back, however—to Jnanesvar, who translated a popular version of the *Bhagavad-Gita* at the end of the thirteenth century A.D., and after him to the famous poet-saint Tukaram, whose verses and lyrics inspired a profoundly pious people.

Rooted deep in the minds of Marathas is the belief that their role in comparatively recent Indian history has vested them with a mystique of leadership about which there cannot be any serious doubt. Others quite naturally do have doubts about this. K. M. Munshi, for instance, says in rebuttal that Sivaji looked upon Gujarat "more as a treasure to be robbed than a country to be governed."[4]

The raging controversy over the bifurcation of Bombay state into Maharashtra and Gujarat was an example of "linguistic nationalism" inherited from history.

The founder of the Sikh faith, Guru Nanak, was born in 1469 in the north, near Lahore. It was the time of the Lodi rule in Delhi. Nanak was the first of the ten gurus who gave Sikhism its scriptures, its literature, its character and lore. As to Kabir, the fourteenth century Muslim saint, to whom "all institutional religions were a hollow sham," so to Nanak, Kabir's admirer, and a philosopher-saint himself, the caste system, the authority of Brahmins, idolatory and such were totally unacceptable. He stressed the common bonds between Hinduism and Islam. Of his two closest disciples one was a Muslim and the other a Hindu. During the pontificacy of the four gurus who followed him, the Sikh order grew. The fourth guru, Ram Dass, built a small shrine near Lahore where now stands the Golden Temple of Amritsar, the Mecca and spiritual home of the Sikhs. The site was donated by Emperor Akbar, the great liberal. But, ironically, the benevolent Mogul's son Jehangir, who succeeded him, helped convert the peaceful reform movement of the Sikhs into one

[4] K. M. Munshi: *Gujarata and Its Literature* (Bombay: Longmans Green and Co.; 1935), pp. 207–8.

of the most militant witnessed in India. What started as an attempt to synthesize the best of two great religions was forced to take to arms in an implacable stand against injustice, tyranny, and the vagaries of Mogul rulers.

The torture and beheading of Arjun, the fifth guru—a scholar and saint and compiler of *Guru Granth,* the bible of the Sikhs—was a tragic turning point in history. Jehangir's brutal punishment of Arjun for harboring his rebel son Khusru was a pyrrhic victory, for out of this senseless murder was born an enemy whose rage carried him into bitter battle with Islam for the next two hundred years and more, until both Muslims and Sikhs went down before the expanding power of the British.

To avenge his father's martyrdom, Arjun's son Hargobind fought the Mogul armies all through his life, till his death in A.D. 1645. The die was cast, for now it was Aurangzeb's turn to behead the ninth guru, Teg Bahadur. The tenth, Govind Singh (who gave the surname *Singh,* or Lion, to all Sikhs), aware of what the Sikhs were up against, proceeded to forge them into a disciplined, battle-tested, militant order founded on concepts of total equality within the fraternity and welded together by voluntary acceptance of a code of ethics framed by the guru.

Guru Gobind Singh's was a far-sighted move. From his death in 1708 to Ranjit Singh's rise to power in 1799, the fraternity he had forged held together through continuous wars with the Afghan invaders from the north and the imperial armies of Delhi from the south.

Then came Ranjit Singh's spectacular reign, a saga of conquests and consolidation. At his death in 1839, Sikh rule extended over Punjab, Kashmir, Northwest Frontier Province, and Sind. But with the restraining hand of the shrewd old leader removed, the decline of Sikh fortunes began. Thirsting for further conquests, his victorious armies, after his death, turned their eyes to Delhi. This was to be the beginning of the end. In a series of fierce battles, and two major wars even more fiercely fought, they finally lost to the British.

From A.D. 1761 the Maratha fortunes were also set on a down-

hill course. Weakened by the defeat inflicted on them at Panipat by the Afghan invader, Ahmad Shah Duranni, the Marathas
never wholly recovered from that major reverse.

> Politically, the chief result of the battle was to pave the way
> for the English conquest; it is doubtful whether the Company's
> forces could otherwise have made any headway. At Poona a period
> of disputed successions, faction and intrigue supervened on the
> death of the fourth Peshwa in 1772. For a time, disaster was
> staved off by the astute policy of Nan Farnavis, "the Indian
> Machiavelli," who was in control for thirty-eight years. But with
> his death in 1800, as the British Resident observed, departed all
> the wisdom and moderation of the Maratha government. . . . In
> 1802, by the Treaty of Bassein, the last Peshwa, Bajirao II, threat-
> ened by a coalition of his rivals, Sindia and Holkar, sacrificed his
> independence as the price of protection. He agreed to be restored
> to his throne by the East India Company, to pay a tribute of 26
> lakhs of rupees, and to accept a British Resident and a subsidiary
> force at his capital of Poona. The arrangement did not last long.
> In November 1817 he tried to shake off his masters, but was de-
> feated on the plain of Kirkee; a few months later he surrendered
> to the British cavalry, and was sent off to exile at Bithur near
> Cawnpore with a princely pension. The descendent of the house
> of Sivaji was restored to the throne of Satara as a British feuda-
> tory.[5]

In 1848, within months of the annexation of the Punjab after
the Second Sikh War, Satara also was finally annexed by the
British.

From the Khyber Pass to Cape Comorin, England was now the
paramount power in India. What had begun with the arrival of
three Englishmen ended with the founding of the British empire
in India.

William Leeds, Ralph Fitch, and John Newbury landed in
India in 1585 with the aim of starting trading operations on behalf of England. They carried a letter from Queen Elizabeth I,

[5] Rawlinson, p. 396.

requesting "liberty and security of voyage" for them and also that they be "honestly intreated and received," so that they could do business "by which means the mutual and friendy trafique of merchandise on both sides may come." The three eventually reached Agra, the capital of Emperor Akbar, and found it "much greater than London and very populous." It was "a great resort of merchandise from Persia and out of India and very much merchandise of silk and cloth and of precious stones, both rubies, diamonds and pearls." Leeds became a jeweler at the imperial court, Newbury took an overland route home and dropped out of the pages of history, while "Fitch returned to England after an absence of 8 years." His report led to the founding of the East India Company.

In 1609 William Hawkins, an English captain, arrived in Agra at the court of Jehangir. He represented the East India Company and came to ask for permission to establish a trading factory at Surat. Hawkins became a boon companion of Jehangir, but returned to England in disfavor in 1612. Next came Sir Thomas Roe, in 1615, as ambassador to India for James I. He was more successful, and returned home in 1619 with major trading rights, which resulted in the first British trading post at Surat port.

The company soon began expanding. It was granted a site for a factory in Madras in 1639 and for one on the Hooghly at Calcutta in 1690. The Company now shifted its headquarters from Surat to the island of Bombay, given to Charles II by the Portuguese as part of his wife's dowry in 1660, and now leased by it for a nominal rent.

At about this time, in 1664, the French formed La Compagnie des Indes under the patronage of Louis XIV, to begin trading operations in India. The first French settlement was founded in Pondicherry around 1674, and from then on, for the next hundred years and more, Britain and France fought continuously to get the upper hand in India. The French finally lost after the Carnatic Wars.

Portuguese influence in India was at a low ebb at the time of the British arrival. The Dutch had made no serious effort to bring India within their orbit of influence; their interest lay in the East Indies.

The consolidation of the British in India under the East India Company is an amazing, involved, and improbable story of battles fought and plots hatched, of treachery and intrigue and savage reprisals, of relentless pursuit of power on the one hand and a decaying society's despairing efforts to resist it on the other. In the end, however, as was inevitable, the fragmented people of India were the losers. As the size and scope of Britain's commitment in India grew, the administrative apparatus of the East India Company changed. From being merely the offices of a trading company, its headquarters were now the seat of governmental power, with all the pomp and panoply of armies and military governors, civil administrators and revenue collectors, allies and feudatories, headed by a governor general vested with extraordinary powers, responsible only to the Company's board of directors in London.

The scientific bent of Western minds and their organizational ability were now applied to the business of governing the country. There emerged the princely states; territorially well-defined units, nominally independent, but in the final count beholden to the British for their existence as well as their elaborate façades. The rajahs, maharajahs, nawabs, and jagirdars were products of typical British genius. Most of them had murky pasts, though the lineage of some went back to distant dynasties and days of glory. A majority, however, received their *riyasats* (princely states) and *jagirs* (estates) from the British for services rendered: for help given in one form or the other when help was needed most. At critical times throughout the period of British subjugation of India, deserters, and turncoats often turned the tide in their favor. Their rewards were handsome, as were the benefits the British reaped. But the manner in which the princely states were used to keep two fifths of India's people in bondage on the one hand, and each other in check on the other, is a remarkable study in statesmanship. (One consequence of the breakup of this elaborate structure at the time of independence was to release vast and vocal multitudes into India's already swollen political main stream, thereby giving a new physical dimension to the responsibilities facing the Central Government at that time.)

The other business the Company undertook between 1800 and 1858 was the framing of legislation as a basis for a uniform system of administration, sanctioned by legislated regulations and procedures. Within the boundaries of provinces, districts were now created, and a system of district administration was initiated. From 1818 till 1850 was a formative period during which details for administering districts were framed and revised and amended in the light of experience gained. In a sense, the system then devised is still in operation in India today. Land policy was also gradually evolved, and in 1858 the first Public Works Department was set up in Madras. But the reforms initiated by the Company in some spheres were partially responsible for the Sepoy Rebellion of 1857, which for a time threatened to bring down British rule in India, and which resulted in the transfer of the colony to the Crown.

Briefly, the reforms resented were those which attacked social and religious customs. The outlawing of "suttee,"[6] the practice of Hindu widows burning themselves on their husband's pyres, was one. Intensified activities of missionaries after 1833 were another major cause of resentment, since they influenced the withdrawal of considerable support the Company had hitherto given to local religious festivals and customs. What was resented even more was the evangelical zeal with which attempts were made to convert people of ancient faiths to Christianity. Lord Palmerston, at a banquet given for Canning on his appointment as governor general, observed: "Perhaps it might be our lot to confer on the countless millions of Indians a higher and nobler

[6] Many sophisticated Indians were opposed to suttee. It was a barbaric practice, but that didn't prevent resentment from being generated by British interference in it.

gift than any mere human knowledge."[7] This belief of the English Prime Minister, possibly no more than a passing thought, was all the same projected on the Indian scene with great fervor.

The priority given to the teaching of English was another contributory factor to Indian resentment. Lord Bentick's resolution to employ appropriations made for education solely for the teaching of English was influenced most by Lord Macaulay, who had arrived in India in 1834 as the first law member of the governor general's council. A passionate believer in the paramountcy of the English language, he had soon formed an opinion of Hindu literature: "False history, false astronomy, false metaphysics which attended their false religion . . . the languages of Western Europe civilised Russia; I cannot doubt they will do for the Hindu what they have done for the Tartar."[8]

Antagonisms were generated by other marginal irritants, too: granting widows the right to remarry, and converts to Christianity the right to retain interest in family property. This reformist zeal was politically unwise. Its cumulative effect was to ignite a situation which had been building up to a flash point. Of interest, however, is the fact that while it was the civil population, of different denominations, which was vociferous about its resentments, it was the army—as the only organized body in the country —which revolted, because "any rebellion among the civil population was most unlikely despite Muslim sermons or the talk of Hindu agents for there was no organisation and no possibility of organisation in a land so seamed by age-old divisions of race and creed and past".[9]

Though there were some signs of unrest earlier in the year in Barrackpore and Berhampore, the revolt began on May 10, 1857, in Meerut. A troop of cavalry mutinied, cut down its European officers, and took the road to Delhi with infantry troops who had

[7] J. Allan, Sir T. Wolseley Haig, H. H. Dodwell, R. R. Sethi: *The Cambridge Shorter History of India* (India: S. Chand and Co.; 1964), p. 558.

[8] Rawlinson, p. 409.

[9] Allan et al, p. 570.

also mutinied. It was over by June, 1858, though in effect the turning point in favor of the British had come earlier with the recovery of Delhi in September, 1857. During the time it took to put the mutiny down it was savage in its intensity, with the British fighting for their survival in India and the Indians fighting for something they were not very clear about themselves. The aftermath of the mutiny was the deposition of the titular Mogul, Bahadur Shah, from the throne of Delhi, and the transfer of the Government of India from the East India Company to the Crown on November 1, 1858. The proclamation of Queen Victoria, on the occasion, extended promise of religious freedom, ample employment opportunities, general amnesty, and a number of reforms meant to quiet an agitated people. British rule in India now entered a new phase.

To a large extent, the foundations of present-day politics in India, the pattern of government and parliamentary practices, the liberalism of the ruling elite, and its preference for representative institutions modeled on Western lines were laid during the next ninety years—from 1858 till British rule ended with the transfer of power in August, 1947. For the British, the first half of this period proved a time for consolidation and reform; for the Indians, the second half was a time in which to give shape and substance to their growing sense of nationalism.

The Indian National Congress, which spearheaded the independence movement, was the brainchild of an Englishman, Allan Octavian Hume. He convened its first session in 1885 and his idea was through it to assemble educated Indians once a year for discussing social and political reforms. The idea took root, but during the first few years the Congress was neither taken very seriously by the Government of India nor did it do much itself beyond asking for larger representation for Indians in the services and in Government. A radical change in its character began about 1900 with B. G. Tilak's emergence on the national scene. Tilak acknowledged the fact that "patriotism is not our national quality, it is the product of the influence to which we have been subjected after the introduction of British rule".[1] But his formula for a burgeoning sense of nationalism was militancy and a return to Hindu orthodoxy. Because his inspiration came from Sivaji, he began by giving a new dimension to traditional Hindu festivals like Ganapathi, so that the militant fervor dormant in the masses could be kindled. To a large extent he was successful in this aim, but its opposite effect was to kindle a sense of uneasiness in Muslims at increasing Hindu militancy. Their uneasiness turned to alarm as the Tilak-inspired Sivaji festival took on a cult-like quality.

As Sivaji had founded the Maharashtra kingdom in the teeth of opposition from the most powerful Muslim Emperor in India, a festival in his honour was well calculated to inspire the masses in Maharashtra. But, as Sivaji and the Maratha power founded by him were rightly associated in the minds of the Muslims with the decline and fall of the greatest Muslim Empire in India, their national vanity was sure to be wounded by doing any honour to the great Maratha leader."[2]

About the time Tilak was projecting his philosophy from Bombay, in Bengal a rather similar movement was under way. Though nationalist in its aims, it was also rooted in Hindu religious beliefs: "The militant nationalism of Bengal was founded upon the twin rocks—the ardent patriotic call of Swami Vivekananda based on the philosophical teachings of Vedanta and *Gita,* and the religious devotion to motherland preached by Bankim Chandra through Anandamath".[3] Though according to some, Tilak's Brahminical orthodoxy was replaced by the nationalist humanitarianism of Gokhale, the crisis of confidence between Hindus and Muslims in any event had begun.

The schism between Hindus and Muslims soon turned into an almost unbridgeable gulf. A restatement of the Islamic doctrine

[1] R. C. Majumdar: *History of the Freedom Movement in India* (Calcutta: Firma K. L. Mukhopadhyay; 1962 and 1963), I, 339.

[2] Ibid., I, 340.

[3] Ibid., II, 16 f.

in a manner more in keeping with the rationalist mood of that time had been made earlier by Syed Ahmed Khan (1817–98). But his later mood, and the voices of some of his successors in the early 1900's, took on aggressive overtones in counterthrust to the increasing militancy of the Hindu majority. There also was a growing fear in Muslim minds of being left behind in the game of political musical chairs which was now being played with increasing verve. Their appeal to the viceroy, Lord Minto, in 1906, seeking proportional representation in the proposed legislatures produced the Morley-Minto reforms of 1909, which embedded the principle of communal representation in the legislature and thus caused a further cleavage between the two communities. Whatever more was needed to articulate the separate aims and aspirations of the Muslims was provided by the Muslim League on its founding in 1906.

From then on, even though some of India's most distinguished Muslims identified themselves with Congress, the Muslim League was able to project itself with increasing success as a party dedicated "to protect and advance the political and other rights of the Mussalmans of India."[4]

The forty years which followed the formation of the League saw the crystallization of the Congress demand for total independence on the one hand, and gradual emergence of the Muslim League as a major political force on the other. While the nationalist movement—spearheaded and inspired by Congress—gathered momentum throughout the country and perfected its organizational machinery, the Muslim League was equally busy developing its personality and program. To begin with its program was largely negative: what the Congress was for, the League was against. But its own more positive ideas were building up toward some sort of coherence, aided partly by pronouncements of chauvinistic and bigoted Hindu elements within the Congress Party, partly by British intransigence.

A great deal of rhetoric has time and again been leveled ac-

[4] Ibid., II, 232.

cusingly at the British for their policy of divide and rule. As if the British were expected to foster lasting love between the different communities in India! The British were here to rule. They were running an empire, not a finishing school. If politics is the art of the possible, Indians made it possible for them to divide and rule. It was expedient for the British to sow the seeds of discontent between the two major communities, but without soil ready for such seed, there could have been no fruit. Expediency is hardly a matter of reproach when the stakes are high.

The Congress itself, for that matter, has been guilty of massive compromises, during the independence struggle and since.

Though India's struggle for independence produced some remarkable leaders like Gokhale, B. G. Tilak, Pherozshah Mehta, Annie Besant, C. R. Das, Motilal Nehru, and a great many more, the man who finally shaped the struggle and took the country through to independence was Mahatma Gandhi. Born on October 2, 1869, at Porbunder in Gujarat, Mohandas Karamchand Gandhi left for South Africa in 1893 to practice law. The years there helped him to shape his own particular political philosophy. It was there he gave form to his concept of passive resistance, or *satyagraha*. It took courage for a puny man to stand up before a rabid society and its hate-filled government, but he faced physical violence as well as other insults and indignities with more than mere courage. His organizational ability also proved remarkable. By the time he returned to India for good in January, 1915, he had forced the reversal of a number of the more obnoxious laws passed against colored peoples, through the mass support he mustered against them. Back in India he first worked under Gokhale, whom he admired as a political guru. But the number of agitations he was able to launch against various repressive measures soon projected him into prominence on the Indian scence. The country recognized his full measure as an all-India leader after he had master-minded the first successful countrywide *hartal* (strike) of April 6, 1919. It was also the first time the Government had an idea of the real dimensions of the country's mood.

Gandhi had a profound awareness of the communal hatreds which lie beneath the surface in India. Few others, except Jawaharlal Nehru, equaled the integrity with which he tried to give India a unified entity in which communal hatreds and regional definitions would cease to be of such importance. Gandhi and Nehru passionately subscribed to this ideal. But many others, men of great stature in most things, were unable to rise above deep-seated religious bigotry. Again, apart from mobilizing many of the intellectual elite of his time to his cause of freedom, it was Gandhi who "shifted politics from the drawing rooms of the educated and the businessmen to the huts of the tillers of the soil."[5]

As the Congress mood between the two World Wars headed toward a demand for total independence, the Muslim League provided the leverage the British needed to stall it.

The League's leadership had gradually passed into the hands of a Muslim barrister from Bombay, M. A. Jinnah. He was born in Karachi in 1876 of parents who came from the Gujarat. His grandfather was a Hindu, of the same Vaisya caste as Gandhi. After a brilliant academic career at the bar in London, Jinnah returned to India to set up a legal practice in Bombay, and soon made it a very lucrative one. In 1906, at the age of thirty, he joined the Indian National Congress and a few years later the Muslim League. To him this was not incongruous since he felt it would help him to bring Hindus and Muslims together, and at the same time co-ordinate their efforts in the freedom struggle. He stayed in the Congress Party till 1920. There are various interpretations of why he left, but the fact is that after the Nagpur Congress Session of 1920, Jinnah ceased to be a Congress adherent. He returned to England to practice but came back on the invitation of Liaquat Ali Khan to head the Muslim League. From then until independence came, Jinnah's attitude toward the Congress Party was bitter. Despite various attempts

[5] Rajendra Prasad: *Autobiography* (India: Asia Publishing House; 1957), p. 131.

at *rapprochement* on Gandhi's part, the bitterness increased, if anything.

The culmination of the struggle for Indian independence has been recorded in fine detail by many of those who participated in the struggle, and many of those who observed it. In this book there seems little point in recording those events again. Much of what is written in this chapter is there because without it one would find it difficult to understand the linguistic and religious problems which beset India today, or the manner in which policy is often subordinated to them. The same applies to the circumstances which led to the massacres of 1947 at the time of India's partition. The blood-letting which attended the division of this country was not as "senseless" as is made out. The savage slaughter made sense to those who had realized from the very beginning that the communal passions injected into pre-independence politics had set the communities on a collision course. And when the collision finally occurred, it made some of the most barbaric periods of Indian history look much less so in comparison.

3

Partition

The general assumption that Pakistan is a concept of the Muslim League is wrong. It was the poet Iqbal who in 1930 first suggested a Muslim state in northwest India; then in 1933 Rahmat Ali, an Indian scholar living in England, came up with the idea of Pakistan. Not until its meeting at Lahore in March, 1940, were the first vague outlines of a new sovereign state spelled out by the League. Its resolution at that time demanded that "the North-Western and Eastern Zones of India should be grouped to constitute 'independent states' in which the constituted units shall be autonomous and sovereign." However, despite impassioned statements and thumping oratory, few were more surprised than the Muslims themselves when what had been a bargaining lever seemed likely to become a permanent fact.

The inevitability of the two-nation concept was fully recognized during the cabinet mission's visit to Delhi on March 24, 1946. This mission, comprising three senior cabinet members of the Labour Government, was sent out to negotiate a solution to the deadlock between Congress and the League. Lord Pethick Lawrence, Sir Stafford Cripps, and A. V. Alexander stayed for over three months. When they left on June 29, 1946, the Indian leaders seemed convinced of one thing: that from then on "It was not to be so much a struggle to wrest power from the British, as a dispute as to how that power, once inherited, should be shared by the parties concerned."[1] If the country was to be divided, the question now was, how?

The Muslim League demanded six provinces: the Punjab, the Northwest Frontier Province, Sind, Baluchistan, Bengal, and Assam. To Congress, the accession of the Punjab and Bengal, with their vast non-Muslim populations, was totally unacceptable. The only alternative seemed to lie in partitioning the two provinces along lines which would give India the non-Muslim majority areas contiguous to it, and Pakistan the Muslim majority areas adjoining it.

Jinnah viewed any such solution as "a sinister move actuated by spite and bitterness."[2] A statement he issued at that time suggested, in substance, that "an exchange of population would sooner or later have to take place and that this could be effectively carried out by the respective governments in Pakistan and Hindustan."[3] But Rajendra Prasad, speaking for the Congress, reminded him that the League's Lahore Resolution of 1940 had endorsed the division of the Punjab and Bengal. He said if there had to be a division of the country it must be thorough, to leave no room for future contention or conflict.

Lord Mountbatten's arrival in New Delhi on March 22, 1941, entirely changed the tempo of events. The new viceroy was of different stuff from his predecessors. Determined to find a solution to the impasse the two political parties had reached, he was a man of tremendous drive and dynamism. Convinced that the deteriorating situation in the country, the alarming spread of communal rioting, and the breakdown of law and order were major threats to the country's stability, he had an outline plan

[1] V. P. Menon: *The Transfer of Power in India* (India: Orient Longmans Private Ltd.; 1957), pp. 279, 355.

[2] Ibid., p. 355.

[3] Ibid.

ready within six weeks of his arrival. Fortunately, this first plan, which proposed transfer of power to provincial governments, was turned down by Nehru, and it became clear that the principle of partitioning the country between two separate sovereign states could be the only basis for any alternative plan.

V. P. Menon, who played an important part at the highest level as a member of Mountbatten's personal staff, writing in his memoirs, *The Transfer of Power in India,* said:

It was late in December 1946 or early in January 1947 that I had a lengthy discussion with Vallabbhai Patel. A united India, under the Cabinet Mission plan was, I suggested, an illusion. The three tier constitutional set-up envisaged was unwieldy and difficult to work; I saw no future for the country under this plan . . . my personal view was that it was better that the country should be divided, rather than that it should gravitate towards civil war. If we agreed to partition, Jinnah couldn't possibly ask for those provinces of the Punjab, Bengal and Assam, which were predominantly non-Muslim. The crucial problem was the basis on which power could be transferred. In a divided India this could best be to two central governments on the basis—a point on which I laid particular stress—of Dominion Status. By consenting to accept Dominion Status, the Congress would be gaining three great advantages. Firstly, it would ensure a peaceful transfer of power. Secondly, such acceptance would be warmly welcomed by Britain and the Congress would, by this single act, have gained its friendship and goodwill. The third concerned the future administration of the country. The civil services at the higher levels, were manned largely by Britishers, and if India insisted on independence there was no question but that the British element had it in their power to create endless trouble at the time of the transfer of power. . . . I pointed out that if the transfer of power took place on the basis of Dominion Status it would enable the Congress to have at one and the same time a strong central government, able to withstand centrifugal tendencies all too apparent at the moment and to frame a truly democratic constitution unhampered by any communal considerations. Nobody could have been better aware of the situation in the country than Vallabbhai Patel; he had already been in charge of the Home portfolio for some months

. . . he assured me that if power could be transferred at once on
the basis of Dominion Status he for one, would use his influence
to see that the Congress accepted it.[4]

With the rejection of Mountbatten's first plan the partition
proposal was revived in May, 1947, and with that a hectic round
of negotiations began. The Congress Party by and large proved
more amenable than the League, but Mountbatten was finally
able to get acceptance of the broad outline of his plan from the
three major parties involved: Congress, the League, and the
Sikhs. With this in his bag he left for London on May 18. The
British cabinet's concurrence secured, Mountbatten was back in
India on May 31, and on June 2, at a fateful meeting at which
Nehru, Jinnah, Baldev Singh, Patel, Liaquat Ali, Kripalani, and
Nishtar were present, the plan was placed before them for final
acceptance. This was accepted on June 3. (In actual fact, it was
accepted much later by Jinnah, who, on Mountbatten's insistance
agreed to nod his head as a token of agreement at the joint meeting but remained adamant in his refusal to say yes or give his
acceptance in writing.)

On the evening of June 3 Mountbatten, Nehru, Jinnah, and
Baldev Singh made a broadcast over All India Radio. In London,
Attlee announced the plan in the House of Commons and later,
in a broadcast that night, he said: "As the Indian leaders have
finally failed to agree on the Cabinet Mission's plan for a united
India, partition becomes the inevitable alternative."

Alan Campbell-Johnson, in his book *Mission with Mountbatten,* recorded the impression Nehru's and Jinnah's talks made
on him. About Nehru he wrote:

Here was neither arrogance nor apology, but a true reflection of
the sadness which accompanies all success—the frustration in victory. Perhaps Nehru's greatest strength is that although he has
reached the heights as a partisan campaigner he retains detach-
ment of spirit. The artist and the scholar in him are always near
the surface. So at this climactic moment he was able to say, "We

4 Ibid., pp. 358–9.

are little men serving great causes, but because the cause is great something of that greatness falls upon us also." . . . Then followed Jinnah. The experts in Moslem League dialectic assured me that his speech was a masterpiece. As one of them put it to me immediately afterwards, "This is the language that will be understood in the bazaars, and it means peace." By objective standards I could not detect the magic. He seemed to me on this occasion to be well below the level of events which he had done so much to create. His opening sentence was devoted to a thinly disguised criticism of the authorities for not having previously afforded him—as a non-official—facilities for broadcast. "I hope that in the future I shall have greater facilities to enable me to voice my views and opinions, which will reach directly to you, live and warm, rather than in the cold print of the newspapers." But I could find no liveliness nor warmth in what he had to say.[5]

The climactic decision was now announced: power would be transferred to the two states by August 15, or in a little over two months. Political commentators and writers have questioned the wisdom of this haste. In their view India and Pakistan were not ready for acceptance of power. It has been suggested that the savage partition riots in East and West Punjab were a consequence of precipitate haste on Britain's part in pulling out. Such criticism does not take into account the communal tensions which existed then. It ignores the fundamental fact that partition was not the cause of communal hatreds; it resulted from them. The beliefs of major religions in India are leavened generously with a sense of moral and spiritual superiority. Each considers others somewhat lacking in quality and substance. It is because of this attitude, with its obvious overtones of deep-seated prejudice, that conflict was inevitable between Muslims, Hindus, and Sikhs. At the height of the killings on September 12, 1947, Pandit Nehru, speaking to the diplomatic corps, specially assembled to hear the Government's point of view and concern at the turn events had taken, said: "The history of India has been one of assimilation.

[5] Alan Campbell-Johnson: *Mission with Mountbatten* (London: Robert Hale Ltd.; 1952), pp. 106–7.

and synthesis of the various elements that have come in. . . . It is perhaps because we tried to go against the trend of the country's history that we are faced with this."[6] But one is compelled through one's own reading of history and recent events to present a different thesis: by and large there never has been any assimilation, there has been only acceptance of the *presence* of alien faiths—and that too through force of circumstance. The assassination of Gandhi is proof of the fact that those who want to synthesize Hindus and Muslims must pay for the ideal with their lives, should a particular situation demand that as a price.

Under the very thin crust of what seemed a civilized social order a vast lava of hate was boiling up in India in 1946 and 1947. It swirled and seethed beneath the surface, fanned and fed by power-hungry politicians for whom the exploitation of communal frenzies was the means to an end. Had the date for transfer of power been put forward by a year or more, the result could easily have been civil war, touched off intentionally or otherwise by those who had aroused communal passions to help them gain political objectives at the bargaining table. In retrospect it is easy for critics to ignore, or even be ignorant of, the pressures which had built up by 1946 and the first half of 1947. There was little then to prevent communal riots from escalating into something much bigger. Strong-arm methods to surpress rioting would have intensified a triangular pattern of hate between Hindus, Muslims, and the British, and set the clock back not only on India's independence but on everything else. All this was realized by Mountbatten and responsible Indian leadership, but unfortunately not by the League's leaders.

I remember a very intense conversation with Dwight Mac-Donald, American author and political commentator, who seemed convinced that it was the Muslims who suffered in the first place from Congress-engineered riots, and when they did strike back it was only in justifiable retaliation. It is a point of view one hears frequently. Facts, however, are quite different and are

[6] Ibid., p. 187.

likely to be blurred in the span of time and distance. The idea of getting those facts straight here is not to apportion blame; it is to show that the communal keg in India is easily set alight. The Muslim League found it expedient to apply the torch to it in 1946–7. Other political and communal opportunists may try to do it again, in the absence of far-sighted statesmanship.

In July, 1946, far-sighted statesmanship was lacking. At a meeting of the Muslim League on July 27, 1946, Jinnah gave the call for Muslims to observe August 16, 1946, as Direct Action Day throughout India. He said:: "This day we bid good-bye to constitutional methods. . . . Today we have also forged a pistol and are in a position to use it."[7]

S. H. Suhrarwardy, Bengal's Chief Minister at that time, was an ardent Leaguer and a member of its Working Committee. (He subsequently became the fifth Prime Minister of Pakistan.) Described as an "outwardly affable but inwardly ruthless politico,"[8] he now set out to show the type of action he was capable of when action was called for. In the August 15 issue of Calcutta's *Statesman* he wrote: "Bloodshed and disorder are not necessarily evil in themselves, if resorted to for a noble cause. Among Muslims today, no cause is dearer or nobler than Pakistan. . . ."[9]

When the August, 1946, carnage of Calcutta, inspired and instigated by the League, got under way, the English-owned *Statesman* was moved to write:

> When we wrote two days ago, conditions in Calcutta were horrifying. They have gone beyond that since. Whatever the appropriate adjective is, they were nothing in comparison with what we have subsequently seen. The latest estimate of dead is 3,000, who have lain thick about the streets. The injured number many thousands and it is impossible to say how many business houses and private dwellings have been destroyed. This is not a riot. It needs

[7] Leonard Mosley: *The Last Days of the British Raj* (New York: Harcourt, Brace and World, Inc.; 1961), p. 29.

[8] Ibid., p. 32.

[9] Ibid.

a word found in medieval history, a fury. Yet fury sounds spontaneous, and there must have been some deliberation and organisation to set this fury on its way. The horde who ran about battering and killing with lathis may have found them lying about or brought them out of their own prockets, but that is not to be believed. We have already commented on the bands who found it easy to get petrol and vehicles when no others were permitted on the streets. It is not mere supposition that men were brought into Calcutta to make an impression . . . thousands have been brutally hurt, smashed eyes, smashed jaws, smashed limbs, of men, women and children—these are the kind of political arguments the twentieth century does not expect. . . . What befell India's largest city last week was no mere communal riot, as we have hitherto understood the sanguinary term. For three days, the city concentrated on unrestrained civil war. Upon whom the main guilt for it rests is manifest. There has been criticism of the Governor. We do not think he has emerged particularly well. But none except a very great man holding his traditionally constitutional office during such a swift crisis could have done so. Where the primary blame lies is where we have squarely put it—*upon the Provincial Muslim League Cabinet which carries responsibility for law and order in Bengal, and particularly upon the one able man of large administrative experience there, the Chief Minister [Suhrarwardy]*.[1] That in the whole of India the only Province where carnage occurred, on the League's professed peaceful Direct Action Day, should have been in Bengal, where a League Ministry holds office, astounds us.[2]

All this despite the fact that Ian Stephens, *The Statesman's* editor at that time, was considered pro-Muslim. A fact of considerable relevance here is that in Bengal the Muslims far outnumbered the Hindus and other communities: 33,000,000 Muslims against 27,315,000 others. When the killings spread from Calcutta to Noakhali in rural Bengal, it was again the majority community which fell upon the minorities. When the communal fever reached the Punjab a few months later, the

[1] Italics mine.
[2] Mosley, pp. 38–9.

pattern of tragedy was the same. The communal killings there in March and April of 1947 were around Rawalpindi, again a part of the province in which Muslims heavily outnumbered non-Muslims. Alan Campbell-Johnson, who accompanied the Mountbattens on a visit to Kahuta, near Rawalpindi, wrote: "We arrived to find that the havoc in the small town was very great. Picking our way through the rubble, we could see that the devastation was as thorough as any produced by fire-bomb raids in the war. This particular communal orgy involved the destruction of Sikhs and their livelihood by Moslems who were proving difficult to track down. The Moslems in the area seemed to be quite pleased with themselves, and to be unable to appreciate that the local Sikh traders were one of the principal sources of their own prosperity. . . ."[3]

A postscript to this could well be the observation of Sir George Schuster, a former finance member of Lord Halifax's Executive Council: "Fifty years of reform and communal co-operation had beeen sacrificed on the altar of Moslem League fanaticism."[4]

This was the stark backdrop against which partition took place. It was a concept conceived in hatred; savage blood-letting attended its final fruition. The bigotry and ill-concealed militancy of Arya Samaj, Hindu Mahasabha, and such groups did a good deal to increase latent Muslim fears of Hindu religious institutions and practices, but for preaching naked hatred, blame must rest squarely on the Muslim League. No responsible Congress leader, least of all Gandhi or Nehru, came anywhere near to making statements of the kind Jinnah and others in the League's hierarchy made in season and out. Their effect quite naturally was to incite primitive passions which any informed and civilized leadership should have considered itself responsible to hold in check, particularly in the light of the frequent and bloody encounters in history between Hindus and Muslims. That responsibility unfortunately was not exercised.

If there was some joy on India and Pakistan's Independence

[3] Campbell-Johnson, p. 79.
[4] Ibid., p. 33.

Days on August 14 and 15, to offset that there was the anguish of millions. Dazed, and with feelings of indescribable hopelessness, they realized that the price for the country's freedom was to be their blood, heartbreak, and misery.

Estimates have varied as to the size of the bill the two countries paid for getting what they did, in the form in which they did. According to one estimate: "In the nine months between August 1947 and the spring of the following year, between fourteen and sixteen million Hindus, Sikhs and Muslims were forced to leave their homes and flee to safety from blood crazed mobs. In that same period over 600,000 of them were killed. . . ."[5] According to another: "It has been estimated that up to the middle of 1948 about 5½ million non-Muslims were brought across the border from West Punjab and other provinces of Western Pakistan. About the same number of Muslims moved into Pakistan from East Punjab (including the East Punjab States), Delhi, the United Provinces, Ajmer-Merwara, Alwar, Bharatpur, Gwalior and Indore. During the same period about 1¼ million non-Muslims crossed the border from Eastern Pakistan into West Bengal. These figures do not of course take into account about 4,000,000 non-Muslims who later migrated to India from Sind. There is today hardly a Hindu or a Sikh to be found in Western Pakistan."[6]

To go back to my friend Dwight MacDonald and others whose emotions and facts often overlap—as in their assessment of the recent history of this subcontinent—the calendar of events which led to the 1947 massacres began with the Calcutta riots of August, 1946, when political action shifted from the bargaining table and public platform to murder and genocide. After Calcutta came the Noakhali (also in Bengal) riots where both Hindus and Muslims were the victims. The third date on the calendar— the Bihar riots—saw Hindus retaliate for what was happening in neighboring Bengal. Then came the "ruthless massacre of the Sikhs in Rawalpindi in March 1947, when the Muslims turned

[5] Mosley, p. 243.
[6] Menon, p. 431.

upon them and, in a welter of ferocity, murdered 2,000 of them."[7]

Soon after the announcement of the Radcliffe Award on August 17, a determined campaign to drive out the Hindus and Sikhs was evident all over West Punjab and the North-West Frontier Province. There were serious disturbances in the Lahore, Sheikhupura, Sialkot and Gujranwala districts. A massacre on an unprecedented scale took place in Sheikhupura in West Punjab. This was followed by a violent anti-Muslim reaction in Amritsar. Therefore communal frenzy gripped the people on both sides of the border, taking a heavy toll of lives and creating an exodus of population between the two Dominions, the like of which, has never before been known in history.[8]

While the frenzy which gripped East Punjab can never be condoned, it can at least be seen in the correct perspective and events seen in the sequence in which they happened:

The uprooted millions [from West Punjab] were in a terrible mental state. They had been driven from their homes under conditions of indescribable horror and misery. Not many had the time to plan their evacuation; most had to move out at the shortest possible notice. They had been subjected to terrible indignities. They had witnessed their near and dear ones hacked to pieces before their eyes and their houses ransacked, looted and set on fire by their own neighbours. They had no choice but to seek safety in flight, filled with wrath at what they had seen, and full of anguish for numberless missing kinsmen who were still stranded in Pakistan and for their womenfolk who had been abducted. . . . The holocaust in Western Pakistan had its repercussions in East Punjab. The streams of fleeing refugees with their tales of woe and suffering made a profound impression on the people. In vain were appeals made to them to remember that retaliation was no remedy. The spirit of revenge was abroad, working up communal bitterness to a frenzied pitch, till all restraint was thrown to the winds. . . . To understand the attitude of this

[7] Mosley, p. 213.
[8] Menon, p. 418.

"over-blamed people," one must appreciate the fact that the Sikhs had been driven out of their homes, contrary to all their hopes and expectations; that they had been deprived of their lands and property, their shrines and holy places; that their losses in men and property had been comparatively greater than those of any other community affected by the communal upheaval; that nearly forty per cent of the entire Sikh community had been reduced to penury and had become refugees with the necessity of having to start life afresh. . . .[9]

The fact that massacres on such a scale took place in East Punjab is no reflection on the Gandhian philosophy of non-violence, or the genuineness of Gandhi's and Nehru's efforts to stop the madness. The intensity of their grief at what was happening was no less than the sorrow of those who were directly affected by the tragedy. It is uncharitable and inaccurate to imply that there was no difference between the leaders of India and Pakistan in their outlook on minorities in the two countries at the time of partition or, for that matter, subsequently. It is this attitude, and to an extent ignorance, on the part of many responsible men abroad, which results in frequent misinterpretation and misreading of the politics of India and Pakistan. What tends to be overlooked is the fact that while Pakistan is unabashedly an Islamic state, India's Constitution—and thus its social and political institutions—guarantee equal opportunities, rights, and freedom to men and women of all faiths. And this is undeniably so in practice.

In evaluating the chronically strained relations between the two countries, observers often tend to gloss over India's genuine concern for the safety of its Muslim minority, which could conceivably become the victim of communal passions if Pakistan's brash policies were to lead it one day into some sort of adventurist enterprise. Since wild and irresponsible statements were once able to provoke indiscriminate and savage communal killings, they could do so again, and the real danger of continuous provocation by Pakistan lies in the distinct possibility of a renewed

[9] Ibid., pp. 418, 419, 432, and 433.

outbreak of communal frenzy within India. Because there are forty to fifty million Muslims living there, this danger cannot be ignored; in West Pakistan the question doesn't arise, since there are no Hindus or Sikhs there. In East Pakistan too the number of Hindus is being systematically reduced. The stream of refugees across the East Pakistan border into India is gradually syphoning off the inconvenient minority. Any observer would agree there is no such exodus of Indian Muslims into Pakistan.

The hysterical reaction against the handful of Chinese in India, following the country's border incidents with China in October, 1962, is proof that mob passions assume dangerous and runaway dimensions when provoked. But the most poignant example, of course, is what happened at the time of partition. One can with justification expect Pakistan to show concern for Indian Muslims, by avoiding policies likely to lead to communal violence against them here. But contrary to any such concern, relations between the two countries have progressively deteriorated through the years, and though India is not entirely blameless, her leaders have come nowhere near equaling the vituperation of their counterparts in Pakistan's successive regimes. The impression Pakistan's leaders tend to create in this country, through pronouncements and policies, is of an obsessive urge to destroy India's internal stability; an aim before which even the destruction of the Muslim community in India, it seems, is considered of no great consequence.

Partition may have solved the problem of internal communal discord in India. But discord has not been eliminated, only externalized. The perpetual strife once found within the country is now found along its borders. Policies aimed at keeping a status quo of hate alive and irresponsible oratory which generates and sustains tensions have succeeded in creating an impasse between the two countries which the absence of a dynamic and courageous program of *rapprochement* has helped to perpetuate. The shrill cries of communalists and communal parties in India, which are heard as soon as someone takes the initiative in trying to break through the deadlock, are as great a deterrent to formulation of a sane policy as the brash utterances of Pakistan's leaders.

The effect of all this is to keep open wounds which are best healed. History's message is spelled out in very unambiguous terms: incitement of communal passions inevitably leads to disaster on a scale impossible to comprehend or contain. This was true centuries ago, and it once again proved itself tragically true at the time of partition. On the brighter side is the fact that once wounds heal, a sound and healthy system can function. Before the communal virus was injected into Indian politics, Hindus and Muslims were an integral part of the Indian scene. A similar situation exists today in India; and if the two countries were to make an effort, this situation might also exist between them.

NOTE: On June 5, 1966, while this book was at the printer's, the rupee was devalued by 57.9 per cent, the new official rate being 7.50 rupees to the U.S. dollar, against the former official rate of 4.76 rupees to the dollar. The old rate of exchange has been used throughout the book.

4

The Anatomy of
a Developing
Economy

Despite the traumatic experience of bloodied and tragic new realities, the mood and momentum generated by the preindependence struggle carried India through the frenzied months of 1947. Conditions slowly returned to normal, which meant that while the resettlement of over seven million refugees[1] was the Government's most pressing concern, its thoughts turned increasingly to the future.

Since the country had been partitioned along communal lines, the withdrawal of personnel from different echelons of Government had also been along communal lines, leaving behind a

[1] According to the Government of India's *First Five-Year Plan:* "Within a few months of the partition of the country in August 1947 nearly 5 million Hindus and Sikhs living in West Pakistan had to leave their homes. Under somewhat different conditions 1.5 million displaced persons migrated from East Pakistan. The disturbances of East Pakistan early in 1950 brought another million or so. According to the 1951 census about 7.5 million persons had moved into India in search of permanent homes: 4.9 million from West Pakistan and about 2.6 million from East Pakistan." (P. 642).

crazy pattern of gaps in the administrative structure. The immediate future therefore meant tying together the truncated civil and armed services and the railways system. Because of the discipline, training, confidence, and administrative experience of these services, and the effective use to which they put their talents during those difficult days, stability was once more restored.

Other major problems which faced the administration were the division of joint assets and the urgent demands of industries suddenly partitioned off from their sources of supplies.

For political leaders, Government executives, economists, and entrepreneurs, the long-term perspective meant finding out exactly what they were up against from that point on when power was relinquished by the British, and the extent to which independent India's agricultural and industrial resources needed developing to satisfy the minimal demands of an emergent people. That India is poor is a fact widely known. What had to be assessed were the true dimensions of her poverty: of malnutrition and mortality, of incredibly low income levels, of a whole people ravaged by famines, floods, filth, and disease.

The forlorn and the forsaken were not fit subjects for debate at the time the transfer of power took place. Outside the cities, in the half million villages of India, beyond the line of New Delhi's imperial vision, were the sick and the starved, like festering sores on the skin of the land. In human terms the depths of poverty at that time were beyond definition.

In more specific terms it was possible to gauge them. Consumption expenditures per person per month around that time were Rs.24.2 (about $5) in villages and Rs.31.55 (about $6.84) in towns.[2]

No farm labor family groups spent less than 80 per cent of their total budget for food, while some spent up to 87 per cent. Such groups did not have even $50 to spend per year per family on all other items of consumption. The average was $25 per year,

[2] Carl C. Taylor, Douglas Ensminger, Helen W. Johnson, Jean Joyce: *India's Roots of Democracy* (India: Orient Longmans Ltd.; 1965), p. 124.

the breakdown of this being roughly $10 for clothing, $2 for fuel, $1 for housing, the rest for all other purposes.[3]

In the sphere of education, teachers in Government schools in 1944 drew an average pay of $5 to $6 per month. In one province the average was less than $2 a month.[4]

In 1950–51 only one per cent of all young men and women from the relevant age group (17–23) were in college. In the same year over 80 per cent of all people in India could neither read nor write.[5]

As for doctors, at the time of independence in 1947 there was only one doctor for every 6,000 persons (as against the United Kingdom average of one for every 1,000). Since nearly three fourths of the doctors served in the cities, the rural average was one doctor for every 25,000 persons.

There was one nurse for every 43,000 people (the United Kingdom average being one for 300). There were only 70 to 80 women doctors in the country with special training in maternity and child welfare work, despite the fact that the majority of deaths in India were among women and children. Madras was the only province which had attempted to organize maternity and child welfare work on systematic lines. School health services did not exist.[6]

The condition of the Indian economy when freedom came was no better or worse than that of any other colony. Colonialists have never colonized for the love of it, the usual aim of the exercise being economic benefit for the former at the expense of the latter. India was no exception. Her mineral and other wealth had for over a hundred years fed the industries of Great Britain, the Indian markets proving most profitable outlets for the finished goods thus produced, with profits accruing yet again to the British business houses importing these goods into India. Some incidental benefits from this merry-go-round no doubt rubbed off

[3] Taylor et al, p. 125.
[4] Ibid., p. 146.
[5] Ibid., pp. 146, 150.
[6] Ibid., pp. 153–4.

on India: a mining industry, a railroad system designed to provide greater accessibility to sources of raw materials and new markets in the interior, ports for handling the increasing volume of passenger and freight traffic, and so on. But by and large the scheme operated solely for the profit of the paramount power.

This was the backdrop for the drama of resurgent India. As the nation's first Prime Minister, vested with immense constitutional authority, Jawaharlal Nehru's thought, precept, and personality were now to dominate the Indian scene. As Gandhi's political heir his leadership had the sanction of the Mahatma, a man who showed unique vision not only in denying himself political office but also in choosing an idealist, secularist, internationalist, and humanist to fill it. Nehru was a man deeply and emotionally involved with his people. A father figure to them for seventeen years, he shared their suffering with an intensity few men are capable of. Yet, paradoxically, their suffering was increasingly to result as much from his own ideological confusion and its imprint on Indian economic thinking as from the demagoguery and disinterest of his advisers and others who entrenched themselves around him.

In India father figures assume a special significance. Etched deep into the consciousness of a people conditioned by the disciplines of a centuries-old joint family system is the belief that the head of the family will make all major decisions, his stature demanding those decisions be respected. In a society so conditioned, there is danger of an adulated leader's pronouncements and practices receiving unquestioned acceptance. Not that dissent doesn't exist in India. It does. But once an Indian leader is able to develop rapport with the masses, their turnout to see and hear him tends to convey an impression of mass support for his ideas and leadership. Such a situation benumbs opposition by reducing it to a ridiculous scale.

Nehru's essential greatness lay in the fact that his impeccable honesty prevented him from exploiting the terrific support he received from the masses. Criticism of him can only hinge on the fact that his economic formulations were weak. His appreciation of India's need for an impregnable industrial base was correct, as proved by recent events, but the means adopted for achieving this base took their toll of state resources. In laying down the guidelines for a social and economic system based on Fabian socialist ideas he had absorbed over thirty-five years ago, he overlooked the fact that Fabian socialism (like many other early socialist parties in Britain such as the Social Democratic Federation, the Socialistic League, and the Independent Labour Party) had itself been swept away by more dynamic and practical forms of economic thinking. Fabianism died because it was unable to stand up to the realities of rapidly changing times. Shaw's manifesto in September, 1884, soon after he had joined the Fabians, stated that "the State should compete with all its might in every department of production."[7] While elsewhere evolution of political thought and recognition of the workers' rights began to render them the benefits of a dawning industrial era without recourse to aggressive participation by the state "in every department of production," in India, decades later, economic thinking was still centered around the Shavian dictum formulated over half a century ago.

The Planning Commission

Since planning of the kind current in India was the means Nehru used in his attempt to shape the country economically, industrially, and socially, it is vital for an understanding of the Indian development effort to trace the evolution of planning from the beginning.

Planning as the basis for economic development after independence was first accepted somewhat vaguely by the Indian National Congress[8] in 1931. Then, in 1938—nine years before

[7] Francis W. Coker: *Recent Political Thought* (Calcutta: The World Press Ltd.), p. 102.

[8] The political party to which Mahatma Gandhi and Jawaharlal Nehru belonged. It spearheaded the independence movement and has been in power ever since. Its name, however, changed subsequently to the All India Congress Committee.

independence—it received a shot in the arm in the form of a country-wide conference called by the Indian National Congress to find a way of dealing with the problem of economic regeneration. The outcome was the setting up of a fifteen-man National Planning Committee with Jawaharlal Nehru as its chairman. Because the Congress wished to associate all sections of thought and specialized knowledge with the development objectives, industrialists, financial experts, economists, and scientists were included on the Committee. (In amazing contrast is the fact that in 1965 the outlay on the private sector in the Fourth Plan was decided *without any prior consultation* with the spokesmen for private industry!)

The Second World War brought the work of this Committee to a standstill. The curtain opened again in 1946. This time the interim Government (headed by Nehru and set up by the British during the period prior to transfer of power) appointed an Advisory Planning Board to assess the work already done in formulating planning proposals, and to suggest objectives, priorities, and the nature of a planning machinery.

The Board's report was a sound, level-headed, and realistic document. It underscored the virtue of learning planning through actual experience. It cautioned against the pitfalls of initiating and implementing extensive controls over industrial, trading, and development activities, and emphasized the importance of a small, compact planning organization to advise the Government on its planning goals.

The Board unanimously suggested a Planning Commission of three to five members, visualizing it as a nonpolitical body free of pressures generated by political motivations and thus able to make objective recommendations. Inclined more in favor of a three-man commission, it specified the broad qualifications of its members: a chairman of eminence with experience in public affairs; one nonofficial experienced in and possessing knowledge of industry, and an official with administrative and financial experience.

But events intervened once again. Within a few months of

the Board's report, independence came to India and the interim Government gave way to the independent Governments of India and Pakistan.

In April, 1948, the new Government of India expressed its economic thinking in an Industrial Policy Resolution. It voiced concern over the problems of poverty, education, and health and affirmed the state's resolve to participate increasingly in developing public sector industries (meaning Government owned and run), and grudgingly acknowledged the role privately owned industries could play in the country's development efforts. Since this resolution, even today, largely forms the basis for the Government's policy of economic development, extracts from it provide valuable insight into the Government's subsequent actions insofar as industrial development of this country is concerned:

> . . . The problem of State participation in Industry and the conditions in which private enterprise *should be allowed to operate* must be judged in this context. There can be no doubt that the State must play a progressively active role in the development of industries, but ability to achieve the main objectives should determine the immediate extent of State responsibility and *the limits to private enterprise.* Under present conditions, the mechanism and the resources of the State may not permit it to function forthwith in Industry as widely as may be desirable. The Government of India are taking steps to remedy the situation; in particular, they are considering steps to create a body of men trained in business methods and management. They feel, however, that for some time to come, the State could contribute more quickly to the increase of national wealth by expanding its present activities wherever it is already operating and by concentrating on new units of production in other fields, rather than on acquiring and running existing units. Meanwhile, private enterprise, *properly directed and regulated,* has a valuable role to play.[9] . . .

While the inherent right of the State to acquire any existing industrial undertaking will always remain, and will be exercised whenever the public interest requires it, Government have decided

---

[9] Government of India: *The Gazette of India Extraordinary.* New Delhi, April 6, 1948; No. 1(3)–44(13)/48, p. 533.

to let existing undertakings in these fields develop *for a period of ten years,* during which they will be allowed all facilities for efficient working *and reasonable expansion.* At the end of this period, the whole matter will be reviewed and a decision taken in the light of circumstances obtaining at the time. . . .[1]

This policy statement was the first attempt at translating "the concept of *The Socialist Pattern of Society* into concrete terms."[2] It was a precursor of the preambles which were to follow in the shape of directive principles of the Planning Commission, the successive Five-Year Plans, the star speeches at Congress Party sessions, and of course the speeches of ministers, officials, party hacks, and such.

Along with countless other holy cows and sacred symbols, independent India was to acquire three more: a Planning Commission, the Five-Year Plans, and a socialistic pattern of society. The first of these made its appearance in February, 1950, the second in April, 1951. The third, the holiest of all, is still to come.

The extraordinary thing is that while talking of promoting a "rapid rise in the standard of living of the people by exploiting the latent resources of the country, increasing production and offering opportunities to all for employment in the service of the community,"[3] Government paradoxically was equally intent on imposing "limits to private enterprise." The first indications of confusion and self-defeating drift were evident in that Industrial Policy Resolution of 1948.

By what yardstick had Government measured the performance of the private sector and found it wanting? What experience of the doings of private enterprise could it have had in eight months in office?

The resolution bore the stamp of Nehru's bias against big business. It was not based on any letdown: personal or national.

[1] Ibid., p. 534.
[2] Government of India, Planning Commission: *The Planning Process.* October, 1963, p. 8.
[3] Government of India: *Gazette,* p. 533.

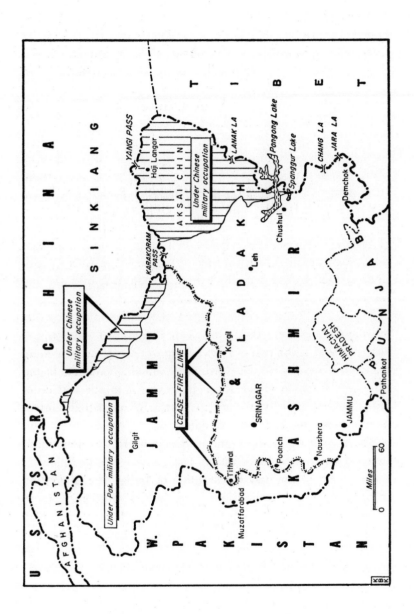

In fact the Congress Party throughout its struggle had been largely financed by big business, and if it was tainted money Congress had shown no qualms about taking it. But now, when the country needed to exploit all its resources and expand production, Government chose to announce to private industry that: (a) it could only be sure of a life span of ten years, (b) from now on it would be Government's pleasure to decide whether it should be "allowed" to operate or not, and (c) it ought to prepare itself for being "properly directed and regulated." If there was anything designed to destroy confidence and incentive, this was it. Instead of rooting out taxation loopholes and energetically enforcing respect for the country's laws, Government seemed set on rooting out the private sector! That it fancied itself capable of training management cadres and running industrial undertakings with their help within ten years showed its inexperience in these things. And if it didn't think it could take over existing industries, why issue unsettling manifestos?

But the really extraordinary aspect of this resolution was that overnight, lines were drawn between Government and private enterprise—as if the two did not belong to the same country and were not moved by similar worthy motivations. It was the beginning of a situation which through irresponsible acts and utterances has over the years led to a state of perpetual tension between Government and free enterprise.

The setting up of the Planning Commission was announced by the Government in February, 1950, in the month following the adoption of the new Constitution of India. The interesting thing is that the founding fathers of the Constitution made no provision in it for a Planning Commission. It was set up by executive action rather than constitutional sanction.[4]

There was good reason for not making constitutional provision for centralized national planning. Any imposition of the Central Government's will on the states would encroach on the federal character of the republic. It was to avoid erosion of the constitu-

[4] By a resolution of the cabinet dated March 15, 1950.

tional relationship between the Central Government and the states that provision for a super-planning body was not made in the Constitution.

In a recent analysis of this aspect, Asok Chanda, former comptroller and auditor general of India, observes:

> It was not intended that a plan or programme should be imposed on the States or that they should be induced by pressure of financial assistance to embark on schemes not directly beneficial to their economy or social needs. . . . Subsequent developments which led to the emergence of the Commission as the economic Cabinet of the country as a whole, able to impose not only policies but also allocate programmes were neither contemplated nor foreseen. The point still remains that there is no constitutional sanction behind planning. The Commission has not been constituted by parliamentary legislation on the authority of the item on "economic and social planning" in the concurrent list; nor has their creation taken away from the States power in regard to planning itself. It is only the prestige and authority of Mr. Nehru and the fact of the Congress party being in power at the Centre and in all the States that have obscured the constitutional deficiency and secured the not unoften reluctant acquiescence of the States. But this is hardly a satisfactory position, nor can it be assumed that this will hold good for all times.[5]

It is not too difficult to trace some of the above charges back to the composition of the Planning Commission. Aside from starting off at the very outset with six instead of three members, its most serious point of departure from the recommendations of the Advisory Planning Board was the high political content of its membership—three of its six members were union ministers,[6] with the Prime Minister as chairman. In consequence the stature and dominant personality of Nehru were to mold the Commis-

---

[5] Asok Chanda: *Federalism in India* (New York: The Macmillan Co.; 1956), p. 277.
[6] Strictly speaking, two of them—C. D. Deshmukh and Gulzarilal Nanda—became ministers within a few months of being appointed to the Planning Commission.

sion's advice increasingly into the kind of cast he preferred. Not only that, but the authority his chairmanship gave to the Commission enabled it to assume amazing powers and immunized it against all contrary advice and criticism. Also, "The partial identification of the Cabinet with the Commission has blurred the constitutional position and made it possible for the Commission to intervene in matters of policy and even in matters of day to day administration."[7]

The amusing aspect of Nehru's chairmanship of the Commission was the anomalous one of a man appointing himself to give himself advice. The disturbing aspect was that of the six members only one had business experience, (G. L. Mehta, who later served as ambassador to the United States). The main qualifications of the others were political and administrative; and the bemused idea that officials and party men are competent to develop large-scale industry and trade took root from that point on. No single fallacy has done more damage to India's economic condition than the absurdity of this premise.

The stacking of the Planning Commission with politicians and bureaucrats has developed into a unique precedent, as can be seen from the composition of most Government bodies and public sector undertakings which have proliferated in time. Men who through training, qualification, and experience have acquired the insight and competence necessary to develop industrial projects, have been excluded from the highest levels of policy-making in favor of officials with no such experience. There can be no other reason for this but Nehru's innate suspicion of private industry, and quite possibly his belief that officials could always be made to do his bidding. An entirely untenable hypothesis has thus over the years grown into a major bogey: that those in Government, or those who talk in season and out of greater state control over everything, are somehow more dedicated and national-minded than others. The Planning Commission, itself a product of such hypotheses, has in turn influenced the coun-

[7] Chanda, p. 281.

try's economic policies by presuming too much on the capacity of the state sector to produce results.

The other disturbing development over the years has been the Planning Commission's total indifference to informed advice. Its insistence on the size of the Fourth Five-Year Plan is one example. While further on in this book the raging controversy generated by the Fourth Plan's proposals is discussed in greater detail, the point at issue here is that what was first conceived as a small, compact advisory body now arrays itself awesomely not only against the voices of experience, but against cabinet ministers too. Even the late Prime Minister, Lal Bahadur Shastri, is said to have expressed doubts about the wisdom of the Planning Commission's proposals for the Fourth Plan. Yet the amazing complexity of the vast system it has spawned enables the Commission to dictate rather than advise, flout rather than admit fault, and scorn all opposed to it.

Who are the people who now run the Planning Commission, sixteen years after its inception? How far has it conformed to the original concept of a highly specialized body of men free from political influence, advising Government rather than making independent decisions?

The present strength of the Planning Commission is a startling figure of thirteen, of which seven are ministers of the Central Government and the rest full-time members—a far cry from the original concept of three. Though the Prime Minister continues to head it, a full-time deputy chairman, Asoka Mehta, who is also the Minister for Planning in Mrs. Gandhi's cabinet, controls the working of the Commission. Because of the power he wields, with its far-reaching consequences on the Indian economy and, in fact, on the stability of the entire country, the logical question to ask is: Is he qualified for the job? The answer is no. His background is entirely political and he is certainly not experienced in spending vast sums of money wisely and well. Yet the amount he proposes spending in the Fourth Plan is somewhere near $45,452,100,000. It is a disturbing situation when a few years in jail for participating in the civil disobedience movement, an-

other few as a labor leader, and a certain amount of economic
theorizing are considered sufficient background for heading a
mammoth organization responsible for framing schemes with profound implications for the millions in this country. Yet this is
what is happening. With the support of elements within and
without the ruling party an economic status quo is being maintained which will accelerate the country's drift toward disaster.
It is not Mr. Mehta's dedication to the economic regeneration
of India which is in doubt, nor his integrity or enthusiasm for
his work. What is open to question is his qualification for the job.

Another strange side of the situation which has developed in
time is the complete absence on the Commission's membership
roster of anyone of stature from the field of private enterprise.
This is a serious omission and one largely responsible for the
imbalance and unrealistic nature of the planning postulates.
Though some of the Commission's members have most impressive records of administrative experience and economic thinking,
their caliber and collective thought cannot compensate for the
absence of valuable experience in the working of large-scale
industrial and financial operations.

The action required of Mrs. Indira Gandhi now is much more
than introducing a member or two with business experience into
the Planning Commission. As Prime Minister of the country
and leader of the party in power, leadership is required of her,
not submission to the voices of unreason which have so far intimidated Government into adopting suicidal economic policies. If
the fountainhead of economic thought is murky, clear ideas cannot flow from it, and that is precisely the trouble with the Planning Commission.

Since India's political stability, productivity, and social objectives all depend on the excellence of her economic policies, any
diagnosis of the country's economic ills must lead to serious study
of the Commission which formulates these policies. It is the most
vital part of India's economic anatomy. Many arguments are
advanced in favor of maintaining the Commission's status quo.
They must each be examined with relentless logic, and if found

unconvincing must be changed. There is no other way the country can be pulled out of the economic morass it is in.

In impassioned oratory, self-appointed protagonists of planning proclaim that absence of it would lead to a sort of free-for-all. The objection is irrelevant. The efficacy of planned development is not in doubt. Planning megalomania is.

What then are the alternatives? Since planning is necessary, as insurance against unco-ordinated growth, what form should it take? Should it be technically competent, based on specialized knowledge and realistic appraisals free from political pressures? Or should it be an assemblage of half-developed doctrines and unreal perspectives imposed on sensitive sectors of the economy by men who lack experience in commerce and industry? Obviously, the latter would be fatal.

The need is for a long-range economic view-finder able to bring resources, requirements, and expenditures scientifically and accurately into focus. Since governments everywhere—and the Government of India is no exception—have the usual heavy complement of politicians, lobbyists, power-seekers, and patronage-touts hanging around, it is necessary to have a body of key economic advisers free from such influences.

Despite ideological differences, serious thinkers have expressed identical concern with the Commission's working. Professor D. R. Gadgil feels that

if the Planning Commission looks upon itself as a technical and advisory body, it can make an effort to make the examination of individual proposals and its total recommendations as objective as possible. On the basis of such objective recommendations, the appropriate political authority will arrive at final decisions which are practicable in political terms. However, if in one and the same authority, both aspects of the process are inextricably mixed, one or the other must suffer. Inevitably, it is the objective approach that suffers. Both the composition and the situation of the Indian Planning Commission have resulted in pushing the aspect of technical expertise and objective examination into the background. . . . What is important is that it should no longer have any executive

functions and should not be mixed up with the essentially political process of final policy-making . . . the relation of the Planning Commission with States and Ministries should be that of an
expert body engaged in brining out the implications of total policy
in relation to the activities of particular organisations or authorities
rather than an authority engaged in bargaining with, or bullying,
or being bullied by another government organisation.[8]

J. R. D. Tata, who heads one of India's biggest industrial
complexes, favors adoption of the French system of planning.
He is particularly impressed by the methodology of the French:

> The details of the Plan are worked out not by the Planning
> office itself, but by as many as 24 planning commissions and in-
> numerable working groups on which officials and non-officials,
> including farmers, employers, workers and others are represented.
> In the Fourth French Plan not less than 3,000 persons were in-
> volved in one way or another in the preparation of the Plan, in
> contrast to the practice in India where a handful of men, no doubt
> able but lacking in practical experience in industry, agriculture,
> commerce, finance and the like are exclusively entrusted with the
> task. Another admirable feature of French planning is the extent
> to which Government and the Planning Office associate public
> opinion and representatives of the private sector in the formation
> of the Plan.[9]

From the vantage position of comptroller and auditor general
of India, Asok Chanda observed the "empire-building proclivi-
ties" of the Planning Commission, which at the last count had
"500 officers, 348 clerical staff and 225 orderlies and messengers.
The Commission employs as many as 45 senior research officers,
81 research officers and 118 economic investigators. The annual
budget provision for the Commission amounts to over $2,114,164.
They now have also a multi-storied building of their own, con-

---

[8] D. R. Gadgil: *Planning and Economic Policy in India* (India: Asia Publishing House; 1965), pp. 163, 170, 171.

[9] An address by J. R. D. Tata to the Central Advisory Council of Industries (New Delhi: *Economic Times*, August 13, 1965).

structed at the cost of a few million rupees to house their establishments. There is also a marked disinclination to disband
organizations which were constituted earlier, like the land revenue division, which have outlived their usefulness."[1] Affirming
that "there still lingers faith in planning as the appropriate
instrument of orderly growth," he gives his view that

> if this faith is to be sustained and strengthened, it is essential
> that the Planning Commission should be reconstituted and stream-
> lined as recommended by the Planning Advisory Board. Their
> advisory role should be reaffirmed and their activities kept within
> the confines of matters of economic and social significance. This
> would imply that ministers should be excluded from the composi-
> tion of the Commission which should concentrate on technical
> aspects of economic planning within the framework of policy laid
> down by government, preferably, the National Development
> Council. The Council should develop into the national economic
> Cabinet. This would be in consonance with the federal concept
> of the State and give the states the feeling that they are equal
> partners in a common national endeavour.[2]

An alternative to the Planning Commission's present mono-
lithic structure is definitely needed. And the answer would seem
to lie midway between Tata's and Chanda's suggestions: a whit-
tling down of the Commission's membership to three, in accordance with the original proposals of the Advisory Planning Board,
and a planning methodology based on the French model. The
soundness of a method which commits specialist groups from the
nonofficial sector to the preparation of a development program
which will inevitably affect them all is indisputable. It will be
disputed, of course. Rabble-rousing rhetoric against any change
is inevitable. But change has to be made—swiftly, and with no-
nonsense firmness—if the promise held out by India's achievements during the early years of independence is to be fulfilled.

[1] Chanda, p. 275.
[2] Ibid., p. 294.

The Plans: Achievements and Failures

There is more to India's credit than is generally realized. For nineteen years a revolution has been under way. Since those leading it have lacked the mountain-moving madness of revolutionaries and showmanship and an understanding of how to communicate in an age of communications, little is known abroad of what India has achieved since independence. Measured by any yardstick, much has been achieved.

The number of times economic progress in India is slowed down by the capricious demands of a democratic system is not often realized. "Villagers have the vote. This is the first time an economy has tried to modernise with a huge peasant population free to save or not to save. There was no choice in Meiji Japan, none in Russia during collectivisation, none in China today. In democratic India, reorganisation in agriculture must be by the slower way of persuasion. . . . In short, the Indian government does not enjoy unfettered action in any sphere. Advance depends on what people can be persuaded to save. The hammer blows of totalitarian government cannot be used."[3]

What Indian economic planning did comprehensively and effectively against the above background was first to spell out in detail the intricate relationship between those essential components in any economy without which a country cannot hope to have a strong economic base. Development was thus viewed in a total perspective. The economic infra-structure—transport, steel, electricity, and so forth—and the agricultural and industrial sectors of the economy were boldly, in fact audaciously planned. And the results in many spheres have been spectacular.

For instance, against 4 billion kw-h of electricity generated in 1947, in 1963 over 22 billion kw-h were generated. The total mileage of roads went up from 240,000 miles in 1950–51 to 465,000 miles in 1961–2. Against 1.2 million tons of steel ingots

[3] "Growth and Government" (editorial), *The Economist* (March 26, 1960).

produced in 1947, production in 1964 was 5.9 million tons, an increase of nearly 400 per cent.

Since the staggering capacity of Indians to increase their number has largely overshadowed the country's capacity to produce food, achievements in this sphere have largely gone unnoticed. There have been many. The area under irrigation was increased from 50.0 million acres in 1948–9 to 70.1 million in 1962–3.[4] By dovetailing industry with agriculture, industrial support to the latter was provided by raising the annual manufacturing capacity of tractors to 14,500 by the end of 1965–6. In 1947 not a single tractor was being made in India. Indigenous production of fertilizers, which was more or less nonexistent in 1947, is likely to be 500 thousand tons in 1965–6.[5]

The efforts to achieve self-sufficiency in production of food, though strenuous, have been largely negated by an exploding population. Since both allocation of resources and the degree of emphasis on different segments of the economy are the responsibility of planners, failure to balance food production with an increasing population must also be their responsibility. As the importance of these two interrelated subjects—food production and population control—is fundamental to the Indian development effort, they will be examined in some detail further on.

The breakthrough in the industrial sphere has been one of the high points of postindependence India. Prior to independence, industrial growth in India was in spurts. The first, around 1850, brought cotton and jute mills, the beginnings of a railway system, and the nucleus of a mining industry. Persistent expansion of these went on till the turn of the century. Out of half a million people employed in industrial establishments in 1900 over 60 per cent were in cotton and textile mills. Another 20 per cent were employed in railway workshops and metal-working factories, and the rest were scattered throughout other industries.

4 *Eastern Economist* (Annual Number, 1965), p. 1349.
5 *Fourth Five-Year Plan, Resources, Outlays and Programmes.* National Development Council, 22nd meeting, New Delhi, September 5 and 6, 1965, p. 16.

The second spurt, between 1900 and the outbreak of the war in 1939, saw the modern steel industry started in India with the setting up by Tata of a steel mill in 1911. Some light engineering industries were also started, and textiles assumed an even more dominant position. But by and large the needs of the Indian market were met by imports, mainly from Britain. "In 1938 . . . there was hardly a machine tool industry worth the name and the country was almost entirely dependent on imports for her requirements of machinery and mill work. In the field of chemicals, too, apart from sulphuric acid and a few other chemicals which were manufactured in small quantities, the pre-war production of most lines was either non-existent or negligible."[6]

The third phase spans the years 1939–45: from the beginning of the Second World War till its end. The First World War, and then the Second, "dramatised the imbalance of India's industrial base. With normal sources of supplies cut off, or severely curtailed, Indian industry was confronted with large increases in the demands for its output and with an inability to tap the usual sources of inputs, especially of machinery and parts. Replacement needs had to be improvised, with limited gain for the plant or for its product. . . . There was a temporary stimulus to certain industries, and for the same reasons. Similarly, it became clear how dependent India's industrial structure was upon sources of equipment abroad."[7]

The new industries set up during 1939–45 included diesel engines, pumps, machine and cutting tools, cables, ferro alloys, nonferrous metals, chemicals (chlorine, caustic soda, bichromates, superphosphates, photographic chemicals, and so forth), bicycles, sewing machines. But industrial production during these years increased only by about 20 per cent.

The demented and demanding period following partition inevitably had an adverse effect on industry. The increase in indus-

[6] G. L. Bansal: "Industrial Development in India," *India 1958: Exhibition Souvenir.*

[7] Wilfred Malenbaum: *Prospects for Indian Development* (London: George Allen and Unwin Ltd.; 1962), p. 154.

trial output slowed down considerably. According to one estimate, between 1946 and 1950 it increased at the rate of a mere one per cent per annum. The determined, dogged, uphill climb toward economic independence began only after 1950. As the First Five-Year Plan was initiated in April 1951, it is a good year to use as a jumping-off point for judging the country's performance since. India's successes and failures from then on have become synonymous with the achievements and shortfalls of her plans. The table on the following page sets out the size of each plan and the relative shares of public and private sectors.

The first Plan reflected concern with agriculture. Eighteen per cent of the total outlay was earmarked for agriculture and community development, and another 21 per cent for irrigation, multipurpose irrigation and power projects, the latter having a direct bearing on agricultural production. Transport and communications, which received a sizable 24 per cent, were also of incidental, and at times direct, benefit to the agricultural effort.

There can be very little criticism of this emphasis on agriculture in the First Plan. Agriculture, after all, contributes 50 per cent to the gross national product and 70 per cent of the country's population depends on it for livelihood. Major industries like cotton, jute, and sugar depend on it for raw materials. India is one of the world's major producers of lac (an agricultural product from which lacquer is made), tea and peanuts, and chronic food shortages have clouded the fact that she is also the world's second largest producer of paddy (unmilled rice).[8]

Some sections have criticized the Government for shifting the emphasis from agriculture to heavy industry in the Second and Third plans. The recent limited war with Pakistan underscored the powerful logic of having a strong industrial base, and chances of a conflict with China in the future reinforce it. There is

[8] According to Food and Agriculture Organization estimates, China produces eighty million tons of paddy annually. India reached a production of fifty-five million tons in 1964. Rice output constitutes 66 to 70 per cent of the paddy output.

TABLE I*: *India's Four Plans in Perspective, 1951–71*

	Public Investment	Private Investment	Total Investment	Relative Size of Each Plan (First Plan = 100%)
1. First Five-Year Plan (1951–6)	$ 3,298,000,000	$ 3,802,600,000	$ 7,103,500,000	100%
2. Second Five-Year Plan (1956–61)	7,887,900,000	6,551,900,000	14,441,800,000	203%
3. Third Five-Year Plan (1961–6)	13,314,400,000	8,663,800,000	21,983,500,000	310%
4. Fourth Five-Year Plan (1966–71)	27,473,500,000	14,756,800,000	42,230,400,000	594%
5. Total (1951–71)	51,978,800,000	33,784,300,000	85,763,300,000	
6. Share of Public and Private Sectors in Total Investment	61%	39%	100%	

* All tables are based on the official statistics released by the government of India; figures are in U.S. dollars.

validity, however, in criticism of a befuddled land policy which placed misguided reformist zeal before productivity, and instead of pressing for a fair deal to the farmers and tillers, drafted incentive-destroying legislation aimed at dispossessing them. Open to question also was the Government's obsessive urge to reserve production of fertilizers for the state sector instead of getting the private sector to expand its production to the limit. Eventually, Government reversed its policy, but not before the embargo's damaging impact had been felt by the industrial sector. There were other resources wasted in the Second Plan which could have supplemented the outlay on agriculture.

First Plan

In planning and performance the First Plan was successful beyond all expectations. Table 2 on page 66 shows the progress in the agricultural sphere.

Production of food grains increased by 22 per cent, cotton by 40 per cent, jute by 27 per cent. "Of the development schemes which contributed to the rise in production during the Plan years, mention may be made of minor irrigation works which accounted for 9.5 million acres of additional irrigation and large and medium irrigation schemes which accounted for about 6.5 million acres. The total consumption of nitrogenous fertilisers in terms of ammonium sulphate increased from 275,000 tons (55,000 tons in terms of Nitrogen) in 1950–51 to 610,000 tons (122,000 tons in terms of Nitrogen) in 1955–56. The consumption of phosphatic fertilisers also increased from 43,000 tons to 78,000 tons in the same period. 1.2 million acres of land were added to the net cultivated area through land reclamation by the Central Tractor Organisation."[1]

While some industries no doubt fell short of the production figures aimed at, others zestfully overshot their targets. The list

[1] M. S. Randhawa: "Indian Agriculture—Achievements and Prospects," *India 1958: Exhibition Souvenir,* p. 31.

TABLE 2: *Agricultural Progress under the First Five-Year Plan*

Crops	Unit	1950–51	1951–2	1952–3	1953–4	1954–5	1955–6
Food Grains	Million Tons	53.0	52.0	59.2	69.8	68.1	66.9
Sugar Cane (in terms of Gur)*	" "	5.7	6.2	5.1	4.5	5.9	6.1
Oil Seeds	" "	5.2	5.0	4.8	5.4	6.4	5.7
Cotton	" Bales	2.9	3.1	3.2	3.9	4.3	4.0
Jute	" "	3.3	4.7	4.6	3.1	2.9	4.2

* A kind of raw sugar.

on the next page (which is by no means complete) shows which industries did exceed their targets and which did not.

On the whole the results at the end of the First Plan were vastly encouraging. The index of industrial production had shown a steady rise and in 1956 stood at 132.6, as against 100 in 1951. Many new industries had started during this period, the most significant being three new oil refineries set up with a total fixed investment of $88,790,000. National income had increased 18 per cent as against the 11 per cent aimed at. Prices at the end of the Plan were lower than when it began; independent analysts agreed with Government's claim that they had come down 13 per cent. The cost of living index was definitely lower in 1955–6 than in 1949–50.

The powerful pressures of poverty[1] were still in evidence everywhere, but employment was up; so was per capita income, by about 8 per cent. Whether morale was up throughout the country is a moot point, but at least the Government and its planners—encouraged by the success of their first large-scale development venture—entered the Second Plan with high hopes.

Second Plan

Their hopes, though not entirely belied, hit serious snags almost immediately. Inflationary pressures, spiraling prices, non-materialization of anticipated increases in national and per capita incomes, a rising population graph on the one hand and indifferent agricultural performance on the other, all began plaguing the Second Plan within a year of its start. To understand what caused this it is necessary to examine the Government's proposals

---

[1] In 1956 average intake of food per capita was 1,880 calories, as compared to 3,150 calories per day in the United States, 3,270 in the United Kingdom, 3,140 in Canada. (The Indian Council of Medical Research recommends a diet yielding 2,700 calories a day for adult Indians.) Per capita income in India in the same year was $59.83 per annum as against nearly $2,114 in the United States. Consumption of energy per capita in India was 1/73 of that in the United States.

TABLE 3: *Table of Industrial Targets and Actual Production during the First Plan*

Serial Number	Items	Production in 1950–51	Target for 1955–6	Level of Production Reached in 1955–6 (Approximate)
1.	Finished Steel (Million Tons)	0.99	1.68	1.32
2.	Cement (Million Tons)	2.7	4.9	4.7
3.	Fertilizers (Thousand Tons)	18	122	99
4.	Petroleum Products	—	403 (Million Gallons)	2.5 (Million Tons)
5.	Millmade Cotton Textiles (Million Meters)	3,380	4,300	4,660
6.	Sugar (Million Tons)	1.1	1.5	1.9
7.	Bicycles (Thousand Nos)	101	530	550
8.	Sewing Machines (Thousand Nos)	33	92	110
9.	Automobiles (Thousand Nos)	16.5	30	25
10.	Electric Motors (Thousand H.P.)	99	320	271
11.	Electric Fans (Thousand Nos)	194	320	280
12.	Electric Transformers (Thousand KVA)	179	450	629
13.	Caustic Soda (Thousand Tons)	11	34	37
14.	Paints and Varnishes (Thousand Tons)	29	366	344
15.	Power Alcohol (Million Liters)	23	82	45
16.	Aluminium (Thousand Tons)	3.7	12	7.6

for raising an outlay of $10,148,000,000 required for the Second Plan:

TABLE 4: *Financial Resources: Second Five-Year Plan*

(United States dollars)

1. Surplus from current revenues		$ 1,691,200,000
A. At existing (1955–6) rates of taxation	$ 739,900,000	
B. Additional taxation	951,300,000	
2. Borrowings from the public		2,536,900,000
A. Market loans	1,479,900,000	
B. Small savings	1,057,000,000	
3. Other budgetary sources		845,600,000
A. Railways contribution to the development program	317,100,000	
B. Provident funds and other deposit heads	528,500,000	
4. Resources to be raised externally		1,691,200,000
5. Deficit financing		2,536,900,000
6. Gap—to be covered by additional measures to raise domestic resources		845,600,000

Total $10,148,000,000

This plan came up against heavy weather as early as 1957. While the private sector moved briskly in raising new capital and stepping up its industrial production, investment in the public sector was less than the figure aimed at. The states also failed to contribute revenue expected from them. The inevitable result was deficit financing and consequent increase in inflationary pressures. Due to massive imports during the first three years of this Plan (mainly of capital machinery and equipment, since consumer good imports had been brought under drastic control by early 1957), the Government's foreign exchange reserves had dwindled considerably. Despite all this, during the last two years of the plan a breakthrough was achieved, due in some measure to two good monsoons, which improved agricultural output and thus the economic picture, and timely additional aid in 1958 and 1959 from the United States, Great Britain, West Germany, and

TABLE 5: *Agricultural Progress under the Second Five-Year Plan*

Crops	Unit	1956–7	1957–8	1958–9	1959–60	1960–61
Food Grains	Million Tons	69.9	64.3	77.3	75.9	81.0
Sugar Cane (in terms of Gur)	" "	7.0	7.2	7.3	8.0	10.6
Oil Seeds	" "	6.4	6.4	7.3	6.0	6.6
Cotton	" Bales	4.6	4.7	4.6	3.6	5.3
Jute	" "	4.3	4.0	5.2	4.6	4.0

Japan. Consequently, when the Plan period ended in 1960–61, the industrial index had risen from 132.6 in 1956 to 181.2. National income over these five years had increased by 20 per cent, (5 per cent less than the 25 per cent target aimed at).

Some of the more spectacular goals of the Second Plan were the setting up in the public sector of three steel plants of one million tons ingot capacity each, increase of finished steel production from 1.3 to 4.4 million tons, cement production from 4.7 to 13.2 million tons, and coal from 30 to 60 million tons per annum. In spite of serious shortfalls in some of these—finished steel production, for instance, increased to only 2.4 instead of 4.4 million tons, and cement to only 8.0 instead of 13.2 million tons—the industrial sphere recorded sustained overall progress.

TABLE 6: *Table of Industrial Targets and Actual Production during the Second Plan*

Serial No.	Items	Target for 1960–61	Level of Production Reached in 1960–61
1.	Finished Steel (Million Tons)	4.4	2.4
2.	Cement (Million Tons)	13.2	8.0
3.	Fertilizers (Thousand Tons)		
	Nitrogenous	388	99
	Phosphate	122	54
4.	Petroleum Products (Million Tons)	4.4	5.7
5.	Millmade Cotton Textiles (Million Meters)	4,890	4,650
6.	Sugar (Million Tons)	2.29	3.02
7.	Bicycles (Thousand Nos.)	1,250	1,057
8.	Sewing Machines (Thousand Nos.)	300	303
9.	Automobiles (Thousand Nos.)	57	55
10.	Electric Motors (Thousand H.P.)	1,250	734
11.	Electric Fans (Thousand Nos.)	600	1,006
12.	Electric Transformers (Million KVA)	1.50	1.39
13.	Caustic Soda (Thousand Tons)	137	101
14.	Paints and Varnishes (Thousand Tons)	61	52
15.	Power and Industrial Alcohol (Million Liters)	136	92
16.	Aluminium (Thousand Tons)	25	18

There has, understandably, been a great deal of debate on what brought this Plan to the brink of failure. Its size had a lot to do with it. In deciding on a Plan more than twice the size of the first, the planners banked on achieving a predetermined output/income figure theoretically reached by keeping it in ratio to the investment made. This kind of approach remains very much of a theory unless the Plan is framed at the district and state level by those who understand the technique of differentiating between heavy long-term investments and short-term ones which produce quick results. The Second Plan was not prepared by any such specialists, since the Planning Commission has made no effort to establish even the nucleus of a planning machinery at that level. What the Commission found on its plate were proposals scrambled up and seasoned by political and bureaucratic know-it-alls, rather than by experts. Their validity can be judged from the fact that most of these proposals had to be halved before they could be fitted into even the doubled Plan.

So the Plan's first major weakness was that its dimensions were not determined by clear terms of reference and equally clear formulations based on them, but by statistical juggling and wishful thinking. Its second was the reliance placed on resources which even in the best of circumstances could not be taken for granted: borrowing through small savings, market loans, additional taxation, and external aid, loans, and grants. In the end many of the resources failed to materialize to the extent and in the time the planners had reckoned on. Yet there was no drastic curtailing of Government expenditure as a result of that, or evidence of attempts at more economic management of investments. Even though most of the mismanaged undertakings were in the public sector, the Plan continued to be given an extraordinary degree of importance[2] in the development programing, despite absence of trained personnel to manage it. Disturbing too was its amazing capacity to mop up scarce resources.

Professor D. R. Gadgil has much to criticize in the Plan, and among the points he makes are: A surprising lack of any price policy in the Plan; insufficient knowledge of conditions in the

---

[2] While in the First Plan allocation of resources between public and private sectors was equal, in the second it was sixty to forty in favor of the former.

field on the part of planners in Delhi; and the fact that Government's much publicized plans and programs acted as a compulsion in pushing it into undertaking an unjustifiably large program. H. Venkatasubbia, on the other hand, questions the wisdom of arriving at a Plan figure by starting at the other end of the planning sequel—namely, national income—and then working the "calculations backwards in order to determine the size of the plan."[3]

Third Five-Year Plan

It is too early to say with any finality whether the Third Plan will confirm its planners' faith, or its critics' fears. It ended in March, 1966, and a balance sheet of its successes and failures will not be available before mid-1967. What is certain, though, is that its rough passage puts the final outcome in serious doubt. The Plan soon ran into head winds in the form of a population increase startlingly higher than the planners had reckoned on.[4] With thirty million more mouths to feed than anticipated, with growth in national income not expected to exceed 3.5 per cent, and with population increase placed at an all-time high of between 2.25 and 2.5 per cent, the net growth in national income for this period is not likely to exceed 1.25 per cent. That leaves a thin margin for a rise in consumption and investment. The effect of the population increase on the food situation was particularly bad, especially with an expected agricultural deficit of 8 to 10 per cent. Food imports increased from $213,500,000 in 1963–4 to $632,100,000 in 1964–5, an increase of nearly 200 per cent in one year.

The combined inflationary effect of stagnant agricultural output and a sky-rocketing population sent prices soaring. The in-

[3] H. Venkatasubbiah: *Indian Economy Since Independence* (Bombay: Asia Publishing House; 1961), p. 294.

[4] The annual population increase was 2.15 percent as against the Planning Commission's estimate of 1.2 percent. The Commission expected India's population in 1960–61 to be around 408 million, whereas the 1961 census turned up a figure of 439 million.

TABLE 7: *Agricultural Progress under the Third Plan*

Crops	Units	1960–61	1961–2	1962–3	1963–4	1965–6 Third Plan Target
Food Grains	Million Tons	81.0	81.0	78.4	79.4	100.0
Sugar Cane (in terms of Gur)	,, ,,	10.6	10.1	9.5	10.3	11.0
Oil Seeds	,, ,,	6.6	7.0	7.1	7.01	9.8
Cotton	,, Bales	5.3	4.5	5.3	5.4	7.1
Jute	,, ,,	4.0	6.4	5.4	6.0	6.2

creases recorded were 9.6 per cent in 1963–4, and 7 per cent in 1964–5; in other words, 16.6 per cent in two years.

With savings down, capital markets sluggish, imports cut drastically because of a foreign exchange position unprecedented in its seriousness (arising partly out of increasing debt repayments), industrial production dropped, too. During 1964–5 the index rose 6.4 per cent as compared to 9.1 per cent in 1963–4. The annual rate of industrial growth in the first four years of the Third Plan registered an annual increase of 7.6 per cent, against a target of 11 per cent.

The impact of all this on specific outputs is reflected in Tables 7–9, which give available figures of actual performance and likely achievements at the Third Plan's end.

TABLE 8: *Agricultural Targets and Likely Achievements in the Third Plan*

Crops	Units		Third Plan Target	Likely Achievement
Food Grains	Million Tons		100	80
Sugar Cane (in terms of Gur)	”	”	11	11
Oil Seeds	”	”	9.8	7.5
Cotton	”	Bales	7.1	6.3
Jute	”	”	6.2	6.2

It would be unfair to draw conclusions on the Third Plan before authoritative assessment has been made of it. But in Government's own words, "in terms of national income growth, the increase of 2.5 per cent per annum in the first two years of the Plan has been considerably lower than the targeted rate of growth of over 5 per cent per annum (compound). . . . Realisation of production targets appears to be lagging behind the investment effort especially in agriculture and in some industries. As the agricultural sector still contributes the largest proportionate share to national income, the trend in agricultural production vitally affects the trend in national income. . . ."[5]

[5] Reserve Bank of India: *Report on Currency and Finance for the Year 1963–64*, pp. 97, 99.

TABLE 9: *Industrial Targets and Actual as Well as Likely
Production during the Third Plan*

Serial Nos.	Item	Production in 1960–61	Target for 1965–6	Likely Achievement in 1965–6
1.	Finished Steel (Million Tons)	2.4	6.6	5.3
2.	Cement (Million Tons)	8.0	13.0	11.5
3.	Fertilizers			
	Nitrogenous	99	587	300
	Phosphatic	54	270	200
	(Thousand Tons)			
4.	Petroleum Products (Million Tons)	5.7	15.3	10.6
5.	Millmade Cotton Textiles (Million Meters)	4,650	5,300	5,300
6.	Sugar (Million Tons)	30.2	32.5	32.0
7.	Bicycles (Million Nos)	1.1	2.0	1.7
8.	Sewing Machines (Million Nos)	0.30	0.50	0.45
9.	Automobiles (Thousand Nos)	55	100	89
10.	Electric Motors (Thousand H.P.)	728	2,500	2,500
11.	Paints and Varnishes (Thousand Tons)	52	142	102
12.	Electric Transformers (33 KV and below) (Million KVA)	1.4	3.0	3.5
13.	Caustic Soda (Million Tons)	0.10	0.33	0.25
14.	Power and Industrial Alcohol (Million Liters)	92	270	270
15.	Coal (Million Tons)	55	98	67
16.	Aluminium (Thousand Tons)	18	73	80

Fourth Plan

The passionate dialogue which took place in India during 1965 was not given its edge as much by speculation on the possible outcome of the Third Plan as by the Planning Commission's outline of the Fourth Plan. The controversy centered mainly around its size. The Planning Commission's intellectual and emotional commitment to a $45,452,100,000 Plan—an expenditure seven times the size of the First Plan and over twice the size of the Third—was opposed by eminent industrialists, Members of Parliament, the press, the World Bank, and other institutions who challenged the wisdom of basing a spending spree on a non-existent rupee.

The Planning Commission not only provides the country with five-year plans but also delivers with each an implied we-dare-you-to-try-and-make-us-change-our-mind ultimatum. Since 1963 Asoka Mehta has headed the no-change phalanx. His reasoning on the size of the Fourth Plan is that it "would require tax receipts as a proportion of national income, to rise from 13 per cent to 18 per cent by the end of the Fourth Plan. Through normal growth the share of taxes would go up to 15 per cent. There is therefore the need to make the extra effort to get 3 per cent more of the rising national income as taxes, to enable us to raise our rate of savings from 10.5 per cent now to 15 per cent and our investments from the current rate of 13 per cent to 17 per cent of the national income by the end of the Fourth Plan. These efforts will not adversely affect the levels of living of the people— the extra effort has to be met from the additional incomes that will be generated. We need to channel 27 per cent of the additional income to investment, through taxation and savings drive, and the remaining 73 per cent would be available to improve our living standards."[6] And everyone would live happily ever after! If only happy endings were as easy to contrive in real life as in fairy tales.

An outsider's commentary on our planning presuppositions is of striking relevance. "Too many of their aims are contingent upon the adoption, by various sections of the Indian community, of attitudes they are exceedingly unlikely to adopt, at least to the desired and requisite extent. If people work harder, if they are less selfish, if they make the Plan their own and contribute enthusiastically and unitedly towards its achievement . . . if the Commission's programmes evoke the planned resources . . . if

[6] Address to the National Development Council, New Delhi, September 5, 1965.

there is more whole-hearted co-operation between the States and the Centre, then we shall achieve our aims: so runs the argument. . . ."[7] This is a fair summing up of the Planning Commission's "if" philosophy.

At another point the deputy chairman talks of "the hard climb this generation will have to make" to raise the level of savings from 10 per cent of the national income to 15 or 16 per cent in order to make the required investment for the plan possible. In the absence of a free competitive market generating its own price checks against an inflationary background of prices rising by 16.6 per cent in two years, talk of raising the level of savings by 5 or 6 per cent is evidence only of a disturbing break with reality.

In the view of India's distinguished industrialist J. R. D. Tata, adoption of a Five-Year Plan "of the magnitude proposed can only lead to failure and disaster. . . ." He continues:

> I remain convinced, as I believe do most people who have to deal with the practical implementation of such plans and not merely with formulating them on paper, that if we persist in going ahead with it, we shall not only fail to achieve our objectives but we shall in the process immensely aggravate our present problems. . . . Let us consider merely the question of resources: as I understand it, the $16,173,300,000 gap in resources is divided between an external resource gap of $8,456,600,000 and an internal resource gap of $7,716,700,000, the former to be filled in *entirely* by foreign aid or investment and the latter mainly by additional taxation. In regard to the external resources gap, the Plan assumes that we shall get $8,456,600,000 in aid from abroad, that is, 50 per cent more than the $5,493,200,000 we got for the Third Plan. I do not know what the basis for such an assumption is, but from all one has read in the papers in the past six months, I would imagine that we shall be lucky if we can get $6,341,200,000. In the Third Plan, repayments including interest on foreign loans amounted to $1,374,200,000 leaving a net accretion of $4,122,-600,000 for investment in new physical assets. During the Fourth Five Year Plan, repayments are estimated at $2,954,600,000.

[7] A. H. Hanson: "The Crisis of Indian Planning," *Political Quarterly*, XXXIV, 1963.

Therefore $6,341,200,000 of foreign aid leaves $3,381,300,000 for investment. Thus, with $739,900,000 less in foreign exchange, we expect to meet the needs of a Plan twice the size of the Third Plan. This does not make good sense to me even allowing for the fact that an increased availability of indigenous equipment, raw materials and components may reduce the foreign exchange needs of each project.[8]

M. R. Masani, M.P., general secretary of the Swatantra Party, was equally critical of it.

Shri Asoka Mehta, Deputy Chairman of the Planning Commission, seems to want us to accept the proposition that the bigger the Plan, the faster the progress of the country or the higher the rate of growth. He thinks we are naïve enough to fall for that kind of simplification. . . . The First Plan had an investment of $7,103,500,000, the second doubled it to $14,441,800,000, the Third target was $21,983,500,000, and now we are told that the Fourth Plan target will be $45,452,100,000. . . . If the claim is true that the bigger the Plan, the faster the progress, I presume the House will expect that while the progress during the First Plan was modest, the progress during the Second Plan was faster and during the Third Plan the national income will go up considerably. But here are the Government's figures: the First Plan had a target of an increase of 12 per cent in national income. The actual increase was 18.4 per cent—a magnificent overfulfilment by 50 per cent. Because it was a small Plan, there was an excess rise of 6.4 per cent. By the time the Second Plan, which was a bad one, came into existence, the target of increase in national income was 25 per cent. But the actual increase was only 20 per cent, and there was a shortfall of 5 per cent. Then came the Third Plan, three times as big as the First. What was the result? The target was 34 per cent increase in national income. But it is estimated that next year, it will be 23 per cent—a shortfall of 11 per cent which the planners themselves expect from this magnificent Third Plan! I don't mind saying that if this pernicious Fourth Plan which

[8] Address by J. R. D. Tata to the Central Advisory Council of Industries in New Delhi on August 13, 1965.

they are now planning is brought before the country, the short-falls will be nothing less than 50 per cent, because it is an entirely unviable plan.[9]

Accusing the Commission's deputy chairman of taking the discussion on the Plan's size "to the market place with the help and abetment from some people who ought to know better and some others who quite obviously are not qualified to talk about such matters at all," S. Mulgaokar, editor of *The Hindustan Times*, says, nobody is "against a big Plan as such. But a lot of people interested in stable progress demand quite rightly that we must give ourselves practical goals within our capacity to attain them, related to available resources and the capacity of the human material to endure strains in a free society without loss of morale."[1]

Frank Moraes, editor of *The Indian Express*, put it more bluntly: "Typical of the quantitative thinking of the Government and its bunch of economic theoreticians, masquerading as practical advisers, is the stress put in the Fourth Plan on quantity, as represented by the investment target of $45,452,100,000 irrespective of qualitative fulfilment."[2]

Very much in favor of a bigger Plan, B. G. Verghese of *The Times of India*, gave the Fourth his enthusiastic though ambiguous support: "The defeatism and inward greed of an essentially small number of individuals has affected a significant number of others to produce a general lowering of morale and consequently of moral standards." He went on to ask: How would "a little over 30 million tons of finished steel which will be available from indigenous production during the next quinquennium"[3] be used if a higher investment in engineering and construction industries was not made now? He didn't explain why the Plan had

[9] M. R. Masani in a speech in Parliament on August 23, 1965.

[1] S. Mulgaokar: "National Affairs: The High Road to Progress," *The Hindustan Times*, August 11, 1965.

[2] Frank Moraes: "The Hundred Days," *The Indian Express*, August 23, 1965.

[3] B. G. Verghese: "The National Scene: No Rebates for Caution," *The Times of India*, July 22, 1965.

to be worked backward from an arbitrary figure of 30 million tons of steel! Since the Fourth Plan target was for 16.5 million tons, the "quinquennium" argument was not of immediate relevance in any case.

After August, 1965, the intensity and urgency of the debate took on different meaning. The Indo-Pakistan fighting, which reached menacing proportions at that time, changed the entire context of the debate. In the shadow of that threat the spotlight turned on the new, greatly increased demands of defense. The position of resources changed too with the suspension of aid by the United States, the United Kingdom, and other principal aid-giving countries. The suspension jolted Indians into re-examining the basic economic postulates of the Fourth Plan. While the aid will no doubt be resumed, the concensus and concern shared by politicians, planners, economists, entrepreneurs, officials, and the public is that overdependence on foreign aid is not compatible with national honor, sound economic planning, or national security. Such an awareness is a good thing, but it remains to be seen whether the Commission's planners will show enough flexibility to modify their approach to the Fourth Plan.

At the time this book was written the shape and size of the Fourth Plan was altogether uncertain. It will be some time before the aid position becomes clear and the defense needs and plan priorities are reassessed.

If India's new Government has a clear understanding of the tasks before it, the size of the Fourth Plan will be modest and the period of the Plan will be used to develop agriculture, bring existing industries up to full production capacity, and start only those industries which are vital to the country's defense requirements. Even more important, the period could be used for drastically simplifying the tax structure and ridding the economy of the controls which are killing initiative and enterprise.

If the new Government lacks understanding of the tasks before it and allows itself to be influenced, as its predecessors were, by the Planning Commission's megalomania, then the economic difficulties will become critical.

Since in the ultimate analysis agriculture will play a pivotal role in India's economic breakthrough, it is fortunate that the food and agriculture portfolio in Mrs. Gandhi's cabinet is held by a very dynamic man. Chances are that a determined bid will be made to achieve self-sufficiency in food during the Fourth Plan. If it succeeds it could well be the take-off point for the Indian economy.

Food: The Continuing Crisis

Man first cultivated cereal crops about ten thousand years ago. He selected wheats from the mountain grasses in the mountains of Afghanistan, Anatolia, and Abyssinia—the earliest cradles of civilization. In the mountainous areas extending from Afghanistan to Caucasus originated the bread wheats, rye, oil seeds, onions, plums, pears, peaches, apples, almonds, walnuts, grapes, strawberries, and Asiatic cotton. From these high regions emerged in due course the river valley civilizations of Egypt, Mesopotamia, Sind, and Punjab. The country extending from the mountains of northeastern India to southern and central China is the home of tea, soybeans, and citrus fruits, while the Indo-Malayan area produces bananas, coconuts, sugar cane and mangoes. Rice also originated here, possibly about the same time as in the Philippines. In India its earliest cultivation was in the eastern state of Orissa, thirty-five hundred years ago. There is evidence of settled village and urban life in India as early as 3000 B.C. Then came the Aryans with their iron plows and bullocks to drive them. Their main cereal was barley. Millet and sorghum came to India from Africa, and grapes were brought from Iraq and Afghanistan by the Muslim invaders in A.D. 1300. In the seventeenth century, from the New World, came tobacco, peanuts, potato, sweet potato, and maize. In the eighteenth century the British brought tea, litchi, and loquat from China, and cabbage and cauliflower from Europe. Planting of American cottons began in the first half of the nineteenth century in Pun-

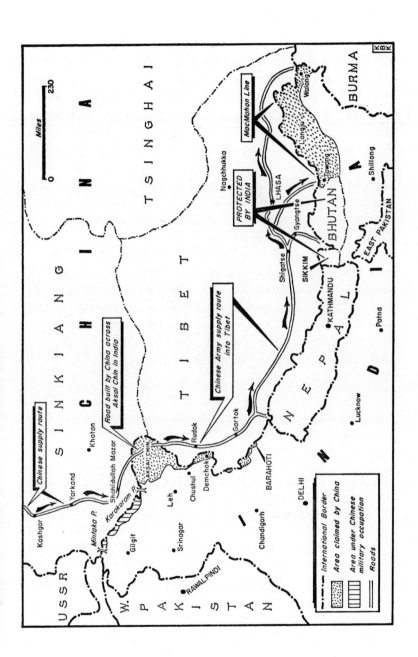

jab, Gujarat, and Uttar Pradesh. The earliest irrigation system in India was built in the second century A.D.[4]

What stands out harshly against this gracefully unfolding story of agricultural evolution in India is the fact that today over 70 per cent of Indians cannot indulge themselves in two proper meals a day. Even more tragic is the perilous rate at which India's population is increasing. The result of this interaction of insufficiency of food and an ever-increasing number of mouths to be fed is a continuing crisis which clouds other achievements and cancels out hopes of a breakthrough until solutions are found to these two deterrents on the Indian economy.

The problem of hunger in India originated many more than eighteen years ago. But in the changed circumstances of today, with a sovereign people steering their own ship of state, it is poignant to realize how low the subsistence level is at which sizable sections of the population live. There is a degree of shame too in the endless reliance on food imports. On the other hand, in the context of history and the chronic record of famines in India, the country has in one way or another succeeded in staving off famines since 1947.

From the beginning of the eleventh century to the end of the seventeenth there were fourteen famines, alomst all of which were confined to small local areas. The frequency of famines showed a disconcerting increase in the nineteenth century. In a period of about 90 years, from 1765 when the British East India Company took over the Diwani of Bengal to 1858, the country experienced twelve famines and four severe scarcities. The frequency of famines showed a still further increase during the first fifty years of the direct rule of India by Britain. Between 1860 and 1908, famine or scarcity prevailed in one part of the country or the other, in twenty out of the total of forty-nine years.[5] Some of the

[4] Excerpted from the research paper, "The Role of Science and Technology in Indian Agriculture," compiled by M. S. Randhawa for a symposium held under the auspices of the Indian Parliamentary Scientific Committee, New Delhi, September 15, 1963.

[5] B. M. Bhatia: *Famines in India* (India: Asia Publishing House; 1963), pp. 7, 8.

more devastating famines during this period were: The Orissa famine in 1865–6, number of deaths 1.3 million;[6] the famine of 1896–7 affecting almost the entire country, during which the normal death rate was exceeded by 4.5 million;[7] and the Bengal famine of 1943, which claimed a million and a half lives.[8]

The causes of famines in India have varied. Some of them are as valid today as they were then; others, viewed in present-day context, have an air of unreality about them. For instance, during the period from 1860 to 1880, famines were mainly due to heavy shipments of food out of India, with a consequent fall in the surplus stocks within the country. The value of rice, wheat, and other grains exported increased from $7,600,000 in 1859–60 to $20,900,000 in 1879–80.[9] The exporting of food grains is a circumstance vastly different from the one which currently faces India.

In other respects too a strange reversal of events has taken place. By about the 1880's it had become clear that the food shortages in the provinces of Bombay, Madras, and Central Provinces were a result of planting more cash crops than food grains.

Estimates recently completed for British India show yield per acre for food grains alone at about the same level in the 1940s as fifty years earlier. For all other crops together, the yield per acre had increased by more than 50 per cent over this period. . . . Indeed, the British devoted much effort to the introduction and promotion of specialty crops . . . production of indigo, teas, cotton, jute, and sugar was encouraged . . . these new investments and developments in rural India . . . showed results in expanded output and in improved yields for specialised crops and areas, but they did not to any noticeable extent stimulate agricultural improvement on a broad front.[1]

[6] Report of Indian Famine Commission of 1880.
[7] Bhatia, p. 242.
[8] *Famine Enquiry Commission Report on Bengal* (1945).
[9] Statistical Tables of British India.
[1] Malenbaum, pp. 125, 129, 130.

The process has since turned full cycle. Now food deficit states are turning increasingly to planting grains in place of cash crops because of the food zones[2] and the compulsions they impose on the deficit states. The inevitable result will be a decline in foreign exchange earnings due to steadily decreasing production of cash crops like cotton, jute, and tea, that are available for export, quite apart from the cataclysmic effect of such barriers on the unity and cohesiveness of the country.

Between the two illogical extremes of exports at any cost during the time of the British, and the present mortgaging of India's own agricultural development to Public Law 480[3] imports, much ground has been covered, most of it in the eighteen years since independence.

TABLE 10: *Land Cultivation*

	1950–51	1961–2
Net area sown	293.4 Million Acres	334.0 Million Acres
Area sown more than once	32.5 "	50.6 "
Total cropped area	325.9 "	384.6 "
Net area irrigated	51.5 "	61.2 "
Area irrigated more than once	4.3 "	8.9 "
Gross area irrigated	55.7 "	70.1 "

But despite the ground covered and the fact that in ten years the gross irrigated area has increased from 55 million to 70 mil-

[2] The creation of food zones in the country is one of the most retrograde steps taken by independent India. Established by the Central Government under pressure from the states, the zones prescribe boundaries, which coincide with existing state boundaries, across which transport of food grains is prohibited by law. There can be no free transport of food grains, for instance, from the surplus state of Punjab to its deficit neighbor Uttar Pradesh. The rationale is that grain prices would increase in surplus states if farmers sold them freely to scarcity states. In effect, there would be a general leveling-off of prices throughout the country, midway between the present extremes. But since the idea of keeping food prices low in their own states is politically attractive to the party bosses in the surplus zones, the Central Government has proved too weak to do away with this step.

[3] Food grains sold to India by the United States under its Public Law 480, against payment in Indian rupees.

lion acres, and the consumption of fertilizers from 7,000 tons in 1947 to 700,000 tons in 1965, food shortages exist, and continue to exercise the minds of consumers and planners alike. Nor is the immediate outlook very encouraging; in fact, it is bleak at its best.

With India's population increasing at the rate of 10 million every year (some estimates place this figure at 12 million), the Agricultural Prices Commission estimates the need for additional food grains at 3 million tons a year to meet the demands of this increase alone. The figure of 3 million tons, added to the existing annual deficit of 6.3 million tons[4] means another 9 million tons per year to reach self-sufficiency.

To meet this need the Planning Commission has set an annual target of 125 million tons of food grains by the end of the Fourth Plan in 1971. An increase, in other words, of nearly 40 million tons annually over the 1965 figures. The population in that year is expected to reach 550 million!

Can India give its agricultural economy the impetus needed to reach the self-sufficiency stage by 1971? Will it be able to galvanize this sector, whose performance so far poorly reflects the dramatic breakthroughs it is capable of? Those dramatic possibilities *are* great. The 120,000 square miles Gangetic basin and the 40,000 square miles of the Indus basin have the potential between them to provide enough food to feed the world. The question is: Will India be able to feed herself within the next five years?

For a country in which 70 per cent of the population draws its livelihood from agriculture, India has proved strangely lackadaisical in dealing with the problem in its totality. Symbolic of this is the fact that half of the growth of food output[5] since independence has been due to more land being brought under cultivation and not to doubling or tripling yields per acre by making technology available to agriculture. Since obviously there

[4] Government of India, Ministry of Finance: *India—Pocket Book of Information* (1965), p. 42.

[5] As pointed out later, this is due entirely to some increase in rice yields.

is a limit to how much additional land can be brought under cultivation, future output growth must largely be from increases in yield. However, there is little in the record on Indian agriculture to give much hope that the yield per acre is likely to go up, unless drastic measures are introduced speedily. Even though it tends to strike too pessimistic a note the observation is valid if seen in the light of past performance.

TABLE 11: *Increase in Yield per Acre*

1950–51 to 1963–4

All Crops	1.58%
Food Grains	1.65%
Nonfood Grains	1.01%
Cereals	2.01%
Pulses	None
Rice	2.19%
Wheat	None
Gram	None
Peanuts	None
Sugar Cane	1.14%
Cotton	2.89%
Jute	None

(Trend lines fitted to agricultural indices maintained by the Ministry of Food and Agriculture.)

What is obvious from the above is that even the modest increase in the yield of food grains in this period is almost entirely due to a higher rice yield. Wheat yields have not improved over a time span of fourteen years.

If examined with relentless logic the main causes of what can at best be called India's indifferent performance are: lack of modern fertilizers, arbitrary ceilings on land holdings imposed by unrealistic land policies, and inadequate rural incentives. Between them they affect the quantity and quality of India's entire agricultural activity.

Foremost among the innovations in modern agriculture are nitrogenous fertilizers. But in India the centuries-old practice of vegetable and animal manuring went right on through the years after the Industrial Revolution until independence. To a limited extent a start was made on the use of fertilizers seventy years ago, but it was mainly for cash crops like tea and coffee. Food grains were touched in passing only during the war as a part of British India's effort to make up food supplies from territories lost in the war. In effect awareness of fertilizer was nonexistent in 1947. Seen from this angle progress has been praiseworthy in the years since.

TABLE 12*

Year	Produced	Nitrogen Imported	Distributed
1952–3	53,067	44,294	57,822
1953–4	52,905	19,346	89,287
1954–5	68,478	19,984	94,810
1955–6	76,859	53,379	107,494
1956–7	78,788	56,768	123,054
1957–8	81,144	110,100	149,019
1958–9	80,766	97,540	171,988
1959–60	83,694	142,335	229,326
1960–61	111,987	171,926	211,685
1961–2	154,326	142,920	291,536
1962–3	194,194	229,462	360,033
1963–4	219,072	235,676	425,872

* SOURCE: "Fertiliser Statistics 1963–64," The Fertiliser Association of India, p. 83; figures are in tons.

But if India's consumption is set against the use of fertilizers in other countries, the tremendous leeway still to be made up becomes disconcertingly clear.

The possibility of making India one of the major granaries of the region need not be discounted on her performance so far. The prospect has to be judged with the idea that lessons learned during this waiting period will be exploited in the future. In a careful and fairly conservative appreciation of India's food crises, a Ford Foundation team in its report said: "If approximately 10 million acres of rice in the selected areas were provided with the

TABLE 13: *Production and Consumption of Nitrogen and Crop Yields in Different Countries—1962–3*

Social Number	Name of Country	Total Production of Nitrogen (Thousand Tons)	Total Consumption of Nitrogen (Thousand Tons)	Per Hectare Consumption of Nitrogen (Kg)	Yield per Hectare (Quintals)			
					Rice	Wheat	Maize	Barley
1.	Netherlands	443.6	294.0	293.4	—	45.5	38.0	43.0
2.	China (Taiwan)	77.2	111.1	127.8	33.1	20.7	19.8	8.8
3.	Japan	1151.4	669.3	110.2	52.6	25.4	24.8	28.2
4.	West Germany	1198.5	768.1	90.8	—	34.8	33.6	32.9
5.	U.A.R.	106.5	191.9*	74.7	58.4	26.1	26.0	26.5
6.	U.K.	513.4	541.0	73.9	—	43.5	—	36.4
7.	East Germany	338.2	253.2*	50.1	—	31.1	19.6	31.1
8.	France	745.9	682.8	31.8	41.9	30.7	21.5	27.6
9.	Czechoslovakia	153.9	146.2*	27.0	—	24.5	23.5	25.3
10.	Italy	722.4	375.1	24.1	54.9	20.9	29.1	13.6
11.	U.S.A.	3427.0	3434.0	18.5	41.8	16.9	40.3	18.9
12.	U.S.S.R.	1170.0	1070.0	4.7	21.9	10.5	16.6	12.0
13.	India	194.2	360.0	2.7	13.8	8.9	9.9	9.5
14.	Pakistan	24.2	62.1*	2.4	15.1	8.2	10.6	6.1
15.	Australia	22.6	37.1	1.1	60.8	12.5	22.2	11.4

* For 1961–2

necessary facilities such as fertiliser (30 lbs. nitrogen and 30 lbs. phosphoric acid per acre), improved seed, pesticides, irrigation, improved cultural practices, etc., it is estimated that an increase of about 2.5 million tons could be obtained."[6] Considering that the present area under rice cultivation alone is 87.7 million acres, the dramatic rewards of increasing yields are self-evident.

Dr. M. S. Randhawa, one of India's outstanding administrators, says it should "be borne in mind that 25 per cent of the increase in crop yields in U. S. A. in the past 12 years has been due to the use of fertilisers." He is of the view that with the judicious use of ten million tons of different chemical fertilizers, India "would increase crop production by 70 million tons of food grains . . . the total gross irrigated area in India is 69.2 million acres, and the area under assured rainfall is about 82 million acres. Present production of fertilisers is adequate for only 11 million acres. This indicates that in the Fourth Plan the production of fertilisers should be 3.65 million tons. . . ."[7]

How much is the production actually expected to be? If 1965 is any precursor of 1971 (the year the Fourth Plan ends), the prospect is gloomy. In 1965, 300,000 tons were produced as against a target of 800,000. C. R. Ranganathan, executive director of the Fertilizer Association of India, attributes the shortfall to "slowness in completion of projects, due in turn to slowness in decision making. The terrific dilatoriness in decision making results directly from the the cumbersome and time consuming procedures.[8] Insofar as 1971 is concerned, however, even with the most determined efforts and optimistic forecasts, production of more than 1.5 million tons cannot be anticipated. One of the reasons for this is that fertilizer plants require extraordinarily high investments with, moreover, a foreign exchange component of 40 per cent. This leaves India with two worrisome alternatives: either to abandon its agricultural targets goals, or to give this sec-

---

[6] The Agricultural Production Team sponsored by the Ford Foundation: *Report on India's Food Crisis and Steps To Meet It;* April, 1959, p. 181.

[7] Randhawa: "The Role of Science and Technology in Indian Agriculture."

[8] In an interview with the author.

tor very high priority in its foreign exchange spending during the Fourth Plan.

One of the major challenges the administration faces is to find resources for raising fertilizer production fourfold during the Fourth Plan. The Food Ministry's demands can always be scaled down by the Finance Ministry, but the hard fact is beginning to be gradually realized that such scaling down will be at a grave cost.

The other modern inputs—pesticides, improved irrigation facilities, better crop varieties, efficient extension services—are all receiving attention; yet the lurking suspicion remains that

> On the side of administration proper, from the highest level downwards, agriculture gets priority in rhetoric but rarely in fact. No Chief Minister in a State has taken over the portfolio of agriculture. The bright entrants to the civil service head for the old levers of power—finance—or for the new prestige areas like industry. No young Collector (the highest official in a District) is likely to feel that his promotion will depend absolutely on raising productivity per acre in his district. The urgency and interest are simply not there. So the known solutions do not receive that charge of administrative drive and follow-through which would help them to get off the ground.[9]

Barbara Ward Jackson feels further that the phenomenon "can be seen in agriculture all round the world." She continues:

> The Cinderella of the colonial services, it has entered Independence in a depressed state and has not yet recovered. The better methods may be known but the men to carry them out are lacking. The result is all too often a tolerant acceptance in agriculture of slackness and inefficiencies which on the railways, in public works, in industry would lead to courts of enquiry . . . agriculture is handicapped by administrative shortcomings and by some lack of

[9] Barbara Ward: *The Plan under Pressure* (Bombay: Asia Publishing House; 1963), pp. 37, 38.

appreciation of the profit motive or, if you like, of incentives. In fact, I believe that many of the particular problems can be only understood in the light of these two wider issues.[1]

Disincentives proliferate in the Indian agricultural system. Almost all states have land ceilings fixed by law to limit the number of irrigated acres individuals can own, usually around thirty acres. In special categories, such as orchids, virtually any acreage of land can be owned. But if an owner puts in a tube-well (a well consisting of a long iron pipe and a pump) his holding is promptly treated as irrigated land, obliging him to sell it to avoid infringing the law. Thousands of acres are lying unirrigated in the Punjab because of the land ceiling policy. Such an anomaly, a serious impediment to land development, reflects the thinking of men who make land laws but have little experience of farming practices.

The extraordinary drive of the North Indian and his love for his land are evidenced by the fact that though a water pump priced at $528 sells for $1,056 in the Punjab and a Massey-Ferguson tractor for $5,284 against a normal price of $3,171, farmers there are queued up to buy them (the normal waiting period is approximately two years), despite their limited resources and the equally limited acreage of land they own. Consequently, it is not their supposed backwardness or ignorance which is responsible for the agricultural slack. The administration grants licenses for manufacture of fans, refrigerators, and air conditioners but limits production of water pumps, tractors, spare parts, and well-drilling equipment. The farmer is no longer the problem. The problem now is the administration and its attitude toward agriculture. Until that changes, until legal instrumentalities are introduced to provide security to landlords and tenants alike, until land laws are rationalized, farms use tractors, fertilizers are fed to the soil, plants protected with pesticides, and prices stabilized through intelligent operation of the laws of pro-

[1] Ibid., p. 36.

duction and demand, the agricultural effort will produce no dramatic results.

Catapulted into the political limelight because of their suspension by the United States as a result of the Indo-Pakistan conflict of September, 1965, wheat supplies to India under Public Law 480 had recently been the subject of fierce controversy. While American timing was undoubtedly poor, the Indian reaction was no less so. It was felt, possibly with considerable justification, that the stoppage was aimed at pressing India into a settlement with Pakistan. Overlooked in the mood of resentment was the fact that India's wheat purchases in the United States (large-scale purchases began in 1956–57), motivated by the need to build reserve stocks, were used instead to keep food prices depressed, a policy the United States could not be considered obliged to support indefinitely. Despite the current popular practice of give and take for political gains, India is not entitled to the Public Law 480 supplies for all time. But the assumption is made at the highest level that this is so. Public Law 480 has become an addiction, a quick way to euphoria, a game of catch-as-catch-can in which the food minister who catches the most from Washington receives the maximum acclaim.

India's continuing dependence on Public Law 480 wheat has cast a shadow on her great development efforts. The irony lies in the extent of the gap which has to be filled to reach self-sufficiency—barely 8 to 10 per cent of India's total food needs.[2] More serious than the damage to India's image is the effect Public Law 480 imports have had on domestic agricultural prices. By marketing the imports instead of using them as reserves against monsoon failures and possible famines, the Government has tried to keep food prices low. This has eroded rural incentives and diverted more farm incomes into trucks, shops, houses, and other external investments. The effect of this trend on internal

[2] In 1964–5, an unusually good crop year, India consumed 93 million tons of food grains, of which 88.4 million tons were produced within the country.

investments in agriculture will be increasingly evident unless the illogic of present policies is realized and they are ruthlessly reversed.

Devastating in its dimensions is the annual waste which drains away 10 to 15 per cent of India's output of food grains. If the rich in India have great talent "for conspicuous consumption" because "this is a part of the world where the rich are rarely discreet,"[3] the talent for waste exists at all levels. The most conservative observers say that the waste of food grains is ten million tons a year.

The causes of this staggering loss in an agricultural economy lamentably lagging behind its production schedules are a mixture of the bizarre and the banal. The population of rats in India, according to the National Institute of Communicable Diseases, is 2,400 million—approximately five to six times the number of human beings. They are known to have a preference for seeds and ripe heads of grain, and their annual intake is anybody's guess. The Institute feels they eat twenty-six million tons of cereals a year, an estimate which reflects a healthy respect for their appetite but is probably correct. Anyway, there is no denying the fact that, between them, rats, monkeys, and cows annually destroy at least as much food grains as the country imports each year to meeet its deficit. Defective handling, careless transportation, and inadequate warehousing account, in all likelihood, for equally lavish figures of waste.[4]

The point then is this: India's potential for agricultural development is incredible. But the catalyst is still to be found. It certainly will not be found in a methodology which ignores the needs, rights, and hopes of farmers and farm laborers. If empty academicism is substituted for incentive, the results will be

[3] John Kenneth Galbraith: "Rival Economic Theories in India," *Foreign Affairs*, XXXVI, 1957–8.
[4] The hundred or so Central Government and 550 state warehouses store no more than one million tons of food grains between them, out of nearly five to six million tons that must be stored.

chaotic. And that would be tragic since the ground has been broken, a good deal of headway made, and a blow struck for the farmer's liberation from the fearsome inhibitions of the past. "The model of the villager as a tradition-constrained, obstinate man of limited aspirations, uninterested in progress, that dominates so much of social science writing on India is not tenable in the face of experience. The accusation that agriculture is backward because the villager has not turned to scientific farming can only be answered by asking for more science from the researchers, and more inputs from the planner."[5]

The Great Debate: Private versus Public Sector

The essential difference between India and most other countries which attained independence in the years after the last war is that India was not a dark continent waking up to new and wondrous realities. It had trained engineers, scientists, and professional men, a network of roads and railways, a hydroelectric and irrigation system, and above all an industrial base which, thought it needed to diversify and enlarge its manufacturing potential many times over, was nonetheless a valuable and promising national asset. India in 1947 was producing about 3,400 million meters of millmade cotton cloth, 1.3 million tons of pig iron and 0.9 million tons of finished steel; 30 million tons of coal were being mined, 4,073 million kw-h of electricity generated, and about 1.5 million tons of cement manufactured. Though as much as a third of private investment in Indian industry was in foreign hands—and understandably so—two-thirds were in Indian hands. This represented experience and involvement in the mechanics of industrial development. It is against this background that India's special position in the context of other emerging nations must be seen.

Since even Indians are self-conscious about comparing India's

[5] W. David Hopper: "The Mainsprings of Agricultural Growth," memorial lecture prepared for the 18th Annual Conference of the India Society of Agricultural Statistics, January 28–30, 1965.

development potential with Germany's or Japan's after the last war, doubts on the part of the outsiders are understandable. These are usually due to one of three reasons: insufficient knowledge, a biased assessment, or a genuine conviction. According to one British view,

> Marshall Aid to Western Europe is often instanced in support of the potential value of foreign aid to poor countries. Its experience suggests the exact reverse. The economies of Western Europe had to be *restored* while those of present recipients have to be *developed*. Western Europe after 1945 was demonstrably lacking in capital resources, but not in human resources and market opportunities. Its people had the attitudes, motivations and institutions favourable to development, as was clear from the past performance of Western Europe for centuries before the second world war. As opposed to restoration, the actual building up of resources involves the development of qualities, attitudes, arrangements, and institutions all of which promote the effective use of the resources generated. When, however, the increase in the resources takes the form of the inflow of free or subsidised resources from abroad, this suggests that suitable human qualities and institutions or market opportunities are locally absent; and the valuable process of generating these is certainly lost. . . . India is perhaps the most familiar example. Thirteen years after the beginning of Western aid and the inception of the five-year plans the country experienced in 1964–65 the most acute of its recurrent, almost annual, food and foreign exchange crises.[6]

Arguments of this kind, with their disturbing tendency to generalize, miseducate responsible public opinion abroad by projecting before it a distorted image of newly independent peoples. Even more unfortunate is the fact that on the surface the projections appear informed and fair-minded.

The use of the phrase "poor countries" is itself misleading. Western Europe, in its devastated form in the years following the last war, was poor too, but not so in terms of the talents

[6] P. T. Bauer: "Does Foreign Aid Really Help?" *Daily Telegraph,* August 2, 1965.

needed to rehabilitate it, or *restore* it, as Bauer would like to see it put. India also emerged materially and spiritually poor from her colonial experience, an experience no less devastating than Europe's in terms of its ravaging effect on the minds and traditions of men. The difference was in time span. Europe's travail was short term; India's was of much longer duration. Like Europe, India had a fund of talent available on which to draw in the postindependence years; the scale of what had to be done, however, was much greater. The difference between Western Europe and India which Bauer fails to mention was not so much a difference of motivations and human qualities as the simple fact that while Europe received Marshall Aid at an annual per capita figure of $13.25, India receives aid at the per capita rate of 80 cents. If "the past performance of Western Europe for centuries before the second World War" (an exaggeration, at best) was qualitatively and otherwise of a high order, India also for centuries had been a many-splendored country of vast wealth and sophistication, and a great many extraordinary trading and technical skills. Bauer tries to clinch his argument by equating it with India's "familiar" example. Since the "familiar" impression abroad of India is one of a country bogged down in a morass of economic difficulties, Bauer's type of reporting, instead of correcting that impression and placing it in perspective, reinforces it further. By not detailing the factors responsible for a country's ills his statements feed familiar misconceptions even more. How familiar are people abroad, for instance, with the fact that India's three Five-Year-Plans—with their capital-intensive investments— are the very reason for the country's foreign exchange crises? They are not a result of spending or import sprees but of trade deficits resulting from heavy purchases abroad of capital plant. Western aid to India has not been give-away aid. It has mainly been in the form of loans, and initially[7] formed only a small percentage of the resources mobilized by India for her three Five-Year Plans (though with the increase in the size of

[7] External financing constituted one tenth of the First Plan's total requirements.

each Plan, external financing progressively increased as well). The fact that in the Third Plan interest on foreign loans amounted to $1,374,200,000 and that repayments during the Fourth Plan will be $2,954,600,000 is indicative that India is paying dearly for the aid it is getting and that the foreign exchange crises are symptoms of growth and not of a wasting economy.

Bauer's passing swipe at India's "recurrent, almost annual" food crises is unfair and misleading. He talks of food shortages thirteen years after Western aid began. Even during a hundred years of rule the British administration in India was unable to meet the country's food needs, and they were the needs of a population only two thirds the size of the present population. In fact some of the most devastating famines in India took place at the turn of this century.[8] India's inability to close the food gap, even after thirteen years of Western aid, is in consequence not so horrifying a lapse. And Western aid in any event has never constituted—even at its best—more than 8 to 10 per cent of India's annual food requirements.

Of relevance to this particular debate is Russia's agricultural experience: fifty years after the revolution and despite staggering scientific and technological achievements, Russia has yet to find a solution to her agricultural muddle. This in a society able to initiate and implement drastic controls and with the problem confined to producing food for a population of 226 million as against India's 480 million. The record of the Chinese is even worse. Despite barefaced and strident claims, Peking bought 187 million bushels from Canada in 1963. Then, in October, 1965, sixteen years after the Communists took over, China and Canada signed one of the biggest wheat sale contracts in history—223.8 million bushels, valued at $403 million. Whatever claims China

[8] The famine of 1896–7 affected every part of the country to some extent and the normal death rate was exceeded by 4.5 million. There was a famine in Uttar Pradesh in 1907–8, and the Bengal famine in 1943; and between 1908–42 there were numerous scarcity areas in India. See Bhatia, pp. 64, 242, 324.

and her apologists may make for her achievements in other fields, insofar as food productivity is concerned the extent of her achievements can be gauged from her increasing reliance on food supplies from abroad. Russia, incidentally, also shopped in Canada for 230 million bushels of wheat in 1963.

The object of this somewhat extended comparison is not to condone India's reliance on food imports—an aspect which is severely dealt with in this book—but to show that import of a small part of a country's food needs for thirteen years is no criterion for doubting all other qualifications of "poor countries."

The constituents of India's tragedy are not, as Bauer makes them out to be, lack of human qualities and motivations (though some allowance has to be made for the not-so-motivated in a society the size of India's); they result, on the contrary, from a politically overmotivated society in which seemingly inspired groups pursue different ideological goals to the ultimate detriment of national interests. That, in fact, has been the worrisome weakness of India's development effort, and nowhere has the ideological pull been more evident than in the great debate over the public and private sectors.

It would be wrong to say that by and large the attitude of those in authority is anti-business. If that were so, private enterprise by now would be on its way out. It is nowhere near that. The hostility is toward free enterprise; and in consequence what policy-framers have done—through design or default—is to create a forbidding and complex industrial policy framework with a maze of rules, regulations, and controls which, because they can be interpreted in many ways, bewilder and discourage the small entrepreneur, and provide unique opportunity for an influential inner group of Indian industrialists to create industrial empires of magnificent size. These empires are a result of rigid industrial licensing laws which encourage monopolies and discourage competition and free enterprise. On the periphery of this inner group is the alert and aggressive new entrepreneur who has access to the politicians and an all-powerful officialdom which frames, interprets, and enforces laws and is able to provide valuable industrial and import licenses almost at will.

The system in India today is anti-entrepreneurial, yet serves the interests of a certain brand of big business. In the sum total it provides the rich with more riches, and the poor with fewer social benefits. There are neither subsidies to contain depressions, nor a policy for containing inflation. There is no social security, unemployment benefits, or social insurance. Under present conditions these latter three are almost impossible in a country as populated and poor as India. But there is nothing to prevent the framing of an industrial policy which through increasing productivity could bring these very valid social safeguards nearer.

The hypnotic influence of the socialist-pattern-of-society mystique has made even intelligent Indians overlook the fact that only a healthy, vigorous system can provide real social benefits, and the building up of such a social system is possible only through bold, not restrictive, economic policies. But because, ironically, the Indian leadership after independence invoked the considerable powers of the state to prevent sane development of private effort, India's performance has never fully reflected the nation's capabilities. This then is what needs to be criticized: this placing of curbs on natural talents and motivations in a futile attempt to impose unreal perspectives on very real possibilities. A standard way of obscuring economic issues is to impose confused political thought on them. In India this process has led to the birth of a myth: the myth that the public sector is a cure-all for the country's economic ills. No reasonable body of opinion can question the wisdom of state control over railways, public utilities, atomic energy plants, and strategic defense industries. But grave misgivings—and all too often they prove well-founded —do arise at the prospect of the Government in the role of an operator of every conceivable type of trading and manufacturing activity, from the manufacturing of antibiotics and newsprint to inn-keeping. There would be nothing wrong with the Government in this role if human nature were to change completely and men were to take to working with as gnawing a concern for

public monies as they do for their own; if profits of state undertakings equaled those of well-run private firms; if their accounts
too were open to public audit and all indirect subsidies and overt
omissions open to searching scrutiny; if interest rates on monies
raised by the public sector were the same as those charged the
private sector by banking institutions; if registrars of companies
had the power to force badly run state undertakings into liquida-
tion as they do private companies; and if the state undertakings
sold on the criterion of quality in highly competitive markets at
a profit—then and only then would one have no misgivings about
the public sector's capabilities. Till such time it is impossible to
have confidence in the dubious doings of the public sector with
its great appetite for large investments, to which, as a branch of
the state, it has continuous access, but for which it is unable to
guarantee even a fraction of the return the private sector can.

There can be no other valid yardstick with which to measure
the capabilities of the public sector except an analysis of its performance so far.

In its Seventh Report, published in April, 1965, the Indian
Parliament's Committee of Public Undertakings made a series of
observations and recommendations on the working of the National Coal Development Corporation, among which was this
excerpt:

> The profitability of the Corporation is even less than 50% of
> that in the private sector and is about 36% of what was envisaged
> by the Coal Price Revision Committee. The Committee consider
> that the present return on the capital and net worth of the Corpo-
> ration is very low. In their various reports the Committee have
> emphasised the need for the public undertakings securing a reason-
> able return on the capital invested in them . . . the Managing
> Director agreed during evidence that the *percentage of net profits
> to capital employed should normally be ten.* . . .

The report found, however, that *"the maximum rate of profitability reached by the Corporation during the last four years was*

in 1960–61, when the percentage of gross profits to total capital stood at 2.8." Another independent observer concluded that

> The coal record is disastrous—simply because coal enters into everything. The private sector, hampered until recently by unrealistic prices and by prohibitions on any expansion beyond contiguous areas, has nonetheless fulfilled its plan target. The entire shortfall—of over seven million tons in 1960–1—has occurred in the public sector:

TABLE 14: *Coal Output (Million Tons)*

	Target for 1960	Actual Output 1960–61	Actual Output 1961–2
Private Sector	44	44.4	45.6
Public Sector	16	10.4	8.7
Total	60	54.8	54.3

> Yet, in the Third Plan, this faltering public sector is allotted the bigger rate of increase and a larger share of capital with which to achieve it. Meanwhile, the coal bottleneck is more responsible than any other single factor for the general slow-down. . . .[9]

The South's prestigious newspaper *The Hindu*, commenting on the Union Finance Minister's prebudget economic survey at the beginning of 1965, wrote; "The investment in Central public enterprises, excluding the railways, ports, posts, and telegraphs, amounts to $1,740,000,000 in 1962–3 and over $803,300,000 of additional investment has been made in the past two years, bringing the total by the end of the current year to nearly $2,536,900,000. That the net profit expected to accrue to the Government in the current year from this enormous investment will be barely $1,060,000 shows how much the performance of public enterprises lags behind the original promise and expectations."[1] The above works out to a profitability ratio of 0.4 per cent on the investment!

[9] Ward, p. 46.
[1] "Performance of Public Enterprise," *The Hindu*, February 27, 1965.

A study of the workings of the Heavy Electrical Project (a Government of India undertaking), delineates overstaffing as one of many reasons for such poor returns. In a total staff strength of about 15,000, the responsibilities are shared in the ratio of *150 persons for administration and supervision to every 100 working on the machines.* In similar industries elsewhere there would be three or four men working on the machines or work tables for each man in the office. The result of this top-heavy management is that while a 75 MVA transformer made by Heavy Electricals costs $211,400 an imported equivalent costs $148,000. Not all of the extra cost is attributable to overstaffing, but it is symptomatic of bad business judgment which is reflected in poor planning, ineffective stock control, idle plants, and indifference to quality control.

The crux of the private versus public sector controversy, therefore, is not the fear of the state making heavy inroads into private enterprise, but the propriety of the state diverting scarce resources into economically unsound investments. Impoverished economies with few resources and great commitments can least afford that. The public sector's lack of commercial experience and managerial and trading skills, its practice of dispersing industries for political instead of practical reasons, overcentralized control, and disinclination to delegate financial authority, make continued diversion of funds into the economically unsound public sector wilful and indefensible.

The assumption that social aspirations can be met only through state enterprise ignores the experience of countries whose rapid economic growth—a result of extensive mobilization of *all* economic resources—has led to wide social benefits faster than other systems. India's economic resources are vast, but doctrinal inhibitions have so far prevented them from being fully mobilized. The most conservative estimates value gold hoarded by the public at $31,712,400,000, an amount close to the entire investment in the first three Plans. Undeclared monetized wealth matches and perhaps exceeds this figure. This tremendous resource lies idle not only because incentives do not exist, but because private wealth is under constant threat of expropriation—a threat which has no real substance and is thus all the more regrettable.

The state sector, as a substitute for the private, has proved less a stimulus to than a drag on the Indian economy. It has not competed fiercely or fairly in the market place but has worked from a privileged position, protected by monopolies and such devices. It has made the consumer a helpless onlooker and progressively reduced his freedom of choice. It has prevented the private sector from being efficient so that its own inefficiencies may remain unnoticed. India cannot afford this. It cannot afford to ignore the experience of countries which have successfully tried the entrepreneurial system, nor can it experiment on the present extravagant scale with what are at best only academic ideas. The current spell of economic stagnation in India results from high prices, which in turn result from shortages that would not exist in a highly competitive and free economy. This continuing denial of freedom to the economy, in the sense of not allowing new industries to develop freely or existing ones to function without being constantly harried by needless limitations and controls, can only be through deliberate political design. And the object of such a design, as always in politics, is power. The appeal of slogans and the spectacular promises they hold out is wide in countries where poverty is a way of life. But they are unrealistic because they promise what their political philosophies are unable to provide in practice. What they do provide politicians with is political influence, and through it, power. Since the public is generally unaware of this detail, it applauds the attractive idea of doing away with the entrepreneur, and his partial eclipse makes the promise of economic breakthrough recede even further.

This is the vicious circle which has to be broken. It will take courage to do it, to dislodge men who have dominated policy for over a decade and a half. But the courageous qualities of the post-Shastri leadership can be judged by no other yardstick.

The Taxation Tangle

India's wildly improbable tax policies have done her as much damage as the wasteful public sector. The slowdown in the country's rate of economic growth in 1964 and 1965 was a consequence of such policies which, instead of sustaining and stimulating, deterred industrial progress. Paradoxically, mopping up rather than creating wealth was given greater importance. Instead of helping income to grow first, and then taxing them hard, an extraordinarily complex and crippling tax structure destroyed incentives, discouraged enterprise, encouraged evasion, and often caused more to be spent on the collection effort than was actually collected.

N. A. Palkhivala, India's outstanding authority on tax laws, warned last year that the "radiating potencies of direct taxes go far beyond mere raising of revenue. They propel tendencies which can obstruct effort, deflect enterprise, constrict growth, and prevent the bringing forth of 'the maximum gifts of each for the fullest employment of all.' Bad economics may temporarily be good politics, but politics should be behind a fiscal law, and not in front of it."[2]

In India, however, politics do cloud most issues of national importance, and tax policies are no exception. The glamour of high taxes in poor countries lies in their assured support by the millions outside the pale of direct taxes, who can be counted upon to applaud measures seemingly enacted for their benefit. The disastrous dimensions of the present tax structure are thus provided by politically attractive though economically unsound policies and equally awesome enforcement regulations. These two have slowed down what could well have been a vigorous, assertive, momentous move forward into industrial self-sufficiency.

Mr. Palkhivala, in his recent book *The Highest Taxed Nation,*

[2] N. A. Palkhivala: *The Highest Taxed Nation* (Bombay: P. C. Manaktala and Sons Private Ltd.; 1965), p. 6.

selects nine countries which top the heavily taxed list, and through comparison shows India as the heaviest taxed of all as far as direct taxes are concerned. In the following table he compares taxes on individual incomes.

TABLE 15

Country	Maximum Rate of Personal Property Tax (Per Cent)	Maximum Rate of Personal Income Tax (Per Cent)	Equivalent in Dollars of the Amount of Income at Which the Maximum Rate of Income Tax Applies
Austria	0.75	55.46*	$79,238.90
Ceylon	2.00	80.00	8,879.49
Denmark	2.30	50.00 (As explained below)	58,300.22
Finland	2.00†	44.00	62,917.54
Germany	1.00	53.00	55,392.17
India	2.50	82.50 (Earned Income)	21,141.64 (Earned Income)
		88.125 (Unearned Income)	15,856.23 (Unearned Income)
Netherlands	0.50	70.50	41,714.58
Norway	1.75‡	60.00	12,220.50
Sweden	1.80	65.00	29,191.34

* Includes 18 per cent surcharge for equalization of burden taxes.
† In addition there is a supplementary tax imposed in 1964.
‡ Personal property tax is also levied by local authorities. Rates vary from district to district. The maximum rate is 0.4 per cent.

Austria, Germany, and the Netherlands levy a personal property tax at a flat rate. The above rates are therefore the flat rates in the case of those countries.

In Denmark there is a theoretical maximum marginal rate of income tax of 105 per cent. But the previous year's income tax may be deducted like any other deductible expense in the computation of taxable income, and consequently the effective maximum rate will almost never exceed 50 per cent for a taxpayer with a stable income.

In actual practice the aggregate of personal property tax and income tax on individuals in India can and does exceed their entire income! This happens in no other country. While it is no doubt an extreme instance of the illogic with which India's tax policy is peppered, there are other equally devastating built-in provisions in it. "So far as middle classes are concerned, the most savage tax is the Gift-tax which has been stepped up from 10 per cent to 40 per cent at $31,712.47 in 1964. No other nation in the world levies a tax on generosity at such a lacerating rate at that level."[3] The queer side of the arbitrarily high gift tax is its disproportion in relation to estate duty, which is complementary to it in the sense that the former is largely meant to prevent evasion of the latter. This disproportion works this way in practice: "If a man of moderate means dies, the rate of Estate Duty applicable would be 8 per cent at the slab between $31,712.45 and $42,-283.29. But if he made a gift in his lifetime, the State would tax his benevolence at the rate of 40 per cent at the same slab. In other words, at the same slab Gift-tax is 400 per cent higher than Estate Duty."[4] Admittedly, the gift tax is designed also to prevent distribution of wealth in the guise of gifts, but by pitching it at a level outside of reason, what it obviously encourages is evasion in one form or the other.

What continuously feeds industry's great appetite for capital in the United States is the ordinary public's constant involvement and interest in investment opportunities in new industrial enterprises. Tax laws in India, in practice if not through precept, discourage this. Not only are the corporate profits out of which dividends are declared fully taxed in the hands of the company—and this tax on companies can exceed 70 per cent—but individuals too are taxed on their dividend incomes at rates which can reach 88 per cent (since dividends are treated as unearned income).[5] A combination of corporate tax and an individual shareholder's income tax can at times take away up to 96 per cent

[3] Palkhivala, pp. 22, 27–8.
[4] Ibid., p. 23.
[5] Prior to 1959 credit was given to shareholders for tax paid by the company.

of the profits earned by a company. Tax evasion thus becomes inevitable. So another aspect of this unhappy situation is that since no company is likely to declare dividends on undeclared profits, these profits swell the personal wealth of insiders in the corporate sector, while the public's income through dividends continues to decrease steadily. Aided and abetted by a tangle of taxes, a monopoly situation, and a favorable climate of scarcities and controls, the rich are getting richer and the poor, poorer.

In the United Kingdom, Germany, and Japan, to take a few examples, legal provisions prevent double taxation of dividends. In the United Kingdom, for instance, till last year a 38.75 per cent tax was deducted at source out of the dividends paid out by a company to its shareholders, and the company—which was taxed at 53.75 per cent—was given credit for this amount. In other words, the company paid only 15 per cent on profits distributed as dividends. This system was abolished in 1965 but companies are now taxed at a maximum rate of only 45 per cent. The United States, Germany, and Japan have equally sensible safeguards which stimulate and encourage the flow of investment. The discouraging effect of the unreasonable provisions in the Indian tax system is to inhibit the flow of badly needed funds into industry. The result: while industrial schemes starve for capital, a good deal of the national wealth remains unutilized for lack of investment incentives.

Then again, probably no other country except India levies both a personal property tax and a higher rate of tax on unearned incomes. The cumulative effect of the resultant tax burden is to encourage—in fact, require—tax evasion, as obviously few individuals are likely to pay more by way of taxes than what they have actually earned. The more scrupulous ones would rather curb their entrepreneurial talents than compromise their ethics.

Since it is the corporate sector which creates a great deal of national wealth in free economies, its functioning ought to be free from factors inimical to its healthy development. Yet the restrictive taxes imposed on it, far from encouraging development, are seriously stunting its natural growth. A stunningly high tax incidence and a maze of complex variants (income tax, surtax, dividend tax, bonus-share tax, plus a series of surcharges) leave the corporate sector with unsavory alternatives: either to evade paying some of the taxes, which is possible in an involved system of endless permutations and combinations, or to continue investing capital in new ventures regardless of the incentive-destroying aspects. Responsible companies are increasingly disinclined to do this.

The following table shows at what a formidable rate corporate incomes in India are taxed in comparison to other countries.

TABLE 16*

Country	Maximum Rate (Per Cent)	Remarks
Algeria	54	Includes 20% surcharge for northern areas only.
Argentina	38.36	Plus emergency surcharge of 20% on profits over $50,000.
Australia	42.5	On excess over £A5,000 for a resident public company. Different rates for other types of companies.
Austria	51.92	
Belgium	30	25% on undistributed profits under one million francs.
Canada	50	Includes old age security tax. 21% on first $35,000. Only 15% on undistributed profits.
Chile	30	On nonresident companies, 50%.
Denmark	44	As 50% of previous year's tax and 50% of taxable income (or 2½% of paid-up capital, if lower) are deductible, effective rate is lower.
Egypt	18.7	Includes 1.7% additional tax for municipalities.
Finland	45	
France	50	
Germany	51	On distributed profits only 15%. On nonresident companies, 49%.

Country	Maximum Rate (Per Cent)	Remarks
Greece	38.2	
Hong Kong	12.5	
India	74	
Indonesia	52.5	On profits over R2.5 million. Slab scale starting at 40%. Further reduced rates (from 25%) for certain new undertaking for 5 years.
Iran	50	On profits over 6 million rials. Slab scale starting at 12%.
Iraq	45	On profits over 15,000 dinars. Slab scale starting at 10%.
Ireland	31.67	Plus 15% profits tax on profits over £2,500.
Israel	46	
Italy	36.22	Plus company tax of 15% of profits exceeding 6% of net worth.
Japan	38	33% on profits under 3 million yen. On distributed income 26%.
Kenya	37.5	Includes 17.5% corporation tax.
Korea	25	On profits over 1 million hwan, reduced rate 20%.
Kuwait	50	On profits exceeding 375,000 dinars. Slab scale starting at 5%.
Laos	25	20% on distributed profits.
Lebanon	42	Plus 10% surcharge for municipalities. Slab scales start at 5%; top rate applies to profits over £750,000.
Malaya	40	
New Zealand	50	
Netherlands	45	
Norway	30	Plus communal taxes of 19 to 23%.
Pakistan	50	On nonresident companies, 60%.
Philippines	30	On first 100,000 pesos, 22%; on nonresident companies, 30%.
Portugal	33	
Saudi Arabia	40	On profits over 1,000,000 riyals. Slab scale of 20–30–35%.

Country	Maximum Rate (Per Cent)	Remarks
Singapore	40	
South Africa	30	
Spain	30	Plus municipal surcharge of up to approximately 10%; plus 4% additional tax deductible from profits.
Sudan	50	On profits over S£525,000. Slab scale starting at 15%.
Switzerland	—	Federal tax of 7.2% plus varying rates (usually dependent on ratio of profits to capital) in each of the cantons.
Sweden	40	Plus local tax of 10–17% deductible from profits.
Syria	49	On profits over S£750,000. Slab scale starting at 8.5%.
Tanzania	37.5	Includes 17.5% corporation tax.
Thailand	25	
Tunisia	24.2	Plus 15% municipal surcharge.
Turkey	20	Plus income tax on behalf of shareholders of 20% of net profits after deduction of corporation tax, equals 16%.
Uganda	37.5	Includes 17.5% corporation tax.
U.K.	53.75	Only 15% on distributed profits.
U.S.A.	48	
Vietnam	24	

* SOURCE: Palkhivala, pp. 34–7.

The strange thing about India's tax policy is that while in other countries the highest rate at which resident companies are taxed is 54 per cent (generally it remains below 50 per cent and in many cases it is appreciably lower), India taxes Indian concerns at a confiscatory rate of tax normally reserved for foreign firms exploiting a country's natural resources.[6]

[6] A case in point is that of Chile: it taxes resident companies at 30 per cent and nonresident at 50 per cent, but in case of two United States corporations mining copper—and thus depleting the country's mineral wealth—it imposes a confiscatory tax of 66 per cent.

Even more devastating than the level of taxation is the paralyzing unpredictability of tax laws. The Income Tax Act of 1961, was amended four times within thirteen months, and on the first day it was in force eleven of its provisions were amended. Then followed a welter of other amendments through the Taxation Laws (Amendment) Act, 1962; Finance Act, 1963; Income Tax (Amendment) Act, 1963; Central Board of Revenue Act, 1963; Finance Act, 1964; Direct Taxes (Amendment) Act, 1964 (which also amended the Estate Duty Act and the Expenditure Tax Act); and finally the Income Tax (Amendment) Ordinance, 1965. In the Finance Act, 1964, one sharp-eyed observer found 68 insertions, 51 substitutions, and 22 omissions in the section dealing with direct taxes. It is doubtful if any other country with established institutions and a rule of law places as great a strain on them and on its legal system as India does by first instituting indifferently reasoned-out measures and then amending them in season and out.

These incentive-killing measures built into India's tax policies are a principal cause of the tragic slowdown in her determined drive toward economic takeoff. Because these policies are in the main framed by men obsessed with theory and confused political thought they have an unreal air about them. Quite unreal, for example, is the assumption that the Government can keep on increasing taxes without crippling the economy just because in the last ten years its tax revenues have increased fivefold against only a 50 per cent rise in national income.

There is always a safe limit beyond which measures cannot be taken without grave risk. That limit in India has been exceeded, and no boom or even an appreciable degree of economic resurgence is possible unless, along with other far-reaching measures, tax reductions are also carried out in dead earnest. Tremendous resistance to any such move can be expected, both from economists who have helped spawn the present tax system and from assorted political groups who consider high taxes a convenient way of discomfiting the business world. These groups remain curiously insensitive to the fact that undesirable elements in business benefit most from irrational tax policies.

Here too the Government's responsibility to the nation can take it in no other direction except toward rationalization of a vital but vilely mismanaged sphere. The steps it takes will be indicative of the extent to which the leadership is willing to go to weed out its wayward advisers, with their confused fiscal and economic perspectives.

In normal times things could have been left to right themselves, but the times have been far from normal for India since Indo-Pakistan hostilities heated up in September, 1965. Simultaneously, it became clear that India could no longer afford to rely indefinitely on aid-givers. The widespread resentment resulting from that awareness ought to crystalize into a national resolve to make the Indian economy self-sustaining. But resolves in themselves don't create self-generating economies. The right conditions have to be created for them. In India they need to be created soon, because at stake are both the domestic stability of India and the prospects of her emerging as a power of consequence in Asian affairs.

5
Foreign Affairs: Policy and Perspectives

If the political actions which paved the way for India's freedom were influenced by the thinking of many men, independent India's foreign policy bore the imprint of one man's thought—Jawaharlal Nehru's. It was tempered by his brilliance and his compromises. For a clear perspective of history credit must go to him, and if at times his policies seemed to lack compassion for victims of some international intrigues, as in the cases of Tibet and Hungary, the blame—if blame can be apportioned at all in these things—must be his too. But by blaming lightly people are less than fair to those who at the time of making great decisions have little choice.

The demands which national self-interest makes on statesmen are harsh, and decisions made in deference to these demands may seem unpalatable to those whose interests are not so directly involved. Nehru's mild stand on the Chinese invasion of Tibet was unpalatable to many countries, but the imperatives of India's internal weaknesses and preoccupations permitted him no other.

America's involvement in Vietnam is equally unpalatable to many, but is necessitated by the dictates of United States interests in the region.

In circumstances of this kind it is very difficult to say who is right or who is wrong, since many algebraic equations can be made out of such situations. India's foreign policy since independence has baffled many countries, irritated an even greater number, and left most others none the wiser. But in the early years it was shaped by fairly clear concepts of goals. If it seemed to falter, this was due less to a confusion of basic concepts than to human foibles, and it was sometimes due to failure to give the concepts concrete shape. In more recent years, however, it has tended to drift.

To understand the shaping of India's foreign policy one has to go way back to the 1920's when serious thinking on foreign affairs on the part of the Indian National Congress first became evident. In 1920 Gandhi wrote: "Common lot no less than territorial homogeneity and cultural affinity is bringing the Asiatic races wonderfully together, and they now seem determined to take their fullest share in world politics."[1]

From that point on the stand of the Congress became specific on the important world issues of the day, though prior to this it had passionately protested against the breakup of the Turkish empire, and after the 1914–18 war had demanded representation at the Peace Conference. In May, 1921, Gandhi made it clear he would openly dissuade the people of India from helping Britain should she decide to go to war with Afghanistan. A month later Congress ratified a similar policy for Indians in the event of hostilities breaking out between Britain and Turkey, and in 1924 it extended its sympathy to the Egyptians and identified itself with their struggle against the British. The significance of these manifestations was far-reaching, because they were more than mere attempts at embarrassing the British. The core of an idea for conducting India's future relations with Asian countries

[1] *Young India*, April 14, 1920.

had begun to take shape. Consequently, what India incorporated in its foreign policy a quarter of a century later was not something it thought up at short notice to checkmate Western or other alliances. It was a final fruition after a long progression of ideas and attitudes, tempered by closely observing the tumultous days the world went through between the two world wars.

In February, 1927, the International Congress Against Imperialism was held in Brussels—a stimulating experience for Indians at a time when they were increasingly identifying themselves with world affairs. One of the members of the presidium of that Congress was Jawarharlal Nehru, who, along with Einstein, Sun Yat-sen, and Romain Rolland, was elected honorary president of the Permanent League Against Imperialism. Brussels afforded Nehru a superb opportunity to come in contact with leaders of nationalist movements in Asian and African countries that was to prove invigorating and invaluable. His presidential address to the Indian National Congress in 1928 gave clear indication of the Indian nationalist movement's growing interest in world affairs. Though the Congress ended its contact with the League in 1931, mainly because the latter took up an irrevocable Communist position, the involvement of Congress leaders with their counterparts abroad was now an important factor in their deliberations. As an expression of the importance it attached to international relations, the Indian National Congress set up its own foreign division in 1928.

In the 1930's, Palestine occupied a dead-center position on the international stage, and it stayed there for almost two decades. First the Indian National Congress and then the Government of India after independence took a ringside seat from which to observe the deepening conflict. India's support went to the Arabs in their stand on the Palestine issue. Since the policy toward Palestine was conceived by the leaders of the Indian nationalist movement at a time when they were outside the sanctums of power, the fact that their stand remained unchanged after coming to power reflects careful deliberation in the first place. What is of interest is that by the 1930's Indian thinking, despite lack of opportunity to follow it through because of British rule, was beginning to come to close grips with international issues. Of one thing there could be little doubt: there were few isolationists among the Indian leaders.

This, then, was the backdrop to independent India's approach to international events. Possibly out of ignorance, perhaps due to indifferent interpretation on her part, the depth or dimensions of India's foreign policy have seldom been correctly gauged abroad. Her stand on various international developments, at least in the early postindependence years, was never impulsive. If at times it alienated other powers, the alienation was due to divergent interests, definitely not to immaturity or insufficient thought.

Nonalignment

The one single aspect of India's foreign policy which has most baffled people—particularly Americans—has been her policy of nonalignment. In the present context this definition has lost much of its original meaning. India was nonaligned in relation to the two opposing world powers, America and Russia. Since now these powers are themselves aligned in their hostility to China, India, because of her own confrontation with China, is obviously in alignment with them. But habits die hard. Not only do Indians still fancy themselves nonaligned, but many in the West still resent India's past policy of nonalignment.

Did this policy deserve the condemnatory comment it received at a time when it had great validity, or the hostility which formed a backlash to that comment? Styles Bridges, chairman of the Republican Policy Committee, apparently felt it did. "I lose patience with those nations which are not only neutralist in their military position, but insist on neutralism in their moral position. I know of no worse offender in this regard than Nehru, who proclaims himself the moralist of Asia. I know of no instance of Nehru having openly and sincerely taken the side of freedom and democracy. I know only of weasel words and idle pretensions."[2] To the American labor leader George Meany, Nehru and Tito were not neutral "but aides and allies of Communism."[3] *The New York Times* saw Nehru "so closely aligned with Soviet policies as to put a large question mark behind his professed neutrality."[4] Dulles defined nonalignment as "an immoral and short-sighted conception."[5]

It was strange for Americans to ridicule India's neutral policies considering that the United States had followed a similar policy from 1789 to 1917. Even after the First World War she withdrew into an isolationist phase which lasted till after the start of the Second World War.

For a fair judgment on nonalignment, however, one must first know something of the motives which made India adopt it as a fulcrum of her foreign policy. Though the chill had set in around April, 1946, the Cold War actually started in early 1947, the year of India's independence. But *as early as 1946,* Nehru, as member for External Affairs in the interim Government, had spelled out the objectives of the future foreign policy of India:

> In the sphere of foreign affairs, India will follow an independent policy, keeping away from the power politics of groups aligned with or against the other. . . . India will uphold the principle of freedom for the dependent peoples and will oppose racial discrimination wherever it may appear. . . . Towards the United Nations, India's attitude is that of whole-hearted co-operation and unreserved adherence, in both spirit and letter, to the Charter governing it. To that end, India will participate fully in its various activities and endeavour to play that role in its councils to which her geographical position, population and contribution towards peaceful progress entitle her.[6]

[2] *Congressional Record, Proceedings and Debates of 84th Congress,* 2nd Sess. (June 27, 1956), CII, 107, 10,039.

[3] M. S. Rajan: *India in World Affairs, 1954–56* (India: Asia Publishing House; 1964), p. 258.

[4] Ibid.

[5] Ibid., p. 259.

[6] *The Indian Annual Register, 1946* (Calcutta: Annual Register Office; 1947), II, 252–3.

This statement was made against the background of an inexorable drift which was carrying the big powers toward uncompromising positions whose openly avowed purpose was the destruction of each other. To India, free at last from the traumatic experience of a long spell of darkness, nonalignment seemed the only hope of survival. If the West expected Nehru to scuttle the future of his country by taking sides in an uncertain contest over which threatening war clouds already hung low, it was asking too much of him. No responsible leader, placed in a similar position, could have taken a very different decision. Nehru realized that even without actively participating in a war, India's unstable economy, cut off by a global conflict from the men, machines, and materials of technically advanced countries, would collapse, bringing in its wake devastation and despair. In the circumstances his best contribution to his country could be to stay out of alignments which seemed headed for conflict, and use the advantageous position of the nonaligned to build up India.

The tragedy lies in the fact that in the Dullesian days of confrontation and fierce rhetoric, policies aimed at national survival were considered immoral. There was great sincerity on Nehru's part, and a hope that he would be understood abroad, when he offered an explanation of his policies in an address to Parliament on March 17, 1950:

> About 150 years ago, the Western world was breaking up on account of all kinds of imperial and revolutionary wars. Having achieved independence by breaking off from the British empire, the U. S. was naturally affected by these upheavals; nevertheless it avoided being involved in the chaotic situation of Europe—although doubtless it had its particular sympathies—because that was the natural thing for a nation in that state of affairs to do. Now this analogy, although it may not be particularly good in the circumstances of today, has a bearing, and I wish to point out that for a country that has newly attained freedom and independence, this is the natural policy to pursue.

Where did India's sympathies lie? Practical considerations aside, India could not even emotionally have honestly taken sides. Her intellectuals, exposed to the political and economic thinking of the West, had a great affinity for it. Her Constitution, as well as other institutions, were modeled on Western lines. "The House knows," said Nehru when addressing the Constituent Assembly on May 16, 1949, "that inevitably, during the past century and more, all kinds of contacts have arisen between England and this country . . . here I am the patent example of these contacts, speaking in the Honourable House in the English language. . . . The fact remains that we are functioning here under certain rules and regulations for which the model has been the British Constitution . . . our educational apparatus has been influenced. Largely our military apparatus has been influenced and it has grown up naturally as something rather like the British Army. . . ."

Yet clouding all this was a recently liberated people's deep mistrust of imperialist practices "arising largely from the imperialist character of most Western powers. There was an obvious snag in the argument that the Western nations were trying to preserve democracy against totalitarian Communism, as long as they themselves sought to retain colonies. The evils of Western imperialism were much more real and obvious to these nations than those of some distant bugbear of Communist totalitarianism. . . . Moreover, postwar American policy was largely concerned with the fight against Communism which, in practice, led to the virtual appeasement of Western imperialism and condemnation, not infrequently, of genuine nationalist movements as Communist or Communist-inspired."[7]

Despite the condemnation by the West of policies whose aim was to avoid involvement in conflicts which threatened national survival, and despite Russia's more sympathetic and understanding attitude in the late 1950's, India has, if anything, been closer to the West. Western diplomacy cannot take all the credit for

[7] *Outside the Contest*, ed. K. P. Karunakaran (New Delhi: People's Publishing House; 1963), pp. 27-8.

this. Even though the frequency with which misunderstandings cropped up did no credit to either side, Nehru's approach to international affairs contributed much toward keeping India's relations with the West stable.

In contrast to the hostility and hardened attitudes which India's policy of nonalignment was evoking in the West (despite continuously expanding assistance to India's development schemes), Russia's attitude toward India began to thaw in 1953. India's efforts in effecting the Korean armistice had been duly noted in Moscow. That war helped veer the attention of the world to the vortex forming in Asia, one result of which was that the expanding might of the Communist world assumed new urgency in United States thinking. The formation of the Southeast Asia Treaty Organization (SEATO), and Pakistan's inclusion in it, strained India's relations with the United States. Her resentment and apprehension at the military hardware America pledged to Pakistan coincided with Russia's mounting concern at the increasing armed presence of the United States in Asia.

Russia's basic policy change, aimed at taking it closer to India in the coming years, dates from after Stalin's death in March, 1953. Till then Russia's relations with India had been cool, patently uncordial, and often suspicious. Relations between Russia and China, on the other hand, were extremely cordial, and the two agreed in their dislike of India. To Russia, Gandhi was a Western lackey; to China, Nehru was "a running dog of imperialism." With a disconcertingly uninhibited, decidedly militaristic power bloc near his borders, Nehru had little option but to strain every nerve to prevent India from becoming the setting for a showdown between her hostile neighbors and the Western powers. The situation was rendered more complex by the fact that the two major Communist states were far from reconciled to the manner in which India had attained freedom: peaceful transfer of power was an anathema to their concept of revolutionary violence. Also, a sharp sense of urgency was given by the series of Communist-inspired revolts in southern India which threatened Nehru's government. Any open alliance with the

West on Nehru's part would therefore only have added fuel to the revolutionary fires within the country.

The power of the two major states in the Communist camp was further demonstrated by Russia's first atomic explosion in 1949 and the victories of the Chinese armies over the United Nations forces in Korea under General MacArthur. These were significant pointers to the power packed by the Communist punch and were not ignored by Nehru in formulating his policy of nonalignment.

There was thus little wrong with Nehru's refusal to relinquish India's right to take an independent stand on international issues. But nonalignment was merely a policy for national survival, not a moral concept. Where Nehru went wrong was in tiresomely treating it as such and in continually irritating those at the receiving end of India's self-righteous moralizing. While India's nonalignment proved useful when opposing powers needed an intermediary, it was unnecessary to peddle it in the international market place on every occasion. It may have been politically irresistible. But it was diplomatically indiscreet. In practical terms it meant little, and it led to a self-hypnosis which brought India close to convincing herself that her policy of nonalignment stood in the way of a global conflict. Since it did nothing of the sort—the big countries taking decisions which suited their power objectives—it frequently caused India to reprimand others at some cost to herself, and tended to make her foreign policy resistent, rather than resilient, to change.

If in pursuit of the nonaligned ideal Nehru was insensitive to American feelings, the United States was equally so in its openly expressed doubts on India's foreign policy. After all, it was clear to the United States throughout that India's nonalignment at no point implied Communism at home. Despite these obvious facts diplomacy of a high order was lacking on both sides. Nothing else can explain why Indo-United States relations have so often hit a new low, even though American aid to India since independence is ten times that from Russia and fifteen times the aid given by Britain.[8] In contrast to the inability of India and the United States to work out an endurable pattern of diplomacy, Britain has not only substantially increased her trade (not aid) with India since 1947, but has also convinced the United States that Western policy in Asia must be based on British, not American, appreciation of the region. A clear example of a remarkable and successful hard sell in the diplomatic field!

The foregoing is history. Today, nonalignment is in need of a momentous redefinition, perhaps even of being discarded altogether as a concept for India to found her future foreign policy on.

If the conflict with China in October, 1962, proved to India that military aid when required could be had from the West without necessarily aligning India to it, the Chinese threat to Sikkim three years later (in September, 1965), proved that even a country about to fight China can be coolly treated by the United States despite her avowed aim to contain China. Another sobering thought to tax the minds of men who frame India's foreign policy is that Pakistan, in spite of her increasing accord with China—which in theory at least means aligning herself *against* the United States but in practice means little since she is already aligned *to* the United States—continues to be treated by the United States on a par with India. And at times with even more favor. This makes equal nonsense of existing alignments as well as of the hitherto heady slogan of nonalignment. Shastri's pronouncement in his first public speech in June, 1964, that "nonalignment will continue to be the fundamental basis of our approach to world problems" was thus pointless. Nonalignment between what, and whom? If through reason and logic India is convinced of the fact that neither the Kremlin nor the White House is now likely to trigger off a war between their two coun-

[8] Authorized United States loans, grants, and aid under Public Law 480 added up to $8,087,200,000, while Russian loans amounted to $811,300,000, and British loans to $524,900,000, up to December, 1962. See *India's Progress Since Independence—A Statistical Bird's-Eye View* (New Delhi: The Eastern Economist Ltd.), p. 24.

tries, then to announce that India is nonaligned between these two makes little or no sense. Indian leadership must relentlessly probe China's Asian objectives and then judge whether they are reconcilable with India's own aims and aspirations. If they are not, then there can be no compromise with the fact that India must be aligned with those who are opposed to China.

Preventing the spread of Chinese hegemony over the Asian mainland is a declared policy objective of the United States and an undeclared objective of Russia. Since India's relations with these two will have a vital bearing on the emerging power patterns in this region, it would be well to examine them in greater detail.

The Indo-United States Link

Robert Trumbull of *The New York Times* once likened India's relations with the United States to the motions of a yo-yo; they have "gone up and down like one," he said. It is a good description. The paradox of this relationship is that though the two have disagreed more often than they have agreed, their mutual involvement has steadily increased. Behind the bickering has been a lively awareness of their importance to each other, but even so a study of their past differences should help to place in perspective Indo-United States relations over the years.

To the United States, India's recognition of China in December, 1949, was an unpleasant shock, the first of many. Nehru's wooing of that country was viewed as being midway between the spiteful and the hostile. His aim, however, was simply to contain China through friendship, through the yet untried avenues of diplomacy. Nonrecognition of China would have implied disapproval of the powerful new regime, and Nehru was reluctant to make that implication since there was no clear reason for him to disapprove of it. Many men have wondered whether he understood the real nature of emergent China. But he was too astute a Brahmin, too steeped in history and learning

not to know that the new flame in China would burn for a long
time to come.

> I have a strong feeling that the future of Asia is rather tied up
> with the relations between India and China. I see that both the
> U.S.A. and the U.K. on the one hand, and the U.S.S.R. on the
> other, for entirely different reasons, are not anxious that India and
> China should be friendly towards each other. That itself is a sig-
> nificant fact which has to be borne in mind . . . what will happen
> to China during the next few years is anybody's guess. But *it is*
> *a complete misunderstanding of the China situation to imagine*
> *that they function like a satellite state of Russia* . . . it is of great
> importance to Asia and to the world that India and China should
> be friendly. How far we shall succeed in this endeavour I cannot
> say.[9]

Prison, it must be remembered, provides opportunity for reflection, and much of Nehru's thinking was shaped by years of
imprisonment. He was also the inheritor of great traditions in
statecraft. When the chroniclers of the past in India recorded a
thousand ways of making love, the sages also put down in the
shastras a thousand ways of practicing the art of diplomacy. In
recognizing Communist China, Nehru showed sharp awareness
of what was happening in that ancient land. It is more than
likely that the United States knew equally well the significance
of those changes and, with vision rooted in self-interest, had
foreseen an eventual Sino-American conflict which made pointless the recognition of a regime it would one day have to fight.

In refusing to be stampeded into precipitate action following
China's menacing moves against Tibet in 1950, Nehru provided
the United States with more cause for worry, though he was being neither timorous nor appeasing toward China. His reaction
was that of a man fully aware of his country's inner weaknesses.
It should be remembered that this was not long after India's war

---

[9] Letter from Jawaharlal Nehru to India's delegate to the United Nations,
Sir B. N. Rau (1950), published in *The Statesman*, December 7, 1965.

with Pakistan over Kashmir, and Indian intelligence reports had warned of another Pakistani build-up along the borders of Jammu and Kashmir. Millions of refugees were milling about the country; the economy had still to find its feet. Later events proved that Nehru not only took sensible cognizance of his own country's weaknesses, but also accurately assessed the strength of his opponent. There was little doubt of this when a few months later—on June 25, 1950—the Chinese armies swept across the Yalu River, over North Korea, and into the south, delivering reeling blows to the United States forces. When three crack divisions of the Chinese army launched an attack on eastern Tibet on October 7, 1950, it was a foregone conclusion that India would be in no position to do much about it.

Nehru's peace efforts in Korea marked another point of difference between India and the United States. His efforts were an extension of his aim to involve China in diplomatic, not just militaristic activity in the region. The United States felt that many of his moves showed undue warmth toward China, but from Nehru's point of view they were silken threads with which he hoped to secure his neighbor. That China snapped them when it no longer suited her purpose does not change the fact that Nehru did gain twelve to thirteen years in which to shore up the country's defenses against an aggressive neighbor. Nehru can be indicted for not putting those years to good use and for his short-sightedness in picking his friend Krishna Menon to head the country's defenses, a man who was too headstrong to see the direction in which danger lay and too incapable to handle a job of such complexity and magnitude. But Nehru cannot be indicted for trying to get along with China in the early years.

His concern at the consequences of United Nations forces crossing the 38th Parallel—which they did on October 8, 1950—though discomfiting to the United States, was to prove well founded. His warning against it; his opposition to the United Nations's "Uniting for Peace" resolution of November, 1950, to the move to brand China the aggressor, and finally to the embargo on shipment of strategic materials to China were moves unpalatable to the United States since it was she who sponsored these resolutions.

Not only was Korea a low point in America's relations with India—even though America eventually approved of India's role as intermediary—but it lead inexorably to that disastrous sandbar in Indo-United States relations: the arming of Pakistan as an offshoot of the Central and the Southeast Asia Treaty organizations alliances set up as a part of the new United States strategy to contain the Communist powers globally. The confluence of this American aim, with the traditional British appreciation of Russia's interest in Gilgit, Jammu, and Kashmir, and Pakistan's willingness to join the pacts, inevitably led to the arming of Pakistan. If, as is generally accepted, the West's strategy in Asia is based on British advice, it is because the United States has often had reason to appreciate British farsightedness in this region. Already obscured by time is the interesting fact that when the Maharajah of Kashmir acceeded to India in 1947 a revolt in Gilgit against the accession was mounted by Major Brown, a British officer of the Gilgit Scouts. Major Brown "hoisted the Pakistani flag there early in November 1947."[1] There was nothing strange in Britain's action in securing Gilgit for the West for its future use as a base against Russia, since countries do what they think is best in their national interests. (The United States's appreciation of Pakistan's usefulness was to be influenced by similar considerations some years later.)

When the expanding power of Russia and China convinced the United States that Southeast Asia was one of the more vulnerable areas in her strategy of containment, Pakistan assumed new importance. In contrast with India's intransigence, Pakistan was willing to join any alliance. It was an important and practical consideration and the United States recognized it as such. The practical lesson India could have learned from this is that when the chips are down, it is not the ideology of a system which is the criterion for judging its usefulness, but the extent to which it is

[1] Balraj Madhok: "The Western Presence," Seminar, September 1965, p. 22.

flexible enough to identify itself with others in its own interests. Just as American casualties in Korea brought that conflict home to all Americans with poignant immediacy, the casualties in India's war with Pakistan brought home to Indians the tragedy of massive American military aid to Pakistan. How far India's resentment is justified can be judged by going into factors which led to the arming of Pakistan, the assurances given to allay Indian apprehensions, and the extent to which those assurances have been honored.

President Eisenhower's pledge, given to Nehru in a letter he wrote to the Indian Prime Minister at the time the United States announced its decision to arm Pakistan, was clear and forthright.

Dear Prime Minister,

... Our two Governments have agreed that our desires for peace are in accord. It has also been understood that if our interpretation of existing circumstances and our belief in how to achieve our goals differ, it is the right and duty of sovereign nations to make their own decisions. Having studied long and carefully the problem of opposing possible aggression in the Middle East, I believe that consultation between Pakistan and Turkey about security problems will serve the interests not only of Pakistan and Turkey but also of the whole free world. Improvement in Pakistan's defensive capability will also serve these interests and it is for this reason that our aid will be given. This Government's views on this subject are elaborated in a public statement I will release, a copy of which Ambassador Allen will give you.

What we are proposing to do, and what Pakistan is agreeing to, is not directed in *any way* against India. And I am confirming publicly that if our aid to any country, including Pakistan, is misused and directed against another in aggression I will undertake immediately, in accordance with my constitutional authority, appropriate action both within and without the United Nations to thwart such aggression. I believe that the Pakistan-Turkey collaboration agreement which is being discussed is sound evidence of the defensive purposes which both countries have in mind.

... We also believe it in the interest of the free world that India have a strong military defense capability and have admired the effective way your Government has administered your military establishment. If your Government should conclude that circumstances require military aid of a type contemplated by our mutual security legislation, please be assured that your request would receive my most sympathetic consideration.

Dwight D. Eisenhower[2]

It is through her failure to honor this pledge that the United States stands indicted in the eyes of nearly all Indians. While self-interest is a sovereign right, it can hardly be furthered by breaking publicly given pledges. Eisenhower's commitment to Nehru was very explicit, and in refusing to honor his predecessor's pledge President Johnson took a step away from what American self-interest could have been best served by: an inflexible and uncompromising insistence by the United States that Pakistan stop using American equipment against India. The American insistence in September, 1965, on acting only through the United Nations, which often means no action at all, was a retraction on the Eisenhower pledge. In any case, what did the United Nations have to do with the use of American arms which it had no hand in giving in the first place?

Moreover, the United States's extraordinary action in also suspending food and economic aid to India caused deep and justifiable resentment in all shades of political opinion. There may be good reason for the United States to insist on economic aid being put to more effective use, and there is justification in the American argument that India has used Public Law 480 supplies as a crutch rather than an interim measure for gaining time in which to set her agricultural house in order. India has so clearly failed to improve her agricultural economy during the period of these supplies that there can be no denying the obvious. The United States is within its rights to insist that India re-examine her economic policies, too. But the timing and length of aid stoppage

---

[2] *Documents on American Foreign Relations, 1954*, ed. Peter U. Curl (New York: Harper & Brothers; 1955), pp. 374–5. The letter was delivered to the Indian Prime Minister on February 24, 1954.

was wrong, as was also the attempt to tie it to the Indo-Pakistan conflict. To Indians smarting from the experience of facing American armor, it was perfidy of sorts that the United States should blackmail them to satisfy Pakistan.

"It is a strange irony of fate," said Y. B. Chavan, India's Defence Minister, addressing a rally of over 600,000 people in Bombay on October 4, 1965, "that Britain and America, which talk so much of democracy should be 'partners' of a dictatorship against the largest democracy in the world. Greater is the pity that America, which talks of crusading against Communism, should help Pakistan, a partner of Communist China." A respected Independent Member of Parliament, Frank Anthony, addressing a public meeting in New Delhi on October 1, 1965, warned the Government against "diplomatic arm-twisting and attempts at pressurizing India." He said that India could not "mortgage her security and existence to the vagaries of uncertain friends" who had joined together to embarrass and weaken India while assisting "a military dictatorship in obvious conspiracy with the ruthless, totalitarian Chinese Communist regime."

Though the initiative rests naturally with the United States in putting India on the spot whenever she wants to, India herself has quite a record of embarrassing the United States on occasions when that country could have done without it. America's involvement in Vietnam is a source of continuing embarrassment to her, and for India to have added to it by publicly denouncing the American bombing of targets in North Vietnam was pointless and shortsighted. By doing so on a number of occasions, Indian spokesmen showed poor concern for Indo-United States relations, as did a number of Indian commentators and columnists who helped to confound further an already complex situation. By equating the reality of the Vietnam crisis with a series of theoretical could-have-beens, official Indian opinion evidently convinced itself that the United States's action in Vietnam was all wrong, since it militated against the North-South reunification under the leadership of Ho, a potential Asian Tito.

The facts of life in Vietnam are quite different. The great

brooding land mass of Russia was not contiguous to Yugoslavia, a fact which prevented Russia from exercising the degree of intimidation which China can against Vietnam. Since China is not unaware of the traditional hostility of the Annamese toward the Chinese, it is logical to assume that powerful pro-China protagonists exist in the power-web of North Vietnam. Then again, China is as capable of subverting a unified Vietnam as she was of getting the North to subvert the South, though in the event of a possible pulling away of the country from China, she would more likely precipitate a showdown in her favor than wait to subvert a hostile regime later.

The practice of large-scale, scientifically planned, sophisticated subversion which plays for high stakes, and which China is developing into a deadly instrument for furthering her national interests, is what India ought to have been particularly careful about in her utterances on Vietnam. In giving legitimacy to the Viet Cong, by advocating suspension of punitive steps against them and pressing for their participation in peace talks, India was treading on dangerously thin ground. Firstly, she couldn't claim to know—nor could anyone else, for that matter—what percentage of the Viet Cong in the South was of grass-roots origins, and how much of it came down from the North. Since it is valid to assume that subversive elements from the North did infiltrate into the South, the Viet Cong can to an extent be equated with the Mujahids which Pakistan sent into Kashmir in August, 1965. It is possible these Mujahids picked up some recruits in Kashmir; it is equally possible that quite a few of them are still lying low in the Kashmir valley. Should this motley crowd surface again and proceed to disrupt law, order, and normal life in the state, would India eventually agree to sit across the table and talk peace with them? What yardstick, then, did India use to measure the Vietnam situation that she found it so different from her own as to feel justified in wagging a finger at South Vietnam and advising it to recognize the National Liberation Front?

One reason India finds herself friendless at her own moments of crisis is because most countries are by now convinced that Indian policies are based on a double set of standards: one set applying to her own interests and the second to the interests of other countries. By condemning American bombing of Viet Cong staging areas in North Vietnam, India was using two different standards for judging analogous issues. In securing Kargil and the Haji Pir Pass in Pakistan in September, 1965, the Indian army took decisive and justifiable action to wrest control of vital points dominating the infiltrators' routes into the Kashmir valley. Yet India saw no contradiction in condemning the bombing of North Vietnam targets, the objective of which was more or less the same. In objecting that it was the United States who carried out the raids, India overlooked the fact that the United States was there at the invitation of the South. To sneer at the Government of South Vietnam was neither good politics nor good diplomacy on India's part.

During the Sino-Indian fighting in the North East Frontier Agency in October and November, 1962, a situation could have arisen when, had the Chinese kept coming down the mountains and onto the Assam plains, India might well have asked for Western air strikes against the extended supply lines of the Chinese in Tibet.

The harsh realities of power politics cannot be subordinated to the temptation to preach and moralize to others *ad nauseum*. The American presence in Vietnam is by any standard beneficial to India's interests. The armed might of the United States is keeping a powder keg burning on China's doorstep, keeping China preoccupied and perhaps preventing her from possible mischief elsewhere. During 1965–6 China has suffered diplomatic reverses in many parts of the world ranging from Algeria, Indonesia, Ghana, and Kenya to Cuba, and she needs to make a demonstrative move to reassert her somewhat shopworn image. She could well decide to make such a move against India in the latter part of 1966 or 1967. Against the background of such a possibility, is it in India's interests to advocate a lessening of the United States's commitment in Vietnam? By criticizing American pres-

ence in Vietnam either directly or through implication, India is
strengthening the hands of those in the United States who are
advocating that America wash its hands of the Asian mainland.
Senator J. William Fulbright, chairman of the Senate Foreign
Relations Committee, feels, for instance, that America has "no
alternative but to seek a general accommodation" with the
Chinese. To achieve this he recommends that the United States
"indicate to the Chinese that we are prepared to remove American
military power not only from Vietnam but from all of Southeast
Asia in return for a similar prohibition on her part." This could
conceivably become a cornerstone of American policy within the
foreseeable future. The Indian Government's assessment of this
possibility must be made with relentless objectivity in order to
gauge whether such a Sino-United States agreement is in the
interests of India's own security. If China did agree to denouncing use of military force, there would still be nothing to
prevent her from concentrating instead on subverting India's
Mizo Hills, the North East Frontier Agency, Sikkim, Bhutan,
and other territories which abut Chinese-held Tibet.

American Columnist Walter Lippmann, who also strongly
favors United States disengagement from the Asian mainland
because he is disturbed by the prospect of Americans fighting in
Asia, draws on a Churchill quote to make his point: "We must
not jump into the water to fight the sharks." Since India, however, is up against a sizable Asian shark herself it ought to be an
article of faith with her policy-planners to have others in the
water helping her fight it! Because the containment of China is
as much in the long-term interests of the United States as of
India, India's pronouncements and policies should logically support and sustain opinion within the United States which is in
favor of a hard line with China in Asia. The Indian effort, in
concert with that of the United States, should be to get China
to denounce subversion as well as the use of military force for
resolving Asian problems. Instead of embarrassing the United
States, India should hammer out an imaginative Asian policy
with her which would ensure peace in Asia, but on condition that

weaker nations are not made a sacrificial offering to their more aggressive and avaricious neighbors.

In a sense India's confused thinking on Vietnam springs from her bemused idea of her nonaligned role—a hangover from the days when she was in fact nonaligned. The confusion was nowhere more evident than in the *The Times of India*'s approving comments on Shastri's criticism of American bombings. According to this leading Indian newspaper Shastri, "in an unusual excess of clarity, has emphasised that meaningful negotiations cannot be possible until the air attacks against the North are halted . . . this is all to the good despite the irritability of an American President, but can it be considered enough either in terms of non-alignment or in those of New Delhi's position in the Afro-Asian world? Disapproval of the air-raids doesn't exhaust the obligations of non-alignment."[3] This is as clear an example of disastrous self-deception as any.

The United States didn't need the Indian Prime Minister or any other commentator in India to tell them that their bombing North Vietnam was somewhat of a damper to negotiations with the North Vietnamese. But to have gone on to say that the irritability of the American President was a lesser consideration than nonalignment or New Delhi's position in the Afro-Asian world was indicative of the kind of break with rational thinking which has damaged Indian interests time and again. When India has to rely on the U.S. for food till at least 1972, the American President's good humour ought to be of some importance to her. Insofar as New Delhi's position in the Afro-Arab world is concerned, the idea that each move India makes must be acceptable there borders on the absurd.

Where was the Afro-Asian world at the time of the Algerian semi-Summit Conference in November, 1965, when absentee China's will to postpone the Summit Conference prevailed, and not India's, who wanted to hold it and was very much present

[3] *The Times of India*: "A Helpful Snub" (editorial signed N. J. N.), April 26, 1965.

to push her case? Where was Jordan and Saudi Arabia's friendship for India when they openly sided with Pakistan during the Indo-Pakistan fighting, or when Iran flew her Prime Minister to Pindi to talk to Ayub Khan in September, 1965? The great solidarity India boasts of with the Arab world was notably absent when the United Arab Republic permitted a ship loaded with explosives to pass through the Suez Canal and head for Pakistan on October 3, 1965, despite India's vigorous protests. This fawning attitude of India toward Afro-Asian solidarity has made her stumble too often for it to be funny.

There is no such thing as an obligation to nonalignment, either. The obligation of any enlightened leadership is to the interests of its own country and people and not to a dated concept made into a godhead.

The second half of the sixties is likely to be a trying time for Indo-United States relations. Though the containment of China will continue to be a major concern of the United States she will have to take a second look at some hard facts. The extent of the American commitment in Vietnam could prove useful under certain circumstances for staging action against China at a later date, but the very scale of the commitment, and the time it has taken to produce very meager results, should convince the United States that it can not "go it alone" in Asia. A strong India can be a useful ally against China. But to what extent the United States will commit herself to aiding Indian efforts toward that end is a key question. Of relevance is the noncommittal attitude the United States took toward the Chinese ultimatum to India on September 17, 1965. According to the Washington correspondent of the London *Times,* American policy at that time was cool toward any conflict between China and India unless it threatened to spread from the Himalayas to the plains of India. Fighting in Sikkim would not be considered as involving American interests in the region. India's national interest, on the other hand, is not only very much involved in Sikkim, but her territorial integrity depends on her ability to demonstrate to the border kingdoms of Nepal, Bhutan, and Sikkim her power to repel Chinese inroads there.

Here, then, is the vicious triangle to which India must increasingly address herself: China's interest in straddling India's Himalayan reaches, the real possibility of United States reluctance to respond in any meaningful measure to China's probings in the region, and India's total commitment to defending the country's outer reaches from China's cupidity.

India needs American help to raise and equip forces on the necessary scale and in the time available. She should therefore take more care in handling her relations with that country. Three or four factors seem to stand in the way of a better appreciation by United States policy-makers of the facts of life in India. One is the belief that the Communist Party's strength in India was weakened by the Chinese aggression of 1962.

> Indian Communism was dealt a severe, if not fatal, blow by the Chinese attack of 1962 and China's support of Pakistan on Kashmir. China's policies have made it impossible for the pro-Peking Indian Communists (the stronger of the rival Indian Communist Parties) to pick up the banner of nationalism. They have also facilitated the Indian Government's repression of the pro-Peking Communists as alleged agents of a foreign power. The pro-Soviet Communist Party in India, on the other hand, has been greatly weakened by the defection of a large majority of the middle and lower ranking Party cadres to the more dynamic pro-Peking Communists, regardless of their weakened status.[4]

Such wishful thinking can be dangerously misleading. Since the above article was circulated in India by the United States Information Service, it needs to be examined in some detail.

To begin with, it is self-contradictory. Indian Communism could not have been dealt a "severe" or "fatal" blow by the Chinese attack if a "large majority" of the Party cadres moved

[4] Donald S. Zagoria: "A World in Mao Tse-tung's Image," Washington *Post*, September 19, 1965.

over from the pro-Soviet to the pro-Peking wing of the Communist Party of India! On the contrary, a recent and most extraordinary phenomenon has been the emergence on the Indian national scene of powerful elements in the Communist Party of India, openly and unabashedly pro-Peking. That they are willing to take an openly pro-Chinese stand despite the general mood of resentment against the Chinese signifies unique confidence in their own strength.

According to E. M. S. Namboodiripad, leader of the Left Communist (pro-Peking) Party of India and former Chief Minister of the state of Kerala: "There has been no lessening whatsoever in the following of the Communist Party of India since October 1962. Absolutely not." He went on to say that "this very morning [December 9, 1965] all the Leftist parties [the two wings of the Communist Party of India, the Revolutionary Socialist Party, and three or four smaller parties] are beginning a three-day session to plan a joint campaign on food, working class and peasants demands. We are sure to agree on a joint electoral campaign too eventually, to contest the 1967 elections."[5] He also told a well-attended rally in Bombay on November 9, 1965, that talk of India recapturing Aksai Chin (India's territory in Ladakh, under Chinese control) was "foolish, stupid and tall." No man in India could say something like that so soon after the Chinese threats of September, 1965, without being confident of receiving support from some sections of the public. Earlier Namboodiripad had advocated "direct negotiations with China on the basis of recognition of China's sovereignty over Tibet." He told this writer that "no serious student of military or diplomatic affairs can consider talk of recapturing Tibet, or even Aksai-Chin, a practical proposition." To support his thesis he referred to an article by John Kenneth Galbraith in the October, 1965, issue of *The American Review*. In it the former United States ambassador, in recalling the limited war the Indians and Chinese had fought in October, 1962, affirmed that the United

[5] In a conversation with the author in New Delhi on December 9, 1965.

States was not interested in "a war in those distant mountains." Under the circumstances, asked Namboodiripad, "do you think India can, or should, talk of capturing Tibet on its own?"

Opposed to those who feel a conflict with China is inevitable, a growing body of opinion in India is beginning to peddle the view that just as the United States and the Soviet Union are learning to coexist, when only a few years ago they were trading nuclear threats, the United States and China too could conceivably reach a similar understanding. Where, the question is then asked, is the logic in India's burning her bridges with China by adopting a hostile and intractable attitude toward her? The following letter in *The Times of India* (November 27, 1965) from a well-known lawyer of Bombay, is indicative of this line of thought:

> Sir. . . . Will it profit us to join in an international crusade against China? . . . The differences between China and the other world powers . . . seem to bear a striking resemblance to those that, a bare decade ago, divided the U.S.A. and the U.S.S.R. That was before the Americans, applying their business maxim "smash 'em or join 'em" but finding that they could not smash, admitted the U.S.S.R. to the "Giants Club." Despite Chinese propaganda exuberance Mao has been astute, as Stalin was, to avoid a premature atomic duel with the U.S.A. If this course continues the result seems inevitable. The trend of contemporary history is towards the composition of differences between the big powers. A sharp change in the U.S. policy towards China may confront us sooner than some anticipate. If that happens and China's differences with Russia are also composed, what would India have gained. . . ?
>
> Danial Latifi
>
> *Bombay*
> *November 15, 1965*

China, ironically enough, is in a position to carry off a major diplomatic coup through the simple expedient of making a patently demonstrative move of friendliness toward India. There are many people in India who, either because they are pro-Left or because they are hostile to the United States on account of its pro-Pakistan policies, would respond favorably to a convincing gesture of friendship by China. Even the dismissal of a general in Tibet, carried out dramatically and ostensibly for the purpose of punishing him for some action against India, could be made to appear an earnest of China's desire for better relations with India! China's interest lies in fanning animosity between India and the United States and in deflecting India from her aim of readying herself to meet the Chinese menace.

Though it is often assumed that the defense forces in most countries are more inclined toward the Right than to the Left, it can do no harm to bear in mind that events influence attitudes. Other resentments aside, the view is frequently heard in defense circles in India that even in the matter of keeping its promises made after the October, 1962, attack by China, the United States has not proved too reliable. The instance is given that as against six mountain divisions the United States promised to help equip at that time, the total percentage of American equipment in the "aided divisions" does not, even three years later, exceed 10 per cent. In 1962 the United States pledged $60 million worth of military hardware to India. It subsequently anted this figure up to $200 million. It is no secret, however, that in actual fact aid has not been permitted to exceed $74 million. To India, with beleaguered boundaries extending thousands of miles along some of the world's most treacherous and inhospitable terrains, this holding back of military aid already pledged is far from satisfactory. It would be wrong for the United States to assume, therefore, that the armed forces in India, who are gaining increasing importance in the country subsequent to the Indo-Pakistan conflict of September, 1965, are a powerful pro-American element. They might be pro-Right in their leanings, but it is doubtful if they will be pro-America for long unless the United States demonstrates her willingness to help them resist the Chinese push.

The last—and quite possibly the biggest—barrier to a better understanding between America and India is the routing of their relations through the "honest broker"—Britain. Unless America learns to deal directly with India in all matters—including and especially defense—no enduring rapport can be established between the two countries. Till such time, the matter of helping India realize her national objective of containing Communist China will remain subordinated to the "usual British ploy in the event of Chinese muscle-flexing in the Himalayas since the beginning of 1963, which has been to rush officials to Washington with charts, maps and diagrams to demonstrate that British forces can be rushed to India's rescue from Cyprus, Aden and Singapore within a matter of hours."[6]

Any dispassionate study of British behavioral patterns toward her former colonies cannot help but come up against the fact that Britain's studied sympathy has been an outward attitude. Often, while diplomacy required Britain to demonstrate she was stoutly standing by those in no position to stand up on their own, her real interests operated otherwise. Her erstwhile colonies know this. The point is, does the United States? So long as the United States continues to be guided by British assessment—often, needless to add, a deeply biased one—of the capacity of India to arrest and resist the southern push of Chinese expansionism, the United States will continue to strike a bad bargain for good money.

Man for man the Indian soldier is as good as any China can put in the field against her. It is also possible to support India's fighting men with a more dependable network of bases and communication and supply lines than China can provide for her forces in Tibet. In any showdown India's air force would disrupt and destroy China's extended supply routes to her farflung garrisons in Tibet. The Tibetans themselves, and their sturdy Khampas, could harry and destroy them from within. The decision America has to make, uninfluenced by Britain's appreciation of the situation, is, does India have the makings of a strong and reliable Asian ally?

America's aim of containing Communist China can severely

[6] K. C. Khanna: "Reorganising the Western Alliance," *The Times of India,* November 27, 1965.

strain her resources of manpower, unless she builds up dependable allies. Recommendations of the American field commanders in South Viet Nam are that the strength of United States forces there "be increased to 480,000 by 1967. If Hanoi responds in kind," say American military planners in Saigon, "a commitment of 600,000 Americans may well be necessary in 1967."[7] If this happens, the United States could scarcely maintain adequate numbers of men at other staging points on the periphery of China, should pressures generated by the Chinese require it. Neither could Britain. India could. But India cannot build up her forces with only half-hearted help from a United States which holds back the hand of friendship out of fear that India might one day become big enough to be a threat to Western interests in the region.

Historically, temperamentally, ideologically, politically, emotionally, and intellectually, India is more aligned to the West than to totalitarianism, whether of Fascist or other forms. Since independence, India has proved that the democratic sapling planted by the founding fathers of her Constitution has begun spreading its roots and is capable of withstanding considerable buffeting. In the last decade and a half there have been *coups d'état,* insurrections, bloody revolutions by the score, and yet the rule of law and respect for constitutional and parliamentary practices have prevailed in India. This should be sufficiently reassuring to those whose own social and governmental institutions respect principles which guarantee personal freedoms and equal opportunities to people.

The Onetime Neighbors: India and Russia

To the odd man in the street, Russia is a country where all men have equal incomes and equal rights. To the dedicated party workers, the Marxist prescription provided a wonder pill to the suffering masses of an oppressed land, making it the land

[7] *Time,* December 10, 1965.

of hope for the hopeless of the world. For the fiercely Marxist armchair intellectuals who do not permit the suffering of fellow Indians to impinge on the splendors of their own living, the ideology of the Soviet system, because of the economic, scientific, and technological success it has achieved, makes it the only sensible system for India to adopt. To the politician who talks Left, Russia is God's special gift to him: what platform would he otherwise have to clamber up to power on? To the Government of India, it is a country to turn to when that other country, America, roughs up her feelings. Because of naïveté or knowledge, experience or expediency, Russia is a major factor in Indian thinking today.

India achieved independence at a time when Stalin ruled Russia. It was a militant Russia. It had proved through force of arms its capacity to mobilize its vast millions in defense of the Soviet system. It was not a Russia which could be expected to admire the finesse of Gandhian thought and philosophy, and it made no show of doing so. It called Gandhi "a charlatan and a mountebank."[8] The *Great Soviet Encyclopaedia* saw him as a "reactionary of the Bania caste who . . . betrayed the people and helped the imperialists against them . . . aped the ascetics . . . pretended in a demagogic way to be a supporter of Indian independence and an enemy of the British . . . and widely exploited religious prejudices."[9]

Gandhi, for that matter, had little love for Communism. To him means were of supreme importance in the attainment of human objectives, and the means favored by Stalin were far from being the ones preferred by the Mahatma. So when Gandhi died on January 30, 1949, "one country, and one only, passed over his death in silence. No message of condolence came from Russia, not a word of comment appeared in Soviet newspapers."[1]

Russian antipathy to emerging India did not end with use of

[8] K. P. S. Menon: *The Flying Troika*, The Political Diary of India's Ambassador to Russia, 1952–61 (London: Oxford University Press; 1963), p. 133.
[9] Ibid., p. 139.
[1] Ibid., p. 18.

language in poor taste. India's independence coincided with Zhdanov's two-camp doctrine, which saw the international struggle as between the imperialists such as the United States and the United Kingdom on the one hand, and the "democratic" forces such as the Soviet Union on the other. To give muscle to the forces of "democracy," a new international Communist body, the Cominform, had been formed. Since India under Nehru and Gandhi was considered imperialist, the protagonists of violence in the Communist Party of India, aided by the Cominform, launched a violent struggle in South India.

These were not events conducive to friendship. There were other jarring notes. Soviet lack of support of India in Kashmir in January, 1948; India's approval of the Dutch-Indonesian independence agreement in December, 1949, despite Russian disapproval; Nehru's announcement at the Commonwealth Prime Ministers' Conference in April, 1949, of India's decision to stay in the Commonwealth—and so on.

But then came Nehru's visit to the United States at the time of Truman's presidency in October, 1949. He and Nehru weren't of the same mold. In fact a more unlikely twosome for laying the foundations of Indo-United States relations would have been difficult to find. Truman was gruff, earthy, of the "give it to them straight" school. Nehru was the opposite. And, as was to be expected, they disagreed. Nehru's plea for slowing down the arms race which had intensified following Russia's first atomic explosion in August, 1949, his attempts to have Communist China recognized, his request for aid without strings and for support for Kashmir were all rebuffed. His visit came a few months after the appointment (in July, 1949) of Dr. S. Radhakrishnan as India's ambassador in Moscow. Dr. Radhakrishnan's efforts, combined with recognition on Russia's part of a diplomatic opportunity to exploit Nehru's mood of disenchantment with the United States, along with Nehru's own receptive frame of mind, made for closer contacts between India and Russia.

But it wasn't easy going even then. There were many high and low points between 1949 and 1953–4 when, with the death of Stalin and the setting up of the Central Treaty Organization and the Southeast Asia Treaty Organization and Pakistan's inclusion in them, the rapprochement between India and Russia was finally sealed. The high points were India's recognition of China and her efforts to have her seated in the United Nations, her role in preventing the spread of hostilities in the Korean war and achieving a truce (though appreciation of this on Russia's part will always remain doubtful considering that "the predicament in Korea, where thousands of American soldiers were being killed and not a single Soviet soldier was involved, was exactly the kind of situation in which Stalin revelled"[2]), the signing of the Indo-Soviet Trade Agreement in December, 1953, and so on. The low points were India's initial support to the United States-sponsored United Nations resolution for collective action against North Korea in June, 1950, and in November–December, 1952, on the repatriation of prisoners of war. Vyshinsky's testy summing up of Indians in a statement on December 2, 1952, was: "At best you are dreamers and idealists, at worst you don't understand your own position, and camouflage horrible American policy."[3]

Since the United States arming of Pakistan in 1954, Russia's support to India, economic as well as moral, has been consistent throughout: a superb example of sustained and even-keeled diplomacy. Considerable confusion nevertheless prevails in the minds of many Indians as to why Russian friendship is so important to India. The Indian Government has not done much to clear up the confusion.

There is, of course, economic aid. But far more important is the fact that a friendly Russia can be expected not only to remain neutral in any showdown between China and India, but even to move actively on India's side at a future date. The neutral role Russia played in the Sino-Indian conflict of October, 1962, was

[2] K. P. S. Menon: "India's Relations with the Soviet Union," *International Studies* (July–October 1963), V, Nos. 1–2.
[3] *The Hindu*, December 3, 1952.

fortunate for India, though at one stage Russia did waver: "On October 25 the Soviet Union indicated that if it came to a choice, it would stand by Peking. It did this in a leading article in *Pravda* which lashed out against the Western countries for giving military aid to India and denounced the MacMahon Line . . . however, on November 5, the Soviet Union returned to its former neutral position in the border dispute between India and Communist China."[4] The objective of Indian diplomacy from now on is to ensure that Russia does *not* waver in the future.

It was fortunate for India that her conflict with China reached crisis proportions at about the same time that differences worsened between China and Russia. Thus Russia's neutral role was not played specifically for India's benefit; but whatever the causes, Russia not only remained neutral through the conflict but in the earlier stages, "in his anxiety to maintain a strict neutrality, Khrushchev withdrew his Ambassador, Pavel Yudin, from Peking after he publicly took the Chinese side in the frontier conflict. The Soviet Premier also rebuked the East German Premier, Herr Otto Grotewohl, when he blamed India for aggression against China."[5]

It is an entirely confused perspective which makes some Indians value Russia's friendship because of her support on the Kashmir issue. Kashmir is a part of India. If Pakistani armor has not been able to change that fact then neither will any votes at the United Nations. Even India's worst detractors cannot accuse her of indifference toward the principles and prestige of the United Nations. But her own interests have to be considered too. In setting great store by Russia's vote in the Security Council, India continues to place herself in a position in which she can always be subjected to Russian pressure. This lever of pressure and persuasion must be removed through India's stating categorically that she is no longer willing to debate the Kashmir problem.

[4] Hemen Ray: "The Policy of Russia towards Sino-India Conflict," *The Political Quarterly* (January–March, 1965), pp. 95–6.

[5] Ibid., p. 93.

By clearing the decks of the Kashmir clutter India could effectively checkmate any future consequences which might result from Russia's moves for closer ties with Pakistan, something India will never be able to do if she is perpetually worried about losing the Russian vote in the United Nations.

Why, after years of hostility because of Pakistan's membership in the Southeast Asia and the Central Treaty organizations, and the fact that America's U-2's took off from a base in Pakistan to spy over her, is Russia now drawing closer to that country? Because, with increasing affluence at home, with stability at the political as well as the leadership level, with the first flush of power over, Russia is taking another long, careful look at her long-term interests in the countries of Southeast Asia. In such an appraisal Pakistan stands out as a country not averse to running with the fox and hunting with the hounds. The fact that she could take $1.5 billion worth of military hardware from America, yet become ecstatic over China, indicates a flexible approach to international alignments. Russia most likely began noticing Pakistan when Ayub started making eyes at China. Pakistan, it must be remembered, is on the southern border of the Soviet Union. It is to Russia's natural interest to secure her border by weaning to her side a hitherto hostile border state. Her objective obviously is to catch Ayub on the emotional rebound from the West, and simultaneously drive a wedge between Pakistan and China before any dangerous collusion develops between them. Pakistan by herself does not present a very serious problem to the Soviet Union, but Pakistan acting along the lines laid down by the Chinese is another and more serious matter.

All of this need not worry India unduly. Russia has staked a lot on India because of the country's size, geographical location, population, and growing strength. It is illogical to assume that Russia would risk weakening her existing ties with India for dubious friendship with Pakistan, especially since the Soviet position in Southeast Asia is totally untenable without a friendly India. Even in the Communist Party of India the pro-Peking elements are gaining strength over the pro-Soviet, a matter of concern to the Kremlin, which must keep its legitimate contacts with India intact.

The question of foremost importance to India is: how real is the Sino-Russian rift? For fifty years the people of Russia have worked, as perhaps no other people have in human history, to build their country up from the backwardness and misery of the Middle Ages to a position where today Soviet Russia is one of the world's two great powers. Any global conflict now—an aim to which China is dedicated—would destroy what the people of Russia have built up in these fifty years. They cannot be expected to view such a prospect with equanimity. There is thus this basic cleavage in their outlook on world affairs: China does not have much to lose and has far more to gain in any war of the future; Russia has everything to lose. Russia is against activities which initiate wars and the type of hysteria which leads to them; China is for war hysteria and for war itself.

The second point of friction hinges on Russia's mass repatriation in July, 1960, of all her technicians in China. Aid had been tapering off much before that, of course. Once it became clear to Russia that Mao's eyes were fixed not only on the territories of other people but on those of her fraternal neighbor, Russia, as well, and once it became clear too that the muscle Russia was helping China to develop might one day be used against her, and even more, that the Russian muscle was expected to start a world war to benefit China, the Russian pull-back began.

There is also the difference in approach between these two major Communist powers toward expanding and exporting Communist ideology around the globe. Russia feels it can be done without recourse to war; China disagrees. Endless rhetoric, voluminous manifestoes, an inexhaustible flow of polemic, have all been part of the dialogue of dissent between the two. The cleavage goes deeper than some would think and the differences between the two countries are too wide to be easily bridged.

It is not likely that the liberal elements in China will surface after Mao's death, once the struggle for power has resolved itself. The Sino-Russian differences are not founded on the personality factor. Khrushchev's exit made no difference to the official Russian attitude toward China. Neither is Mao's death likely to make any difference in China's attitude toward Russia. China's present policies were framed by a collective leadership in the caves of Yunan decades ago, and Mao's exit from the Chinese scene is not likely to make any material difference to them.

But the vital fact which India cannot and must not overlook is that on October 25, 1962, Russia indicated, however briefly, that in a showdown between India and China, she would stand by China! Indian national interest requires the continuation of Russian hostility toward China as a balancing factor to the latter's adventurist ambitions.

If it comes to a showdown between the United States and China, would Russia ally herself with China? Would she remain neutral? Are there convincing reasons to assume she might even side against China? Would she acquiesce to a limited operation, such as the destruction of China's nuclear complexes? Though these questions are of more concern to the United States and the Soviet Union, they are of extreme interest to India because on the answers to them must rest the content, shape, and purpose of India's foreign policy in the coming years.

It can never be India's intention to threaten the existence of China, but it is conceivable—and India must reserve herself this right—that at a future date she will question the Chinese presence in Tibet. When the British established the two Tibets, Inner and Outer, there was farsightedness and vision in their move. They felt it was important for them to have a buffer between Imperialist Russia and their own Indian empire. The exigency still exists. Only the villain in the piece has changed; it is now China instead of Russia.

The scope of joint and meaningful diplomacy between India and Russia is limitless. Russia might frown on any armed disciplining of China but she is certainly interested in extending her own orbit of influence to as many countries in Southeast Asia as possible. Since this clearly implies the containment of China's influence in this region, India's and Russia's interests are identical. Here again is opportunity for preparing a well-conceived long-term blueprint for a joint containment of China.

The Russia of today is manned by hardheaded men. Technocrats by nature and training, precise and specific in their appreciation of situations, the less sentimentality expected of them the better. India should distill emotionalism—and Russia's vote on Kashmir and her growing friendship with Pakistan are no more than emotional issues—out of her relationship with them. The new relationship has to be on the basis of an equal partnership in which Russia helps India economically and militarily in any conflict India might have with China, while India respects Russia's interest in Southeast Asia.

An important point on which the Indian leadership gets confused, and where future confusion must be avoided, is that friendship with Russia does not oblige India to ape Russia's pattern of economic development. There are many ardent, utterly confused, and thus potentially harmful enthusiasts in India who from the vantage positions they occupy in public life tend to interpret India's friendship with Russia as meaning India should "go Russian." Economic strength can not come to India the Russian way. Russia pulled herself out of the darkness of despair and developed the sinews of her economy through her own efforts and not through massive aid from other Western countries, but she did it with the help of a ruthlessly efficient system. India has neither a ruthless nor an efficient system. Hers is a far cry from the system which was able to develop Russia. This is ignored both by the pseudo-Marxist intellectuals and the practicing demagogues in India. Only private initiative, sustained by the dynamics which operate in a free, open, and competitive economy, and motivated by the legitimate profits which are the reward for grit, drive, and entrepreneurship, can snap India out of the somnolence of ages.

The Kashmir Dispute

When on September 6, 1965, the three crack divisions of the Indian army's Eleventh Corps swept across India's border with Pakistan in a thrust toward the prestigious city of Lahore, it was the climactic act of a long and bitter wrangle over the former princely state of Jammu and Kashmir. This climax had been anticipated. The only surprising thing, when it came, was that it had been so long in the coming.

The bitter story of the beautiful valley of Kashmir began in October, 1947, when Maharajah Hari Singh signed the letter of accession making his state a part of the Republic of India. Over five hundred other princely states had already acceded, and the fact that Hari Singh was one of the last of the rulers to do so was because he felt he could negotiate a unique status of some sort for his kingdom. But not being a very perceptive man, he failed to take account of events which were moving relentlessly toward a showdown.

On Saturday, October 25, at a meeting in New Delhi of the Government of India's Defence Committee—which included, among others, Lord Mountbatten—General Sir Rob Lockhart, the Commander in Chief of the Indian army "read out a telegram from the Headquarters of the Pakistan Army stating that some 5,000 tribesmen had attacked and captured Muzaffarabad and Domel and that considerable tribal reinforcement could be expected. Reports showed that they were already little more than 30 miles from Srinagar."[6] Muzaffarabad and Domel were towns in the state of Jammu and Kashmir. Shaken by the invasion, completely unnerved by the proximity of the advance columns from Pakistan which were rolling toward his capital, Hari Singh acceded his state to India and departed from Srinagar the same day with his wife and son. That was on October 26. The troops in the city of Srinagar on that day consisted of one squadron of cavalry.

[6] Campbell-Johnson, p. 224.

New Delhi now moved fast. Officially accepting the accession, India proceeded to meet Pakistan's challenge, and at dawn the next day, Monday, October 27, the first troop transports began landing at Srinagar's airfield with men of the First Sikh Battalion. Bloody battle was soon joined to push the raiders back, who by then were within four miles of Srinagar.

Alan Campbell-Johnson, in *Mission with Mountbatten,* made an interesting note in his diary at that time on Gandhi's reaction to the fighting which had erupted in Kashmir. "At yesterday's Prayer Meeting the Mahatma struck an almost Churchillian note over Kashmir. His line was: the result was in the hands of God; men could but do or die. He would not shed a tear if the little Union force was wiped out like the Spartans bravely defending Thermopylae. Nor would he mind Sheikh Abdullah and his Moslem, Hindu, and Sikh comrades dying at their posts in defence of Kashmir. That would be a glorious example to the rest of India; such heroic defence would affect the whole sub-continent and everyone would forget that Hindus, Moslems and Sikhs were ever enemies."

Was the Maharajah's accession valid? The answer to this question has been blurred by time. On October 28, 1947, Alan Campbell-Johnson noted that "the legality of the accession is beyond doubt. On this particular issue Jinnah has been hoist with his own petard as it was he who chose over Junagadh, to take his stand on the overriding validity of the ruler's personal decision."[7] Even the Security Council was in no doubt about the legality of the accession.. Speaking in the Council on February 4, 1948, the United States representative said: "External sovereignty of Jammu and Kashmir is no longer under the control of the Maharajah . . . with the accession of Jammu and Kashmir to India this foreign sovereignty went over to India and is exercised by India and that is how India happens to be here as a petitioner." The United Nations Commission's legal adviser came to a similar conclusion, and the Commission itself recog-

[7] Campbell-Johnson, p. 225.

nized it in its report submitted to the United Nations in which it defined its resolutions of August 13, 1948, and January 5, 1949.

An interesting fact now also obscured by time is that it was India who decided to refer the Kashmir dispute to the Security Council. She did that on January 1, 1948, "in order to avoid any possible suggestion that India had taken advantage of the State's immediate peril for her own political advantage, the Dominion Government made it clear that once the soil of the State had been cleared of the invader and normal conditions were restored, the people would be free to decide their future by the recognised democratic method of plebiscite or referendum, which, in order to ensure complete impartiality, may be held under international auspices."[8]

Militarily, India was firmly in the saddle by that time. She had the situation well in hand. The raiders were being rolled back, the lines of communication between India and the state were open, the build-up of troops and equipment had reached great proportions, a government under Sheikh Abdullah was functioning, and there was little cause for India to ask the United Nations to intervene or to voluntarily offer self-determination. Whatever reasons may be imputed to it, there is no denying that India made a civilized decision, and it was taken neither in panic nor out of weakness.

The instrument of accession was accepted by Mountbatten, as the governor general of India. India did not force the state to accede to her. Ironically, Kashmir was forced to accede to India by Pakistan because of the latter's faith in and reliance on violence, a recourse which precipitated a situation which otherwise might have turned out in Pakistan's favor.

Of the raiders Pakistan sent into the state in October, 1947, Robert Trumbull of *The New York Times* wrote: "There was never any doubt that Pakistani provincial authorities, perhaps unofficially but certainly not without the knowledge of Karachi, supplied the blood-thirsty tribal *lashkars* (war party) with truck

---

[8] Government of India: *White Paper on Jammu and Kashmir*, p. 77.

transport. And Pakistani army officers, alleged to be on 'leave,' led the contingent."[9] The most revealing admission, however, came from Pakistan's governor general, M. A. Jinnah himself, in a conversation with Mountbatten in Lahore on November 1, 1947.

> Mountbatten advised Jinnah of the strength of the Indian forces in Srinagar and of their likely build-up in the next few days. He told him that he considered the prospect of the tribesmen entering Srinagar in any force was now remote. This led Jinnah to make his first general proposition, which was that both sides should withdraw at once and simultaneously. When Mountbatten asked him to explain how the tribesmen could be induced to remove themselves, his reply was, "If you do this I will call the whole thing off", which at least suggests that the public propaganda line that the tribal invasion was wholly beyond Pakistan's control will not be pursued too far in private discussion.[1]

It was not Jinnah alone who was hoist with his own petard through Hari Singh's accession to India. India too has since been hoisted with one of her own making: her submission of the Kashmir case to the United Nations. The only positive result of that move to date has been the cease fire, which was made possible through the United Nations Commission's efforts, and the posting of United Nations observers along the cease fire line. Had India not taken the Kashmir issue to the United Nations, had she settled it instead, once and for all, through force of arms, she would have avoided being put on the spot time and again.

What are the underlying factors which have bedeviled the Kashmir question over the years? How important is Kashmir to the two countries who have so bitterly contested its ownership? Is there justification in assuming that India's pledge to hold a plebiscite remains unaffected by the events of the last nineteen

---

[9] Robert Trumbull: *As I See India* (New York: William Sloane Associates; 1956), p. 89.

[1] Campbell-Johnson, p. 229.

years? Under what conditions could the pledge have become operative? Will the Kashmir caldron continue to simmer, or is some solution possible? These are the vexing questions around which much of the mystery and mystique of Kashmir is woven.

The propaganda blasts from Pakistan, aimed at projecting the entire plebiscite question in distorted perspective, have not been the only reasons the Kashmir question has stayed in the news. Being factors beyond India's control they are of lesser consequence. But it was within India's power to ensure efficient administration of the state. Her glaring failure to do so helped greatly to aggravate the Kashmir question. First an adventurer, then a man utterly corrupt, was allowed to shape the destiny of a beleaguered state with a vigilant enemy across its borders and an attentive world watching all that went on within them. This neglect will remain one of Nehru's most extraordinary lapses, though in a sense it was characteristic of his inability to pick the right man for the right job.

Sheikh Abdullah, Nehru's friend and Kashmir's first popular Prime Minister, was a man who had nursed great ambitions over the years and was obsessed with them when he came into power in October, 1947. During his term of six years in office, Abdullah, through irresponsible action and oratory, not only alienated himself from the Indian leadership but fixed world attention on the state through his irresponsible politicking. The tragedy of it all is that, through omission, the Indian Government connived with Abdullah's adventurism. It observed the drift and failed to arrest it. And when the drift came to a head, with Sheikh Abdullah openly flouting Nehru's authority, he was unceremoniously arrested and removed from office.

Nehru can be indicted for not insisting, when he easily could have, that only the most brilliant and hand-picked men of proven merit and integrity fill all important positions in the state government. He could and should have initiated an imaginatively prepared crash program to develop the state educationally and industrially and pull it out of its centuries-old backwardness. He could have opened it for resettlement of a million refugees from

West Pakistan who, with their grit and guts and undisputed drive, could have brought the state not only prosperity but security. Nehru had absolute authority to accomplish this at that time, both in India and in the state. His decisions were prone to acceptance without question; yet he and his cabinet showed signal lack of vision in not taking such actions.

To appoint Bakshi Ghulman Mohammed to succeed Sheikh Abdullah was even worse. During his regime of over ten years as Prime Minister of the state, while his own family made vast fortunes, the misfortunes of the Kashmiri people were removed with only half the sense of urgency they deserved because of the political importance of the state. New Delhi's reaction was that of an indulgent observer—untouched by the rampant corruption, undismayed by the decline in the morale of the people of Kashmir, uninterested in acting swiftly to remove the corrupt politicians and the decadent institutions built by them in the valley.

The time lapse, poor administration, and the bumbling manner in which India has projected her case have all confused the central issue in the Kashmir debate. The impression many countries abroad have formed is at best one of two grownups incessantly squabbling, and at worst one of India holding on to something she is not entitled to. The facts are quite different. When India filed a complaint in the Security Council on January 1, 1948, she herself "made it clear that once the soil of the State had been cleared of the invader and normal conditions were restored, the people would be free to decide their future by the recognized democratic method of plebiscite or referendum." There could be no stronger proof of her intentions, or of the spirit in which she approached the United Nations. But the operative term was *"once the soil of the State has been cleared of the invader."* This was not inserted as a loophole. This was based on the assumption that international opinion would compel aggression to be eliminated first. The United Nations did recognize this principle when the United Nations Commission for India and Pakistan (UNCIP) passed a resolution on August 13, 1948—which, incidentally, was accepted by both India and Pakistan—that "As the presence of troops of Pakistan in the territory of the State of Jammu and Kashmir constitutes a material change in the situation since it was represented by the Government of Pakistan before the Security Council, the Government of Pakistan agrees to withdraw its troops from that State." But today, eighteen years after that resolution was accepted, Pakistan is still in illegal occupation of 40 per cent of the state's territory. The portion which was under her occupation—or under the occupation of the "tribesmen," as she preferred to call them then—at the time of the cease fire, is still held by her. Pakistan calls this portion Azad (Free) Kashmir, and has planted a puppet President at the head of it. It is against the background of this cynical flouting of the United Nations resolution of August 13, 1948, that the demand for a plebiscite in Kashmir must be seen. It will take time to determine the price the West will eventually pay for pampering Pakistan with regard to Kashmir. The first instalment was paid when Pakistan gave 2,700 square miles of strategic Pakistan-occupied Kashmir territory to China in an agreement signed between them on March 2, 1963.

China's interest in Kashmir is a direct consequence of Western moves which have centered around it. China was led toward what it now considers fair game. The quarry was sighted by the West, but soon China was also in full pursuit. "Kashmir is near the borders of four countries, India, Pakistan, Afghanistan and China," said Peking Radio in a broadcast on September 13, 1965. "Its position is strategic and its mineral resources are rich." These are ominous words. And very revealing, coming as they do from a regime which is selective in its use of words.

If the West encouraged Pakistan in the United Nations, China encouraged her outside it. It can be a heady experience to be supported on all sides, and it went to Pakistan's head.

On the morning of August 7, 1965, a fleet of cars turned in at the gates of the presidential palace in Rawalpindi. The new Indian High Commissioner, Kewal Singh, had arrived to present his credentials to President Ayub. The usual sentiments were expressed, though when Kewal Singh appealed to the president for his country's friendship Ayub's thoughts were probably far away on his plans for Kashmir, which were at that very moment being put into action. But Kewal Singh was in dead earnest. He was born and brought up in West Pakistan at a time when it was still a part of India. Later, as a member of the Indian Civil Service, he had served there. Many of his friends and colleagues were in powerful positions in Pakistan. He was determined to convince them of his belief that the existence of the two countries depended on an enduring accord between them.

But the die had been cast. A massive, specially trained force of infiltrators had begun to move on August 5. As the pleasantries were being exchanged that morning of August 7 in Rawalpindi, Pakistani commandos with grenades, guns, and detonators were taking up positions throughout the valley of Kashmir. On August 9 the news broke that major moves had been made across the border into Kashmir. Within a few days it was open knowledge. Writing from Rawalpindi the London *Times* correspondent reported on August 31: "There can be no doubt that the guerrilla action in Kashmir results from infiltration from this (Pakistan) side in an operation conceived, planned and directed by the Government of Pakistan." London's *Daily Telegraph* reported that the "most likely reason for Pakistan's action in sending the infiltrators into Kashmir seems to be the realization by Pakistan that it was futile to place any reliance on the local population and that the only way to keep the Kashmir question alive was to send in groups of well-armed intruders for sabotage and general guerrilla warfare." Analyzing Pakistan's strategy later, in its issue of October 13, 1965, William Patterson, associate publisher of *Saturday Review,* wrote: "The armed infiltrators Pakistan began sending into Kashmir last August were to inspire local uprisings . . . the Pakistan army, poised and waiting, was then to respond to pleas from our Kashmiri brothers for protection against Indian brutality, and was to sweep through Kashmir on a mission of mercy right to the Indian frontier. There it was to halt while President Ayub Khan presented the world with a *fait accompli* . . . the strategy was to mix force with appeals to the United

Nations for peace—in order to consolidate politically the armed seizure of Kashmir."

On the night of August 24–5 detachments of the Indian army crossed over into Azad Kashmir to occupy the Pakistani outposts in the Tithwal sector, and on August 27–8 they moved into the Uri-Poonch area to secure vantage positions, among them the Haji Pir Pass, which overlooks the routes the infiltrators took to come into the state. These were operations India could no longer avoid. In a sense they were analogous to the American pounding of Viet Cong bases in the North that support their activities in the South.

Events now moved with breathtaking speed. At dawn on September 1, 1965, tanks of Pakistan's Armoured Division rumbled across the Indian border in the Akhnoor sector in Jammu with the objective of cutting off Jaurian, India's main link with Jammu and the entire Valley of Kashmir, and beyond that, Ladakh. India's reaction was swift and decisive. She called in her air force to strike at the attacking tank columns, and ordered the Eleventh Corps to mount a major three-pronged attack toward Lahore. On the morning of September 6, the Eleventh Corps struck. On September 9, Indian troops opened two new fronts: against Pakistan's Sialkot sector, and across the border at Gadra in Rajasthan. It was a war of savage intensity on the battlefields and in the air. It was a war in which cities were blacked out, places of worship razed to the ground (St. Paul's Cathedral in Ambala in the Indian state of Punjab on September 20), hospitals bombed (the Military Hospital in Ambala on September 18 and Jodhpur Jail Hospital in India's Rajasthan state on September 22), and densely packed civilian areas pounded from the air (Amritsar and Jodhpur). On September 15 as many as ten raids were made in a single day on India's holy city of Amritsar. It was a war in which the conventions of international protocol and diplomatic behavior were contemptuously trampled upon. The Indian Chancery in Karachi was searched for seven hours on September 13 in violation of all norms nations have established and respected for centuries. On September 11 every nook and cranny of Kewal Singh's residence in Karachi was searched, a treatment no civilized country has meted out to an envoy in recent years.

When at 3:30 a. m. on September 23, 1965, the order to cease fire became effective, it silenced the guns. But the dispute remains. Whether the agreement signed at Tashkent[2] between President Ayub and India's late Prime Minister Shastri, is able to extinguish the smoldering fires of hate between the two countries, remains to be seen. But there have been other changes, radical and revolutionary, which have transformed the context and meaning of this dispute.

The first of these is the jolt India's friendship with the West received. Within two months of the October, 1962, war between China and India, Russia was delivering helicopters to India, along with other arms and equipment. Five months after the shooting had stopped in September, 1965, neither the United States nor the United Kingdom had resumed either arms or their economic aid, whereas the Russian response was once more generous and immediate. "Ironically, the Indian Government was finding its sole response in the Soviet Union, while the West, which had so often decried India's neutralism in the cold war, was being very stiffly proper and neutral in a hot war. . . . The Soviet Union has gained enormous prestige in India by remaining steadfast to her commitments. The United States and Britain

---

[2] In the Tashkent Declaration signed on January 10, 1966, India and Pakistan agreed to: 1. Exertion of all efforts to create good neighborly relations and settle disputes without recourse to force, in accordance with the United Nations Charter. 2. Withdrawal of all armed personnel to positions held prior to August 5, 1965. 3. Noninterference in each other's internal affairs. 4. Discouragement of hostile propaganda, and active promotion of friendly relations. 5. Return of the high commissioners to their posts. 6. Restoration of economic and trade relations, communications and cultural exchanges, and implementation of existing agreements. 7. Repatriation of prisoners of war. 8. Discussion of problems of refugees and eviction of illegal immigrants, prevention of exodus of people, and the return of property and assets taken over by either side during the conflict. 9. Meetings at all levels to discuss matters of direct concern to both countries, and the setting up of joint India-Pakistan bodies to report to the two Governments.

have lost face throughout Southeast Asia, as well as a magnificent opportunity to gain urgently needed prestige by honoring our commitments to India. . . ."[3]

The American action reflected misjudgment of the central issues involved in the Indo-Pakistan dispute. In attempting to equate the differences between the two countries with those of other tiresome neighbors elsewhere in the world, United States policy-makers showed colossal ignorance of the high stakes the West has in seeing India's free institutions emerge intact from the power struggle which is beginning to develop in this vital Asian region. "People seem incapable of grasping the unique importance of Indian democracy and even those who do realise what a miracle it is—and what measureless disaster its destruction would be—cannot see the connection between India's freedom and integrity of India's federal union," wrote John Grigg, the former Lord Altrincham, in *The Guardian* on September 9, 1965. He continued:

Yet the two are inseparable. Let no one doubt that this is an issue in the present war—an issue which, as we now believe, justified Abraham Lincoln in fighting one of the bloodiest wars in history. At that time, of course, sophisticated British opinion was strongly opposed to Lincoln and his cause. Gentlemanly Southerners were preferred to scheming Yankees. But in the perspective of history, true merits of the struggle are more clearly seen. North's victory preserved American democracy to be the salvation of the Western world. India's victory would have the same vital significance for the East. I am not suggesting that democracies can do no wrong, dictatorships no right. But it is a good principle that democracies should stand together and make generous allowance for each other's faults. We cannot afford to treat a secular state, with a freely elected Government and a free press, on a par with a theocratic state, ruled by a military dictator and with a controlled press. . . . If India loses, fissiparous tendencies in the country will soon get out of control and the light of freedom will

[3] William D. Patterson: "A View from India," *Saturday Review* (October 30, 1965).

be extinguished in Asia. Either way, those in the West who are now failing to support India will have a massive cause for regret.

Another effect of the September, 1965, events will be that the Indian public will increasingly resent any debating of the Kashmir issue. Unless, of course, an Indian Prime Minister with a penchant for discussing it would like to see himself removed from power. The reasons for this changed attitude, apart from the purely emotional ones, now center around a fuller appreciation in India of the strategic importance of Kashmir and Ladakh to the national objective of containing China's thrust into Pakistan and along India's borders.

Ladakh is of supreme importance to China. Through a corner of its Aksai Chin plateau runs the new Yeh-Ch'end-Tibet highway which China built in 1956–7. It connects Yarkand and Khotan in Sinkiang with Gartok in Tibet. This was not a factor for consideration in 1947 when India offered to hold a plebiscite in Jammu and Kashmir. Today it is. China's concern is to keep this highway open so that it continues to "bring into Western Tibet from Sinkiang the supplies of foodstuffs and livestock which the large Chinese garrisons now posted there require, freeing the roads from China to Eastern Tibet for the transport of oil, petrol and munitions."[4] She can secure this link, of vital importance to her occupation of Tibet—ideally, by ousting India from Kashmir; alternatively, by ensuring India remains weak and preoccupied there. If, in collusion with Pakistan, Kashmir is kept in a state of ferment, conditions might deteriorate to the point where the idea of an independent Kashmir can be successfully promoted. China's strategy, therefore, is to keep the subcontinent strife-torn, restless, and divided.

Firstly, it prevents India from concentrating on wresting back from China the area she now occupies illegally in Ladakh. Secondly, it keeps India economically burdened by the vast outlays her simultaneous confrontation with Pakistan and China require.

[4] L. F. Rushbrook William, C. B. E.: "The New Phase in India-Pakistan Relations," *Asian Review* (July 1960).

Thirdly, the continuous preoccupation of India and Pakistan with Kashmir keeps them from uniting against China. Fourthly, by keeping the valley in despair the frustration of its people can be exploited.

The roads which provide logistic support to the Indian divisions facing the Chinese in far-flung Ladakh converge from the outer rim of this territory to Leh, the capital of Ladakh. From there, through great mountain ranges, the road link leads to Srinagar. Then it winds upward to the Banihal Pass, down again to Jammu, and from there into Pathankot and the rest of India. To expect the Indian Government to ignore its commitment to safeguard this vital route into India is tantamount to expecting it to abdicate its most fundamental responsibility to the country. China realizes the unique advantage of controlling this deep and potentially dangerous wedge in the Indian subcontinent, through which India and Pakistan could both be threatened at will.

India has special treaty arrangements with both Sikkim and Bhutan which place responsibility for their defense on her. By effectively defending Ladakh, India can demonstrate to these border kingdoms her ability to defend their sovereignty from Chinese hegemony.

Another aspect, no less important than security, was underscored by a senior editor of *Newsweek*, Arnaud de Borchgrave, in a radio interview in New York on October 20, 1965: ". . . the Indians, if they concede anything at all in Kashmir, are running the risk of seeing the Indian Federal Union fly apart. In other words, if they concede some kind of autonomy to Kashmir, they could very well—the next step would be agitation for self-determination or self-government or separate language states in other parts of India, and the whole thing could collapse. The great experiment of Indian democracy could collapse, and the only people who could stand to gain from that would be the Chinese, and you might even see a local brand of Chinese Communist regimentation in India. It could well bring down democratic forces, and that is what is at stake in Kashmir." About a plebiscite, de Borchgrave said: "There is no question of a plebiscite now. I know they did agree to it originally, but today to expect the Indians to stick to that pledge of seventeen years ago is as unrealistic as expecting President Johnson, for example, to accede to would-be Mexican demands for a plebiscite in Texas. It is just not in the cards."

One of the more unfortunate casualties of the miserable doings in the latter half of 1965 was the United Nation's stand on India. "When future historians get down to the job of examining the Security Council's bona fides and its claims to sit in lofty judgment on the destinies of smaller peoples the record will reveal as shoddy and sordid a tale of backstage intrigues and manouvres as ever soiled any Chancery with James Bond around. On Kashmir the Security Council's record is luridly dishonest . . . the odium for the unconscionable prolongation of the Kashmir dispute attaches to the U. N. for its initial insistence on refusing to distinguish between the aggressor and the party attacked. . . ." wrote Frank Moraes, editor in chief of *The Indian Express,* in his paper on September 6, 1965. A sober, responsible, pro-Western journalist, Moraes was provoked into writing in this manner, and he was no exception. The Indian press reacted sharply to the obvious attempts of the United Nations to equate India's defensive actions with Pakistan's aggressive ones.

If the United Nations had set its record straight by a long, clear look at the implications of Pakistan's action in sending infiltrators into Kashmir in August, 1965, and made no bones about naming Pakistan the aggressor in early August, not only might the inevitable escalation of hostilities have been avoided, but India's shattered confidence in the United Nations might have been to some extent restored. By attempting once again to keep the balance even between the aggressor and the attacked, the United Nations damaged still further its standing in India.

The *coup de grâce* to India's disenchantment with the United Nations, an institution she has supported diligently over the years, was appropriately dealt by Z. A. Bhutto, Pakistan's foreign minister, in his address to the Security Council. His behavior reached its nadir when he said: "The Indian dogs have gone home but not in Srinagar, only in the Security Council." It is doubtful if the United Nations in the worst of its haranguing, tirading, shoe-pounding days saw more unbecoming behavior then that of the foreign minister of Pakistan that night of October 25. The tragedy of that unfortunate episode was not so much that decency and decorum were violated as that Hector Acpaysee Reyes, the Council's chairman, was reluctant to rule against such conduct.

Canadian correspondent Richard Purser of the *Winnipeg Free Press,* who witnessed Bhutto's performance, summed it up in his report to his paper. "On the basis of Mr. Bhutto's performance here in the small hours of Wednesday," he wrote, "he could best serve his country's cause by staying at home with his mouth taped shut. His diatribe was a catalogue of verbal excesses delivered with a high-pitched emotion in a voice sometimes nearly breaking in sobs of passionate hate. . . . This is a technique of gross exaggeration carried to Hitlerian extremes. It was the most violent attack by a civilised country's representative against a neighbour that this correspondent has ever heard."

India has acquitted herself well over the years with both Pakistan and the United Nations. The moderation of India's leadership in its dealings with Pakistan was evident as early as 1948 when she gave $118,400,000 (about £44 million) to her (as part of the financial agreements between the two) at a time when Pakistan had laid siege to the state of Kashmir. That sense of fair play has continued throughout. In October–November, 1965, within weeks of the cease fire, India released an amount of $16,910,000 to Pakistan as annual payment under the Indus Water Treaty, and she also released water from her eastern rivers.

No ending to the Kashmir story is likely in the foreseeable future. Just as the world learned to live with the Cold War, the Berliners with the tension along the wall dividing them, and the Malayans with the bullying by Sukarno, India too will reconcile herself to living with the Kashmir crisis. It might help if other countries would appreciate the fact that Kashmir is an integral part of India. Otherwise, India will most likely learn to live without that appreciation.

India and Southeast Asia

China's outward push all along the perimeter of Southeast Asia will be the biggest threat to this part of the world in the coming years, creating a situation that brings this region sharply into focus for India. Here converge the vital interests of India, China, and Japan, the three major Asian powers. India's tragedy is that while China, through manipulation and militancy, and Japan, through her excellence in the sciences, finance, and industry, have created their spheres of influence in most of the Southeast Asian countries, India, through desultory and indifferent diplomacy, has lost the status she gained in the first ten years of independence. In the absence of any fundamental political objectives in Southeast Asia, India's attempts to get a firm foothold there have lacked drive. In Indian estimation Arab and African countries overshadowed Southeast Asia in importance— though no tangible gains accrued from her great flirtation with the Afro-Arab world—while little was done to prevent China's shadow from hanging low over the small but vital countries of Southeast Asia.

India's conflict with China in October, 1962, brought home the true dimensions of the Chinese menace, but failed even then to provide a new direction to her policies toward Southeast Asian countries. Tunku Abdul Rahman, the Malayan Prime Minister, was in India when China attacked her in 1962. Considering that there was a large Chinese population in his own country, the Tunku took a remarkably unambiguous stand in India's favor. He denounced Chinese adventurism as "aimed at showing Communist China's strength and might to impress the smaller nations," and on his way back home was even more explicit when he stated in Singapore on November 1, 1962, that in the event of war between India and China, his country would give India "all-out support." He said he was against any half-hearted policies on such questions. That, however, is not the case with India. In no recent crisis in Southeast Asia, a crisis-prone, strife-torn, and restless region, has India taken a firm and unequivocal stand on any issue. Her weak and vacillating policies have lacked China's militancy and Japan's economic vitality.

In contrast, Mao's basic dictum, which he outlined in a speech as far back as 1937, reveals the kind of Chinese tactic India is up against: "Processes change, old processes and old contradictions disappear, new processes and new contradictions emerge, and the methods of resolving contradictions differ accordingly." Translated into practical politics, this means that "Mao's domestic and foreign policies alike are constructed around this theory of contradictions, in which one antagonistic force is used to overcome another in the classical thesis-antithesis-synthesis progression, which Mao views as unending. It provides for many shifts and devious routes, in foreign affairs particularly."[5] India's inability to effectively counter China's diplomacy in Southeast Asia can be better understood against this background of Chinese strategy. India's policies are too rigid to stand up to the flexibility of Chinese diplomacy.

One of the most grievous examples of Indian diplomacy is the manner in which India avoided taking a firm position at the time of the formation of Malaysia. In a report on the Indian Parliament's proceedings on February 23, 1963, *The Times of India* said:

> The Prime Minister carefully avoided any direct comment on the merits of the issue of Malaysia but said that the paramount thing from India's point of view was that "those British territories would cease to be colonies." The rest is for them to decide! Mr. Kamath [Opposition Member of Parliament], referred to the "bellicose postures" of Indonesia and said that the "new Imperialism" of Jakarta constituted a threat to the peace of the region. Mr.

[5] O. Edmund Clubb: "China's Position in Asia," *Journal of International Affairs*, XVII, No. 2 (1963), 115.

Nehru replied that the statement of Mr. Kamath disguised as a question did not help the cause of peace. "It is a complicated question. There are two points of view and recently a third country, the Philippines, has entered the picture. India can only hope that mediation by the U. N. Secretary General would succeed in securing an orderly and peaceful transfer of power by the U. K. What more can I say", he added.

India's hesitancy, characteristic of her foreign policy, placed her at a clear disadvantage in respect to the pliable Chinese. The fact that a great Asian country like India was unable to take a decisive stand on Malaysia did little to enhance the Indian image in Southeast Asia. If there were "two points of view" with regard to Malaysia's formation, the Sino-Indian differences were not so simple, either. Yet the Tunku took an unequivocal stand, not in favor of militant, ultranationalist, and expansionist China, but in favor of India.

If the Opposition Member of Parliament's question in the Indian Parliament "did not help the cause of peace," neither did India's reluctance to support Malaysia's right to federate with other territories. Peace is seldom secured by submitting to unprincipled bullying, and Indonesia, as later events proved, was not unduly enamored by India's initial reluctance to support Malaysia. On the contrary, India's record of indecision encouraged Indonesia to treat her contemptuously at the time of her conflict with Pakistan in September, 1965, when a stage-managed Indonesian mob burnt India's Information Office in Jakarta on September 9, 1965.

There is an influential section of opinion in India which subscribes to the theory that "In spite of all the unprincipled moves Indonesia has made and her tactical alignment with China, she remains the inspiration for dynamic nationalism in the region. This nationalism is built around the Malay race—stretching from southern Thailand to the Philippines—and contains strands of Islam and a strong, if mixed-up, radicalism. This mixture, as events will prove in the future as they have in the past, is a heady brew for some 150 million people in South-East Asia."[6] The first half of this appreciation, concerning Indonesia's efforts at becoming the beacon light for nationalism in Southeast Asia, is correct. What is doubtful is whether the common denominators of race and religion are sufficient to hold together the different countries of the area. The animosity between the Thais and the Cambodians and the conflicts betwen Arab countries, despite Islamic ties, prove the weakness of this theory of religion. If the Tunku has now become lukewarm in his approach to the Kashmir question, despite his representative's spirited defense of India's case in the United Nations, it is due to India's equivocal support of the formation of Malaysia. To attribute the Tunku's changed attitude to a rising tide of nationalism in Malaysia is to pick a pet premise out of context. If there is a mood of narrow nationalism in Malaysia, a hesitant India has helped it along. Parties like the Pan-Malayan Islamic Party and Party Rakyat, who were opposed to the Tunku's earlier support to India, found their chauvinistic opposition strengthened by India's wavering stand on Malaysia.

If China and Pakistan can settle their differences when it suits them, and Malaysia and Indonesia can replace confrontation with co-operation, as some observers expect them to,[7] there is no reason to assume that support of Malaysia would necessarily prevent India from entering into a more meaningful relationship with Indonesia in the future. But for any relationship to be meaningful it has to be founded on a clear appreciation of each other's strength and capabilities. So far, India has only shown her weaknesses.

Decisive support of Malaysia would have prevented the mis-

[6] S. Nihal Singh: "New Delhi Must Think Anew on Southeast Asia," *The Statesman*, August 24, 1965.

[7] "The winds of Malay-Indonesian nationalism are likely to prevail over others. Given Indonesia's radicalism, minus its Peking-oriented Communism, India can only hope that the religious element in this future coming together of Malays and Indonesians will not dominate their political thinking." S. Nihal Singh: "Conflicting Pulls in Southeast Asian Politics," *The Statesman*, December 9, 1965.

understanding now being created in Kuala Lumpur through India's friendliness toward the breakaway state of Singapore. Ultranationalist elements in Malaysia are misconstruing that friendliness, and the task before Indian diplomacy is to counter such efforts.

On the other hand, while there should be no illusions in India's mind about the loyalty to mainland China of predominantly Chinese Singapore, so long as it is feasible India should use her friendly relations with Singapore to their mutual advantage. India can gain nothing by alienating herself from or isolating Singapore. She should carry both Malaysia and Singapore with her.

If the Islamic tie is played up at some future date, Singapore's non-Islamic character could be of advantage, as could those of Buddhist Burma and Thailand, part Buddhist and part Roman Catholic South Vietnam, and the predominantly Roman Catholic Philippines. India's inexplicable failure to involve the vast numbers of Buddhist peoples in Southeast Asia with the land where the Buddha was born is an unpardonable lapse. By doing so India could in no way be accused of expediency. She would only be emphasizing the fact that India is the fountainhead of a great philosophy from which the gospel of wisdom and peace fanned out across Asia and beyond. A vividly imaginative move for India would be to declare the holy city of Gaya a gift to Buddhists around the world, with a special status somewhat like that of the Vatican City in Rome. Within its confines could be developed the world's biggest center of Buddhist teaching and a library of books and historical records supplemented by an outstanding center of research manned by distinguished Buddhist scholars.

Something on the above lines, had it been in existence during the last decade, might have exercised an emotional pull on Buddhist Burma; hopefully, it might even have made her ally herself with India in order to resist invidious colonizing by China. Instead, Burma's behavior toward India has been strange; but stranger still has been the fact that India has questioned neither the Burmese Government's right to expel Burma's Indian settlers nor the expropriating of their businesses and entire personal wealth. When India's Minister of State for External Affairs, Mrs. Lakshmi Menon, went to Burma to explain the Indo-Chinese conflict in 1962 to General Ne Win, her comment on her return home was: "We put our case before him and he listened with great interest and asked many questions about which he was doubtful. He never expressed sympathy or non-sympathy and we never expected him to do so"—a demeaning statement for the representative of a sovereign country to make. If Burma had to be told anything, it was to demand compensation for the unprincipled manner in which she had taken over Indian assets. Burma could never have done what she did had India not continuously projected a flabby image of herself before her Asian neighbors.

As against the Burmese rebuff, Thailand—which had often been at the receiving end of India's caustic criticism because of her membership in the Southeast Asia Treaty Organization—came out squarely for India. So did South Vietnam. Yet India kept advising South Vietnam's ally, America, to stop bombing the bases and staging areas from which the North was trying to overrun the South. Insofar as Korea is concerned—a country for which India staked all her diplomatic efforts in 1950, antagonizing both America and Russia in turn; where she made substantial contributions in defense personnel as well as civilians—it now finds hardly a place in the calculations of those who frame India's Asian policies.

And lastly, Japan, a country which in the final count holds the key to the future of Asia. Japan has reached a dazzling position of economic, scientific, technological, and financial pre-eminence. Her industrial growth rate is the highest in the world. Not only does her per capita income surpass that of any other country in Asia, but it continues to increase at a rate higher than all others. In technological sophistication she has bettered international standards, and through the drive and dynamism generated by the successive regimes of Shigeru Yoshida, Ichiro Hatoyama, and

Nobusuke Kishi her industrial productivity has been placed on an unassailable base. Her businessmen, bankers, bureaucrats, politicians, and even her premiers have traveled extensively through Southeast Asia and secured for Japan a pivotal role in the development projects of most countries in the region. She has scrupulously avoided all controversies, initiated technical assistance programs through the Colombo Plan, offered teaching, training, and financial help to Southeast Asian trainees, played an assertive role in the Economic Commission for Asia and the Far East, contributed to the Mekong River Project, become a member of the Organization for Economic Cooperation and Control, and—most important of all—has a reliable record of having taken a hard line against Communist China for years. In an interview on October 14, 1958, Kishi said: "Japan must do everything it can to prevent Taiwan and Korea from being subjugated by the Communists. For the sake of Japan's security we must not allow this to happen. The situation in the Taiwan Straits is not a civil war. It is an international battle against Communist aggression."[8]

Japan's defensive concerns are with Northeast Asia. "Southeast Asia seems to have been conceived differently. This was the region of economic opportunity. This was the community within which Japan was destined for economic leadership . . . everywhere the Kishi men stressed Japan's peaceful purposes, its intent to cooperate fully with the free world and the United Nations, to which it had been admitted, and deep concern for Asia. The peace and prosperity of Japan were dependent on the peace and prosperity of Asia. . . ."[9]

For Indian diplomacy this can be the factor on which to hinge a new relationship with Japan: their mutual interest in ensuring peace in Asia, so that the prosperity of Asian countries, and their own, can be achieved. Since peace and prosperity in Southeast Asia are far from being the concern of expansionist and militant

[8] James W. Morley: "Japan's Position in Asia," *Journal of International Affairs,* XVII, No. 2 (1963), 147.
[9] Ibid.

China, this fact too has to be emphasized in their relationship.

In much the same way as powerful voices are beginning to be heard in India in favor of arming the country with a nuclear deterrent, "the Japanese mood may change when China begins producing atomic or hydrogen weapons."[1] Japan, however, is at an advantage. She has a security pact with the United States which guarantees her protection without necessitating substantial outlays on her part. But that guarantee can not help Japan protect her vast economic interests in Southeast Asia. In the ultimate analysis any form of threat to national interests can only be met by a similar counterthreat. Beneath the surface, despite the chastening experience of the last war, there is already a resurgent militarism. It is difficult to believe that Japan's moderate leadership can keep this latent spirit in check in face of the growing Chinese menace.

What is required of India on the basis of the foregoing is a determined economic and diplomatic reorientation toward Japan, much closer industrial and investment collaboration, the setting up of a supply mission in Tokyo, training of military personnel in Japan, and eventually perhaps even a defense treaty. One of the ways of intensifying Japanese interest in all this is by enabling her to raise her stakes in India.

Any purposeful political and diplomatic drive by India in Southeast Asia can be successful only if it is founded on sound economic strength and military power. The two are complementary because one is not possible without the other, and without these two to back Indian efforts in Southeast Asia, her diplomacy will continue to lack realism. All along the periphery of China are nations which need economic help; India must be willing and in a position to give it to them. Preaching the gospel of peace and noninvolvement is not enough, no matter how much passion is put into it. In view of the fact that not only the public but even India's governmental institutions show no grasp of national perspective and do not work as an integrated team to

[1] Allan B. Cole: "Political Contrasts—China, India and Japan," *Journal of International Affairs*, XVII (1963), 166.

achieve those perspectives, it is difficult to visualize how India can introduce a new dynamic into her Southeast Asian policies unless a dedicated and inspired leadership determinedly puts things right.

An elementary principle any sensible and successful politician follows is to secure a firm hold over his own constituency before attempting to wield power nationally. India tried to exercise international influence without first securing her home base. Thus, the tragedy of her political effort abroad has been that undue importance was given to the Afro-Arab world, while Southeast Asia was neglected. This showed poor political judgment on India's part, a fact confirmed by the manner in which her standing in the Arab and African world, Europe, and the United States has suffered in recent years. India is no longer considered to have any great influence in Southeast Asia, and because she is unable to influence events in one of the world's most vital regions, she is not taken as a power to be really reckoned with.

The need for pluralism in India's policies in Southeast Asian countries requires much more of her then economic and military strength. In failing, for instance, to develop educational institutions at home on the scale required, the Indian Government is not only denying Indians the necessary opportunities through which they can acquire qualities of leadership, but is also neglecting the tremendous scope which exists for offering outstanding educational facilities to the countries of Southeast Asia in every branch of learning. That Indians in their attitudes and interests are largely oriented toward the West is the result of British far-sightedness in bringing to Britain for their education the elite she knew would eventually inherit power and condition thinking in India. India must view her role in Asia in this perspective. True, she has a number of institutions teaching African, Arab, and Southeast Asian students, but their number is ridiculously low. The excellence of her educational institutions should also become a factor of importance in Indian diplomacy. It is a suggestion sure to be hooted down at the present time, since national objectives abroad are not considered a concern of the entire cabinet of the Union Government but only of the Foreign Affairs wing of the Government of India, a situation which exists in neither China nor Japan.

Since analysis of India's entire foreign policy is not the purpose of this book, no attempt is made to examine in detail her diplomacy in the Afro-Arab world, or the successes and failures achieved there. The point which nonetheless needs making is that India has without doubt given exaggerated importance over the years to the Arab world and the emerging countries of Africa, at the expense of Southeast Asia. Despite the fact that there are protagonists in India passionately in favor of even closer ties with the Arab and African worlds, and despite the fact that moves to lessen the importance given to these countries would be firmly resisted, the fact remains that until India has secured her position in Southeast Asia and developed sufficient economic strength to talk seriously of securing the markets of Arab and African countries for her products, she must lessen her involvement with West Asia and Africa. She must maintain her contacts, and nothing more.

Sooner or later India will also have to re-examine her stand toward Israel. The hypocrisy of allowing a consulate general of that country to operate in Bombay, yet drawing a fine line between that and the establishment of a full-fledged embassy in New Delhi, does India no credit. She has allowed fear of Arab displeasure to shape her attitude toward Israel long enough. The bias some of the Middle Eastern countries displayed in favor of Pakistan in her fight with India in September, 1965, showed that India had not gained much by ostracizing Israel. It was one thing for them to express views on Kashmir contrary to India's, or to express solidarity with Pakistan, but it was clearly a hostile act on the part of Saudi Arabia, Jordan, Iran, and Turkey to have sent arms and other equipment to Pakistan. And sufficient reason for India to re-examine her past and reassess her future Middle East policies. Closer contacts with Israel could prove useful to India for securing arms supplies in the future and could favorably dispose world Jewry toward India, especially

American Jewry which has great influence in the banking and financial circles in the United States. Apart from the technical, scientific, and agricultural skills with which Israel could help India, the most important thing is that by drawing closer to Israel, India could pave the way for securing for that country a place in the comity of nations. Indian diplomacy could successfully turn Israel's gratitude to India's advantage.

In all her external policies India's thinking must be conditioned by the national imperative of strengthening the country for the confrontation with China. It is going to be a continuing confrontation, and on its outcome will depend the shape of things in the world for generations to come.

6
India and China: The Continuing Confrontation

We, in India, have had 2,000 years of friendship with China. We have differences of opinion and even small conflicts, but when we hearken back to that long past something of the wisdom of that past helps us to understand each other," said Nehru on a British Broadcasting Corporation program in December, 1949. He was giving his reasons for recognizing the Chinese Communist regime.

Two months earlier Peking, the other half in this friendly twosome, had expressed *its* views: "British imperialism and its running dog, India, through their officially controlled publications, have declared in unison that Tibet never acknowledged China's suzerainty over it, and that Britain never acknowledged China's claim that Tibet is part of China. . . . Nehru, riding behind the imperialists, whose stooge he is, actually considers himself the leader of the Asian peoples. Into his slavish and bourgeoisie reactionary character has now been instilled the beastly ambition for aggression. . . . The bourgeoisie of India

. . . have learned the ways of the imperialists, and are harbouring intentions against Tibet and Sikkim as well as Bhutan . . . the victory of the Chinese people has brought dawn to the oppressed peoples of Asia and sealed the fate of Nehru and betrayers of his ilk. The Chiang Kai-sheks of India, Burma, Indonesia and others of their ilk must march on the same road to death as Chiang Kai-shek has done."[1]

From this love-hate relationship India and China, the two most populous countries in the world and potentially very powerful, set out to forge a friendship of convenience. Its professed aims had wide appeal for other emergent countries: Asian resurgence, liberation from foreign domination, an opportunity to stage a dramatic entry onto the world's stage. On the reverse side of this outward façade were two wary and traditionally hostile powers maneuvering for positions. For the sake of convenience China decided to cloak her hate for India with outward love. India did the same for China, but somehow allowed herself to become inwardly infatuated. A fatal error, as it turned out.

There was little wrong with Nehru's strategy of trying to cultivate China's friendship at that time, because the strategy had a purpose. The purpose was to gain time for preparing India to face China, should such a confrontation become inevitable. This fact was lost sight of. In the time gained, India failed economically, militarily, and politically to gear herself to meet the growing menace of Communist China. During the heady days of the great *play* the countries made for each other's friendship, India began rationalizing each menacing move of her friend, attributing it simply to Asian resurgence, a dangerous oversimplification. "The only area where our interests (China's and India's) overlapped was in Tibet and . . . I had, even before I started for Peking, come to the conclusion that the British policy (which we were supposed to have inherited) of looking upon

[1] Girilal Jain: *Panchsheela and After* (Bombay: Asia Publishing House; 1960), pp. 7, 8, 10.

Tibet as an area in which we had special political interests, could not be maintained. The Prime Minister had also in general agreed with this view."[2]

China thought otherwise. In her coldly calculating way she was in no doubt about her national interests, or the manner in which India would further them. "China's problems are complicated, and our minds must also be a little complicated," Mao Tse-tung observed soon after V-J Day. Then, in a letter to the Communist Party of India which *The Communist* of Bombay published in January, 1950, he voiced the hope that "relying on the brave Communist Party of India and the unity and struggle of all Indian patriots, India certainly will not remain long under the yoke of imperialism and emerge in the Socialist and People's Democratic family. That day will end the imperialist reactionary era in the history of mankind." From China's point of view her own and India's interests did not overlap in Tibet only: the very existence of India in her constituted form was an affront which could be set right only by "the brave Communist Party of India"!

China's aims, despite the proverbial inscrutability of the Chinese, had been articulately expressed even earlier. In December, 1939, Mao had said: "The imperialists have taken away many Chinese dependent states and a part of her territories. Japan took Korea, Taiwan and the Ryukyu Islands, the Pescadores Islands, Port Arthur, England seized Burma, Bhutan, Nepal and Hong Kong; France occupied Annam, and even an insignificant country like Portugal took Macao."[3] These ominous and unambiguous words left China's Asian ambitions in no doubt. They spelled out the numerous other areas in which her interests overlapped with India's. A solution to set the situation right was also provided: "The great People's Liberation Army

[2] K. M. Panikkar: *In Two Chinas* (London: George Allen and Unwin Ltd.; 1955), p. 102.

[3] Mao Tse-tung: *Chinese Revolution and the Communist Party of China* (Bombay: People's Publishing House Ltd.; 1959), p. 9.

would march to further victories until the liberation of all Asia was completed."[4]

Countering the clear, unwavering, and fixed aims of China was India's belief that the only area where her interests with China overlapped was in Tibet. At least this was the wishful thinking of Sardar K. M. Panikkar, India's ambassador to Peking during the crucial years of 1948 to 1952. Ambassadors play a key role in influencing their government's attitudes and policies toward the countries to which they are accredited, and this remarkable simplification by the Indian ambassador of so complex an issue must have had some impact on Nehru. According to Panikkar it did: "The Prime Minister had also in general agreed with this view."

Since Panikkar's ambassadorship in those early and vital years undoubtedly influenced India's policies, it is interesting to study his own mental attitude toward China. It reveals an extraordinary amalgam of idealism and naïveté.

> My knowledge of Communism was only from books . . . all my training had been in the liberal radicalism of the West and consequently, though I was in some measure familiar with the economic doctrines of Marx, I had no sympathy for a political system in which individual liberty did not find a prominent place. But as against all this, I had a deep feeling of sympathy for the Chinese people, a desire to see them united, strong and powerful, able to stand up against the nations which had oppressed them for a hundred years, a psychological appreciation of their desire to wipe out the humiliations which followed the Western domination of their country and to proclaim the message of Asia Resurgent. . . . It was my mission, as I saw it, to prove it to him [Mao Tsetung] that a neutral position was also possible.[5]

Here were the zealot's fervor, the intellectual's confusion, the reformer's ardor, all rolled into one. Panikkar's desire to see the Chinese strong and powerful and united was as misplaced in an ambassador as an itch in a soldier to teach his enemy how to shoot

[4] Chu Teh in an address to a huge gathering in Peking in 1950.
[5] Panikkar, pp. 72, 73.

straight. His eagerness to prove to Mao that neutralism was also possible was equally unrealistic.

Panikkar's confusion and the contradictions in his thinking were evident from the outset: if he had no sympathy for a political system such as the one which had emerged in China, there was no question of wanting to see it strong and powerful, because the regimentation a system like that is capable of was bound one day to pose a dangerous threat to his own country and to her liberal institutions. If China's entire imperial history points to anything, it is this: China's main concern has always been with herself and with the cultural superiority of the Chinese people over all others. To them, the people on the periphery of their frontiers will always be barbarians. For that matter, all those across the seas will too. There never has been any question of China showing any interest in, or being involved with, Asian resurgence. A Chinese saying, "yi yi chih yi," means: "Use barbarians to control barbarians." So much for China's emotional involvement with Asia or her desire to see it resurgent.

As for Panikkar's hope of getting Mao to like the idea of neutralism, he apparently wasn't put off by the fact that Mao had himself quite tersely stated his views on it in 1949: "Neutrality is a camouflage, and a third road does not exist."

Though Indians may not readily admit it, the Chinese game of outwitting them most likely began from the time the gullibility of India's envoy—and through him, of India—became obvious. If the Indians were so eager to think well of them, the Chinese were not going to let the opportunity pass. "Peking had realised just how valuable India could be in reaching the other Asian nations who might in other circumstances, without so respected a sponsor, have shied away from so militant a neighbour with suspicion and distrust."[6] If India felt that the fact of being "in" with the isolated Communist regime of China gave her prestige and standing with the Afro-Asian world and some Western countries, it was all right with China. It was all right with her too

---

[6] George N. Patterson: *Peking Versus Delhi* (London: Faber and Faber; 1963), p. 112.

if India wanted to sponsor her at the Bandung Conference. But consequences soon showed it was not all right for India. In the years between Bandung (1954) and the abortive Afro-Asian Conference in Algeria (November, 1965), Chinese political strategy succeeded in isolating India—the very same country which had tried to draw her out of her isolation and introduce her to the various clubs of which India herself was a respected member. Those were the years of great successes for China. While the fiction of Sino-Indian friendship kept India bemused, Tibet was annexed, the state of North Vietnam was established, South Vietnam was laid siege to, Indonesia turned hostile toward India, Pakistan was wooed and won, India was defeated militarily, and Southeast Asia, was set atremble by the might of an aggressive and militant China. This, then, is what the "united, strong and powerful" China which Panikkar desired has meant to India.

Whereas the years of *panchsheel*[7] were used to superb advantage by China, India did precious little in this time to weld either domestically or diplomatically her economic, military, and political resources in preparation for the imminent struggle with China. It is futile to argue that India *did* prepare for the struggle in those years. When the showdown came, the outcome told its own story. India's defeat at the hands of the Chinese in the eastern sector of India in October, 1962, was proof of the fact that India *had not* prepared for a confrontation with China.

The Indian army had been gradually denigrated in the years since independence. Its position in 1962 was such that it had no real say even in the framing of policies concerning national security. The politicians and civil servants had between them used the sound principle of civilian control over the defense forces to invidiously lower the importance of the armed services. This may have been done out of a feeling that because the army

---

[7] *Panchsheel*: Five principles of peaceful coexistence first announced in the preamble to the Sino-Indian Trade Agreement over their relations with Tibet, in April, 1954. They are: (1) mutual respect for each other's territorial integrity and sovereignty; (2) mutual nonaggression; (3) mutual noninterference in each other's internal affairs; (4) equality and mutual benefit; (5) peaceful coexistence.

was the prestigious right arm of authority in British times, it had to be shown its place now that the times had changed. The irony in this is that the civil servants too had been trusted lieutenants of the British, yet in order to secure their own position, they willingly connived at undermining the vital functions of the armed services. The appointment of V. K. Krishna Menon as India's Defense Minister in 1957 was the final flaw in the chain of events which kept India in a state of unpreparedness. No more haughty, headstrong, or unsuitable man could have been found to head such a sensitively balanced or finely tooled instrument of national policy as the defense machine. Not only was he responsible for deep and dangerous rifts in the armed services, but he also convinced Nehru that the danger lay, not in the direction of China, but toward Pakistan and, to an extent, even toward the Western powers!

For China, on the other hand, *panchsheel* was providential. In those balmy days she got down to the business of ruthlessly subjugating Tibet and establishing major bases there from which to threaten and perhaps at a future date secure Sikkim, Nepal, Bhutan, and Burma. And who knows, maybe even India and Pakistan, with the help of fifth columns and friendly pro-Peking elements operating from within.

What was India's reaction to these obvious moves? Nothing. India could only rationalize. And so long as it suited China, she helped India rationalize. She fed her with logic of the Chinese variety and secured from her acceptance of China's annexation of Tibet. On April 19, 1954, an agreement was signed between India and China in which for the first time the phrase "the Tibet region of China" appeared. No one can say that China had not used time to *her* advantage.

China's edge over India lies in the fact that she has clear goals for which her leadership has formulated equally clear tactics. As Mao said: "We have formed the concept for a long time that strategically we should slight all enemies and tactically we should take full account of them . . . in war, battles can be fought one by one and the enemy can only be annihilated two by two. . . .

Strategically, although we slight the eating of a whole meal, we can finish the meal. But when actually eating, we do it a mouthful at a time. It would be impossible for you to swallow the entire feast in a single mouthful. This is called the one-by-one solution. In military literature, it is called smashing the enemy one by one".[8]

China's other great advantage is that the country's tough, closely-knit Communist system permits the massive potential of that vast land to be exploited and channeled at will. Her leaders have hammered out policies and programs aimed at global objectives. To achieve the grand design for which her leadership feels China is destined, the political, military, industrial, and economic functions of government are under the command of a strong, central, unified authority in Peking. There are no dissenters, as there are in India, no federation of states resentful of the power of a central authority, no divergent pulls, no cliques working at cross-purposes within the Government, no shadings of political coloration, no regional loyalties, no interministerial wrangling. Instead there is an integrated, dedicated, cohesive, and obsessed leadership demanding of the system, and securing from it, what it knows is in China's national interests.

On the other side of the Himalayas, in India, are a people split and divided and riven by a hundred hues of religion, regionalism, caste, customs, political creeds, ideological schisms— eternally conciliating and temporizing, rejecting absolutes, accepting equivocation almost as a moral code, and facing all dangers with eyes blinkered by dated beliefs.

No wonder, then, in a land in which compromise is almost a code of existence, that Nehru in time allowed his original appreciation of China to be compromised. For India, as so often has been the case, time lost all meaning. The time gained was not used to clarify the fundamental internal as well as external political objectives of emergent India. Instead of encouraging and

[8] V. C. Trivedi: *China and the Peace of Asia,* ed. Alistair Buchan (London: Chatto and Windus Ltd. [for the Institute of Strategic Studies]; 1965), p. 132.

supporting moves for the unification of India so that the country could face unified China, bickering in different regions was quieted by creating new linguistic states. Instead of creating economic power on which to found the nation's political strength, precious time was wasted in manipulating the vital financial, agricultural, and industrial sectors of the economy, with shattering effects on productivity and output. Time was not used to build up formidable and forbidding military power to deter China. Nor was it used to diplomatically undermine China's aims and motivations in countries around or beyond her periphery.

The strangest enigma presented by Nehru was that even though he sensed with uncanny perceptivity the real nature of the new China, his actions were contrary to what that awareness required of him. One example was India's initial refusal to recognize the South Vietnamese regime of Bao Dai, on the grounds that it had colonial overtones. Peking was the first to recognize Ho Chi Minh's government in North Vietnam. That was obviously in its national interests, but strangely enough India's action too furthered not her own but Peking's interests. India could have continued her outward show of friendliness toward China, but there was no reason to delay recognition of South Vietnam. Such recognition would have strengthened a regime hostile to Peking, and that would have been in *India's* interest. All of India's political actions should have had as their aim the generating of anti-Chinese lobbies in countries in which elements hostile to China could have been encouraged. In much the same way as China has generated hostility toward India in many countries— including Pakistan, Nepal, Burma, Indonesia, and, till recently, even Ceylon—India's principle and paramount effort throughout should have been the exposing of China's aims in Asia. That this was not done is not so much the failure of Indian diplomacy as failure of the Indian leadership to give it direction.

India has sent out many able envoys to represent her since Independence. Her careermen in the Foreign Office, with some exceptions, are of a high caliber. But diplomats cannot formulate policy, they can only implement it. Whereas China's diplomatic missions doubtless had clear instructions from Peking regarding their country's policy toward India, Indian missions for years have been left bewildered by New Delhi's inability to provide them with a coherent policy toward China. India knew of China's expansionist aims, yet managed to convince herself that conciliation was still the best thing, even when the propriety of many Chinese moves was in grave doubt. China's aggressive diplomacy in many world capitals was countered with weak and vacillating diplomacy. The result was that India's missions abroad, which could have effectively checkmated China's flood of false propaganda, were never given a chance. Even when the countries finally came to blows, India's missions were no better prepared than her armed forces to meet the challenge.

The October 1962 Showdown

One thing is clear: the major clashes between the Indian and Chinese armies in Ladakh and the North East Frontier Agency in October, 1962, need not have caught India napping. Chinese intentions had been obvious for over eight years, and it was only self-deception which led Indians to believe that the conflict of interests could be settled by negotiation. The events of October, 1962, were conclusive proof of the fact that Nehru's shrewd assessment of the momentous changes taking place in China had not been put to full use: "It is a complete misunderstanding of the China situation to imagine that they function like a satellite of Russia. . . . It is of great importance to Asia and the world that India and China should be friendly. How far we shall succeed in this endeavour I cannot say."

His efforts in the years since expression of this view in 1950 had been concentrated on promoting friendship with China—an admirable aim, if only he had also made some provision in the event of its failure. That he didn't is an unforgivable omission. If the Indian armed forces had been told in unmistakable terms, when evidence of Chinese duplicity first became clear, to prepare for a military showdown, the outcome of the October, 1962, collision would have been different.

When did India first become aware of China's encroachment into Indian territory? India, who has a curious knack of being carried away by her own enthusiasms and effusiveness, did not realize it but the first storm signals were up within weeks of her playing gushing host to Chou En-lai in June, 1954. On July 17 the Chinese officially protested against the presence of Indian troops in Barahoti, in the Indian state of Uttar Pradesh. They even gave Barahoti a Chinese name, Wu-Je. Here was the first claim being staked to what was indisputably Indian territory, and staked soon after India's sentimental toasting of Sino-Indian friendship. The Indian reaction was typically hesitant and uncritical. It was neatly summed up by the Government of India itself, in a press handout: "In the Agreement of April 29, 1954, the Government of China, far from laying claim to any part of Indian territory, had given a solemn undertaking to respect the territorial integrity and sovereignty of India. In view of this, the Government of India concluded that the claim to Barahoti was made by the Chinese in ignorance, particularly as they did not seem to be aware of its exact location." As if the devious and calculating Chinese would do something like that out of ignorance!

But this was only a foretaste of what was to follow. Chinese maps around this time began telling their own extraordinary story: they showed 50,000 square miles of India as Chinese territory! During an official visit to China in October, 1954, Nehru brought these cartographic inaccuracies to Chou En-lai's notice. Chou, naturally, played them down. He said the maps were reproductions of old Kuomintang maps, and because the People's Government had been rather busy it had not had time to revise them!

India swallowed the story.

In April, 1955, at the Asian-African Conference in Bandung, while Nehru toasted Chou En-lai and introduced him to the heads of the 29 nations assembled there, China got set to feast some more off India. Within weeks of a great show of amity, China made its next militant move.

In June, 1955, Chinese troops established camp at Barahoti, came down ten miles south of the Niti Pass, and challenged Indian patrols. The next year, in April, 1956, they entered the Nilang area, which is also in Uttar Pradesh. Six months later, they come into India across the Shipki Pass. India declared no national emergency, ordered no major troop movements, took no inflexible stand to discourage Chinese adventurism, did nothing to tighten up the Indian economy to meet the obvious and growing threat from the north. She sent protest notes. And when Chou En-lai visited New Delhi in November, 1956, and again in January, 1957, "It was decided that while there were no disputes regarding the border, there were certain petty problems which should be settled amicably."

Encouraged by the flabbiness of the Indian response to their probings, confirmed in their belief that they could now lay their hands on the prize they coveted, the Chinese got down to real business. With the conquest of Tibet complete, the next logical Chinese moves were: firstly, to consolidate their hold over Tibet; secondly, to acquire control of the mountain passes and high ranges from where, in a militarily advantageous position, they could threaten the plains of India, infiltrate into Indian territories, and begin the process of subjugating the Indian subcontinent.

To understand the physical dimensions—the scale and topography—of the remote and desolate regions which constitute the frontiers of India and China, the first staggering fact to note is the length of the frontiers: 2,640 miles. This includes the boundaries of Sikkim and Bhutan with Tibet, since the external relations and defense of these states are part of India's responsibility. This long boundary has three divisions: the western, middle, and eastern sectors.

The western sector begins at the tri-junction where the boundaries of India, China, and Afghanistan meet. It ends in the region where the Indian states of Kashmir, Punjab, and

Himachal Pradesh form a common boundary with Tibet. From here starts the middle sector, which ends at the tri-junction of Uttar Pradesh, Nepal, and Tibet. Then begins Nepal's boundary with Tibet. Where it ends, at the tri-junction of Nepal, Sikkim, and Tibet, begins the eastern sector, which covers Sikkim, Bhutan and the North East Frontier Agency frontiers with Tibet, and ends at the tri-junction of the North East Frontier Agency, Tibet, and Burma boundaries.

The line which divides the North East Frontier Agency from its junction with Bhutan up to the point where it meets the Burma border is known as the MacMahon Line. It was accepted by the representatives of the Governments of India, Tibet, and China in a conference in Simla in 1913–14. It is a long-dormant frontier, accepted through tradition, custom, and administrative convenience by India, Tibet, and China.

Direct access to Tibet is easiest from the east, but these roads run through difficult terrain and are subject to attacks by Tibet's Khampa guerillas, who are even now not reconciled to Chinese rule in Tibet. They were much less reconciled in the mid fifties. The southern roads pass through Bhutan, Sikkim, Nepal, and India and are thus not available to China. The major trade route from the northwest goes through Leh, the capital of Ladakh, and is also unsatisfactory from China's point of view since it traverses Indian territory.

The ideal alternative for China was to build a major highway over the Aksai-Chin Plateau, in the Indian region of Ladakh. She could thus come in to Lhasa from the north, linking her industrial might in Sinkiang to her needy garrisons in Tibet. "The road that the Chinese first built in 1956–57 across Ladakh was important to the maintenance of their control over Tibet. Without such a supply route, the officially acknowledged Khampa revolt in Eastern Tibet might have reached disastrous proportions. . . . It soon gained the status of a major road, connecting Yarkand and Khotan with Rudok, Gartok and finally Taklakot, a trade and agricultural centre of long recognised strategic interest just

North of the point where the borders of Tibet, Nepal and India meet."[9]

In the days of Sino-Indian brotherhood the Chinese could hardly tell the truth about their maps. But it is extraordinary that India should have accepted the lame excuse offered and, worse still, put so much faith in it that when the showdown came eight years later, she had no major military deployment in the disputed areas.

While the 14,000 to 16,000[1] square miles in Ladakh are vital to China for her highway into Tibet, some 36,000 square miles of the North East Frontier Agency (almost all of it) are important to her as high ground from which she can dominate the rich plains of the Indian state of Assam, with their oil fields, timber, tea, and mineral resources. Not only Assam, but Sikkim, Bhutan, parts of Bengal, and the Indian territories abutting on Burma all become indefensible with the North East Frontier Agency under enemy control. As far as India is concerned, the North East Frontier Agency in Chinese hands can spell the beginning of a process of Balkanization of the entire Indian subcontinent.

The eight years between October, 1954, when Nehru first spoke to the Chinese about their maps, and October 20, 1962, when the inevitable collision came, were marked by legal quibbling and a series of dreary protest notes on the part of India; and by acquisition of territory, consolidation of their hold over it, and the drawing of the first blood on the part of China. (In October 1959, Chinese forces came forty miles into Ladakh in the Chang Chen Mo Valley and killed nine members of an Indian patrol.)

While New Delhi talked, Peking acted. The absurdity of it

[9] Margaret W. Fischer, Leo E. Rose, Robert Huttenback: *Himalayan Battleground—Sino-India Rivalry in Ladakh* (London: Pall Mall Press Ltd.; 1963), pp. 7–8.

[1] A new Chinese map in 1960 claimed 2,000 square miles more of Indian territory in Ladakh because more territory was required for a second route through Aksai Chin, since completed. The Chinese have also made known their intention to build a railroad alongside this highway.

is that whereas China, with an unswerving sense of purpose, was possessing herself of Indian territory and preparing for a show-down, India was gleefully totting up 630 items of evidence to prove her claims, against 245 of China's, and patting herself on the back that their "qualitative superiority [of the claims] . . . was even greater than the quantitative superiority."[2]

In 1961 war clouds began gathering over Ladakh and the North East Frontier Agency. In April of that year the Chinese intruded into Sikkim, in May into the Chushul area of Ladakh, in July into the Kameng division of the North East Frontier Agency, once more in Ladakh in August—this time to establish three check posts, one at Nyagzu and two near Danbuguru. In January, 1962, they crossed over near Longju in the North East Frontier Agency; in April, May, and June they went into the Chipchap and Spanggur areas of Ladakh; and in July they sur-rounded an Indian post in Galwan, Ladakh. On September 20, 1962, the Chinese forces crossed the MacMahon Line in strength near Thagla, in the North East Frontier Agency. Characteris-tically, India kept making overtures and sending notes "in the interests of a peaceful settlement," a phrase which by then had become monotonous as well as meaningless. The Chinese were spoiling for a fight so they could legitimize what they had already secured, claim what they coveted, and serve notice on the world that Communist China was a power to be reckoned with.

On October 20 the Chinese armies struck. In the North East Frontier Agency the strength of their attacking forces reached "three Divisions, two from the direction of Tawang and one Division in the direction of Kibithoo. To launch such an attack on such a large scale, one can imagine the amount of preparation they must have undertaken. They must have been planning this for a long time in considerable detail, and these actions in over-running our post in Dhola Bridge and in occupying Thagla Ridge, must have been with the specific aim of forcing us to react so as to give them a good excuse for launching an attack

[2] Government of India, Publications Division, Ministry of Information and Broadcasting: *China's Betrayal of India*, p. 29.

on us,"[3] wrote the late General K. S. Thimayya, India's retired army chief of staff. They also attacked in the Chipchap Valley and the Pangong Lake areas of Ladakh. Within three days major fighting was in progress in five main areas extending from far-away Ladakh in the northwest to Kibithoo at the tri-junction of India, Burma, and Tibet. By October 24, the Chinese were well across the MacMahon Line and eight miles into Indian territory through a sector twenty-five miles wide. At the eastern extremity Kibithoo had fallen.

On the same day, October 24, China made a peace offer in the form of a three-point proposal which, under the circumstances, displayed a somewhat macabre sense of humor: the Chinese said the Sino-Indian border question should be settled peacefully; they talked of the sanctity of a "line of actual control," and suggested that the Prime Ministers of the two countries should get down to talking once again. Chou En-lai disarmingly asked: "What issue is there between China and India which cannot be settled peacefully?" He went even further. "China doesn't," he said, "want a single inch of India's territory."[4]

Nehru's reply to the Chinese proposals, said in part: "There is no sense or meaning in the Chinese offer to withdraw 20 kilometres from what they call 'line of actual control'. What is this 'line of actual control'? Is this the line they have created by aggression since the beginning of September? Advancing 40 or 60 kilometres by blatant military aggression and offering to withdraw 20 kilometres provided both sides do this is a deceptive device which can fool nobody."[5]

In the meantime, the fighting raged on. On October 26 India declared a state of national emergency. By October 31 the Chinese had consolidated their position in the North East Frontier Agency and were poised to threaten the plains of India.

[3] General K. S. Thimayya: "Chinese Aggression and After," *International Studies*, V, Nos. 1–2 (July–October, 1963), p. 51.

[4] *White Paper No. 8, Notes, Memoranda and Letters,* an exchange between the Governments of India and China. October, 1962–January, 1963; p. 1.

[5] Letter of the Prime Minister of India dated October 27, 1962: *China's Aggression in War and Peace.*

On November 16, they launched a second, brilliant operation in the North East Frontier Agency, and when they offered a cease fire as of midnight November 21-2 "the Chinese Communist armies were in possession of mountain gateways into the plains of Assam . . . were in command of the natural approaches through the mountains to the Brahmaputra Valley and threatened the whole of Assam and its oil fields. The entire North Eastern Frontier Agency area now lay under the threat of Chinese conquest. . . . The Chinese in lightning conquest had seized the crest lines and now controlled the key passes and were moving down-hill, towards the crowded plains."[6]

In Ladakh, India fared better, although some of the Indian posts which stretched from faraway Karakoram Pass to Demchok were vacated.

> . . . none of these outposts were capable of fighting any kind of serious battle; they were meant to demarcate our forward line so as to discourage the Chinese from expanding any further . . . Chushul [India's supply base for her garrisons in this region] on the other hand, was a strong point, capable of tough resistance which could be reinforced and maintained by air for considerable time. So when the Chinese launched their main offensive in October 1962, the outlying posts had no alternative but to withdraw to their bases. The Chinese however learnt their lesson when they attacked our outposts in Chushul. Our men were entrenched in strong positions and put up a very gallant defence, giving the Chinese a bloody nose who because of the heavy casualties they suffered gave up any idea of capturing our main post at Chushul.[7]

Nevertheless, the fact is that India came out second best in the first major clash of arms between emergent China and independent India. Many explanations have been offered for India's poor performance. According to V. K. Krishna Menon, India's Defence Minister at that time, the Chinese had a "very considerable superiority in numbers and fire power." The appreciation of

---

[6] S. P. Varma: *Struggle for the Himalayas* (New Delhi: University Publishers; 1965), p. 159.

[7] Thimayya, p. 50.

others is that at places Indian troops "hurriedly called to the front and completely unfamiliar with the terrain held . . . a Chinese army five times larger in number, preparing this attack for months and possessing fire power at least thrice more effective."[8]

Why was India in such a state of military unpreparedness? Because the political naïveté of the Indian leadership made it assume that the Soviet Union would restrain China from any adventurist enterprise. It couldn't reconcile itself to the fact of an eventual armed showdown with China. Also, the Indian intelligence system was unable to warn the administration in time of the massive Chinese build-up across her frontiers.

Though the smoke and the din subsided and the Chinese and India troops began moving back to their old positions on December 1, 1962, the myth of Sino-Indian friendship lay shattered. The demands of national security assumed new urgency and the defense services new importance. But the scales are still tipped in China's favor: while a hard-headed, centrally directed, single-minded system plans and directs the strategy and tactics of expansionist China, in India the dogmatists are still able to deter the doers. The economic base on which alone her military might can confidently rest is still weak. And the leadership, instead of sweeping aside the dogmas and getting down to doing things, continues to equivocate.

In the final analysis, however, the most encouraging of the consequences which flowed from the October, 1962, showdown is that an awareness of India's commitments to her own security and that of the region was brought home.

Areas of Future Conflict

To some extent the foregoing is history. As 1965 drew to a close a sharper awareness was evident in India of the imminence of another Sino-Indian conflict, a conflict whose scale cannot be foreseen—firstly, because the Government of India, on the defensive both militarily and politically, is still unable to think in

8 Varma, p. 159.

terms of wresting the initiative from China; and secondly, because the true nature of the collusion between Peking and Rawalpindi is unknown.

No confrontation with China is possible unless the sinews of India's economy are revitalized through rejection of dated economic dogmas and the military potential developed in order to confront China not only at places of her choosing but to threaten her at places of India's choice. Only if action is initiated in these spheres can India really look China in the eye diplomatically. Even though it will take time to reach that stage, there is little reason for India to be eternally conciliatory in her dealings with China. It was entirely unnecessary, for instance, for India to have even replied to the Chinese ultimatum of September 17, 1965, in which she impertinently demanded that India demolish structures allegedly built by her on the Tibetan side of the Sikkimese border. India should have ignored the note. Contemptuous silence would have had far greater effect on world opinion than the weak and conciliatory reply she chose to send ("If any structures are found on the Tibet side of the border there can be no objection to their being demolished") and her offer of "a joint inspection of those points of the Sikkim-Tibetan-Indian border where Indian personnel are alleged to have set up military structures in Tibetan territory. The Government of India on its part is prepared to arrange such an inspection as early as possible."

Why did India reply? Surely it wasn't her past experience with China that encouraged her to think that China would respond to a reasonable suggestion. By hastening to reply—in effect, to conciliate—India showed the same lack of firmness which has characterized her dealings with China ever since that country took to harassing India. No one was going to believe for a minute that India's note was "A cool, well-reasoned, even conciliatory diplomatic manoeuvre, aimed at depriving China of any pretext to launch an armed aggression against India."[9] Cool and well-reasoned moves have not deterred China from aggression in the

[9] *The Indian Express,* September 18, 1965.

past, nor will they in the future. All they do is encourage her to further excesses. Only through resolute rebuffs will China get the message that India is no longer in a mood to be trifled with. The world will realize it too, and it is important that it should because India's international standing since her open rupture with China is far from high. The dispute

> . . . has had a profound influence on the image of Indian leadership of the Asian neutrals—a truth not readily admitted in Indian Governmental circles—and smaller, more vulnerable Asian powers have drawn from it the lessons which the Chinese no doubt desired. It has shown China's disposition to resort to force in a situation which did not seem to require it, as well as revealing, in the amoral world of power politics, the hollowness of reliance upon moral platitudes. India's limited military capability has been revealed and the reluctance of her Government to proffer assurance to India's weak neighbours. The arguments that India is too preoccupied with her own difficulties at present, harm the prospects of an Indian leadership of the neutral states in mainland Southern Asia.[1]

The main focus of Indian political objectives must be once more to burnish her image as an Asian power. There is a special urgency for doing this in the eyes of Nepal, Bhutan, Sikkim, and Burma, and thereafter those of Afghanistan, Malaysia, Singapore, Thailand, South Vietnam, Japan, and eventually Korea and Outer Mongolia.

China's coveting of the states along India's borders by no means begins with Mao's pronouncement that "England seized Burma, Bhutan, Nepal," with its implied threat of repossession. Though the earliest history of Nepal is somewhat of a mystery, Chinese travelers began writing about it in the seventh century and in the same period, in A.D. 643, a Chinese mission visited Nepal for the first time. The contacts increased through the centuries and were at times friendly, at others hostile. In 1788 Nepal subjugated Tibetan territory near her borders, and

[1] D. E. Kennedy: *The Security of Southern Asia* (London: Chatto and Windus Ltd. [for the Institute for Strategic Studies]; 1965), pp. 24–5.

though that was sorted out, in 1791 Nepalese forces marched on Tibet, causing the emperor of China to send his army to repel the invasion. One of the humiliating terms of the truce treaty Nepal signed with China required her to send tribute to Peking every five years. It was also stipulated "that Nepal's tribute status was to be like that of various other dependencies of China, such as Annam, Korea, Siam and Burma."[2]

Though the status changed subsequently and at one point it was Tibet which paid tribute to Nepal, and even though after the Nepalese-British war in 1814–15 Nepal was closer to British India, the Chinese memory is long and capable of reaching way back into history at its convenience. It has been doing just that. China's actions in the last few years have been aimed at reversing history and making Nepal much more than a dependency of China. Her ultimate aim is to make Nepal a region of China.

Nepal need never have been alienated from India, which is what did in fact happen. India's help to Nepal in the last sixteen years has been considerable. Her encouragement to the Nepali Congress, a movement of democratic forces in Nepal, helped to break the strangle hold of the Ranas, the traditional prime ministers who ruled Nepal for over a hundred years under titular kings. On November 6, 1950, pro-Indian King Tribhuvan, along with the royal family, dramatically sought refuge in the Indian Embassy at Kathmandu and was flown out to India under Indian protection. When he returned to Nepal a few months later the Rana's monopoly of power had been smashed, a coalition government was in the process of being formed, and the democratic forces of the Congress were for the first time involved in the administration of the country. These were significant developments, for which the royal family as well as the Nepali Congress had reason to be grateful to India. But, tragically enough, India was unable to consolidate her position. Through indifferent, often heavy-handed diplomacy as well as lack of appreciation for the sensibilities of the Nepalese—though Indians are more sensitive

2 Patterson, p. 131.

themselves than most other peoples—India's influence by 1952 was beginning to irk the Nepalese. Anti-Indian feelings "mounted through 1953 and 1954 as crisis followed crisis in the administration until even the Nepali Congress, born and nurtured in India and placed in power by the help of India, adopted a Resolution in 1954 demanding the withdrawal of both the Indian civilian experts and military mission in the interests of what it called 'the healthy relations between India and Nepal' because 'the experience of the last two years, particularly the last eight months during which the participation of foreign advisers has been maximum, has not been happy.' "[3]

With King Tribhuvan's death on March 31, 1955, and King Mahendra's ascension to the throne, Nepali politics went through another dizzying spiral of change. Not all for the better. On December 15, 1960, King Mahendra took direct rule into his own hands, dismissed the cabinet, herded his Prime Minister, the council of ministers, the speaker and the leader of the Opposition into jail, and generally swept out of the way anyone with contrary political opinions. Nehru said: "This is a complete reversal of democracy, the democratic process, and it is not clear to me that there may be a going back to democratic processes in the foreseeable future. That is the main thing and naturally one views such a development with considerable regret." Nehru's criticism of the king's action in Parliament so angered the king that "a full-scale propaganda blast was released in Nepal against India, notably by four leading newspapers. They even warned Sikkim and Bhutan of Indian designs, asked them to free themselves from Indian interference and called for a federation of Nepal, Sikkim and Bhutan, with Nepal taking the lead."[4]

For the observant Chinese, already intent on wooing the Nepalese, this was a heaven-sent opportunity. They proceeded to settle their border dispute with Nepal, even magnanimously conceding half of Mount Everest to the Nepalese—something which had always belonged wholly to Nepal but which the

3 Ibid., p. 142.
4 Ibid., p. 152.

Chinese had with commendable foresight laid claim to earlier. King Mahendra was invited to China where on October 5, 1961, a treaty was signed between him and Liu Shao-chi, chairman of the Chinese People's Republic. It straightened out the border disputes, accepted China's claim to half of Everest, wiped out Nepalese privileges in Tibet, secured from Nepal recognition of Tibet as "an integral part of China," and gave China the right to build a £3,500,000 road linking Tibet with Kathmandu, the capital of Nepal. This was China's supreme reward for political strategy wisely and assiduously practiced. For the first time in history the natural northeastern barriers of India were to be penetrated, giving China immense military and strategic advantage over India.

The road has since been completed. Of profound interest to India are some of the facts concerning it which were disclosed by Huang Jung-sheng at a press conference in Taipeh on June 2, 1965. Huang worked on the construction of the road from April, 1962, to April, 1964, before defecting to Taiwan.

> The bridges along the Kodari-Kathmandu road are secretly being built to accommodate heavy vehicles—such as 60 metric tons rather than the 8 metric tons specified by the Nepalese Government. They are large enough to accommodate heavy trucks and tanks. . . . Technical personnel working on this road have been obliged to spy for the Chinese Communist Military Attaché in Kathmandu. They turn over to him all topographical, geographical and geological information on the road and its vicinity, which he in turn sends to Peking for use in compiling military maps. . . .[5]

Earlier, a report by the *Daily Telegraph* had pointed out that "The Chinese technicians who roamed Nepal prospecting for lime deposits turned out to be the same who appeared as specialists in brick and paper. This had led to the deduction that the Chinese are more interested in surveying the country than anything else. . . . The 400 road technicians, to judge from their

[5] A. Kashin: "Nepal: Chinese Stepping Stone to India—II," *The Indian Express,* September 8, 1965.

unwillingness to face the camera, are probably military engineers."[6]

Nepal is a vulnerable, potentially explosive sector in which Sino-Indian interests clash head on. China has secured a dramatic lead: while India tried to help Nepal out of the darkness of the decaying feudal system of the Ranas, China cashed in on the sensibilities of a people on the emotional rebound.

A showdown in this region could result from any number of factors.

Almost 20,000 Tibetans are scattered along Nepal's northern border with Tibet, almost half of them former rebels, who fought against the Chinese during the 1956–59 revolt. At present they are short of everything—food and medicine as well as arms and ammunition—but should they become a nuisance to China in their marauding raids on Chinese convoys in West Tibet as they have been doing, or should these attacks increase due to a mysterious increase in their supplies of arms, etc., or should the situation in Nepal not develop to Peking's liking, then the presence of this large, armed, attacking force on Nepal's northern border could give Peking the excuse it wanted to take direct action to absorb the country. Or it might even be that starving, freezing, despairing and frustrated at being left and ignored, these 20,000 Tibetans might be won over to the Chinese once again, and be a formidable striking force to be used against the increasingly vulnerable South.[7]

Nepal's relations with India have stabilized greatly in the last two years, and the three-week state visit to India of the king and queen of Nepal—in November–December, 1965—climaxed a growing understanding between the two countries. To what extent they are able to enlarge the area of agreement between them, and how far India is successful in creating confidence in her good faith in Nepalese minds and in easing China out of the advantageous position it occupies in Nepal at present, are tests for Indian acumen and political finesse.

[6] *Daily Telegraph*, London, June 16, 1964.
[7] Patterson, p. 154.

Both Bhutan and Sikkim, because they were under the suzerainty of Tibet for hundreds of years, are from the Chinese point of view regions which rightly belong to her. The inference, of course, is that since Tibet now belongs to her, all territories which at any time in history ever belonged to Tibet now rightfully belong to China. The Tibetans overran Bhutan between the seventh and tenth centuries. After a few hundred tumultous years they claimed suzerainty over it in 1728 on behalf of the Chinese emperor. British contact with the Bhutanese was established when the latter attacked the small state of Cooch Bihar in Northeast India. This state being a dependency of the British Indian Government, the British intervened and pushed back the Bhutanese, an action which led to the first Anglo-Bhutanese treaty in 1774. According to it Bhutan agreed to return the territory of Cooch Bihar overrun by her, and to pay a nominal tribute to the East India Company. Throughout this period the Bhutanese remained under the suzerainty of China and paid tribute to the emperor, sometimes even paying fines for some lapse or neglect. From 1828 onward relations between the British Indian Government and Bhutan deteriorated steadily. In November, 1864, Britain declared war on Bhutan. After the capitulation of Bhutan, a treaty was signed on November 11, 1865.

Though China showed little concern for the goings-on in Bhutan at that time, by 1905 her interest in Bhutan had revived considerably. To make their position quite clear to the Bhutanese, the Chinese Amban (Resident) in Lhasa addressed them a letter which began: "The Bhutanese are the subjects of the Emperor of China, who is the Lord of Heaven. . . ."[8] In view of China's increasing interest in it, the British also felt it was time to consolidate their position in Bhutan, and in January, 1910, a new treaty was signed between Bhutan and Sir Charles Bell, the British political officer. One of the conditions of the treaty was that "The British Government undertakes to exercise no interference in the internal administration of Bhutan. On its part, the

[8] Sir Charles Bell: *Tibet—Past and Present* (Oxford: The Clarendon Press; 1924), p. 100.

Bhutanese Government agrees to be guided by the advice of the British Government in regard to its external relations."[9] Sir Charles Bell's own appreciation of the significance of the treaty was that it

> can be used effectively to prevent Chinese colonisation in Bhutan. China had already, in 1909, made strenuous efforts to populate the inhospitable tracts around Batang in Eastern Tibet with Chinese colonists. She was looking towards South-Eastern Tibet which is not far from Bhutan, with the same object in view. Bhutan has an ideal climate for the Chinese from southern and central China. Owing to the decrease of its population from monasticism, diseases and war, three-fourths of its land is uncultivated, and would quickly respond to the touch of Chinese agriculturalists.[1]

This treaty, together with the earlier one of 1865, formed the basis for a new treaty which was ratified and accepted by the Governments of India and Bhutan on August 8, 1949—a wise move on India's part when seen against the background of the imminent rise to power of Chinese Communists.

During a visit to Bhutan on December 23, 1958, Nehru pointedly said: "In the event of any aggression against Bhutan by any country, India would consider it an act of aggression against herself and act accordingly." On February 15, 1961, he told the Indian Parliament that "any kind of incursion into Sikkim or Bhutan will be considered an incursion into India, and we shall abide by the assurances we have given to them."

Between Nepal and Bhutan lies Sikkim, adjacent to the beautiful Chumbi Valley, which was once the seat of Sikkim's rulers but was taken over by Tibet in the eighteenth century. To Sir Charles Bell the inverted triangle of the Chumbi Valley was "a dagger aimed at the heart of India"—not only a very graphic but a prophetic statement, since this valley is presently bristling with one of the heaviest concentrations of Chinese troops in the region. This valley was also the setting for the Chinese ulti-

[9] Ibid., p. 297.
[1] Ibid., pp. 105–6.

matum of September, 1965, which accused India of setting up posts on the Tibetan side of the border. For India it is one of the most vulnerable of her Himalayan reaches. Five strategic passes lead from Chumbi Valley into Sikkim: the Cho-La, Yak-La, Nathu-La, Jelep-La, and Dongchui-La passes. From Sikkim two vital highways lead into India: the Nathula-Gangtok-Siliguri and the Jelepla-Rhenoch highways. Indicative of the importance of these passes and the two highways is the fact that if the Chinese are able to wrest control of them from India they could pour down into the Indian plains and cut off the jugular vein at Siliguri, isolating completely the vast eastern areas of India comprising parts of Bengal, Assam, the North East Frontier Agency, Nagaland, and the kingdoms of Bhutan and Sikkim. Against this grim background rests the great importance of peaceful little Sikkim to India.

Sikkim's history, like that of Bhutan, is closely identified with Tibet, and because of that, with China. According to some reports, the rulers of Sikkim are descended from Tibet's seventh-century kings. Others suggest that the Tibetans shrewdly introduced Buddhism into Sikkim in the seventeenth century, and that through conversions of the easy-going Lepchas (the inhabitants of Sikkim) and the raising to positions of power of monastic leaders, the Tibetan lamas secured the loyalty of the Sikkimese people and rulers. But the ties were subjected to many strains. In the eighteenth and nineteenth centuries strife between Sikkim and Tibet, invasions of Sikkim by Nepal and Bhutan, and disputes within Sikkim's ruling family eventually led to British intervention in 1826–8 and again in 1850. In March 1861 a treaty was signed between British India and Sikkim. Finally, a treaty establishing Sikkim as a protectorate of the British Government was signed in 1890 between Britain and China. Article 2 of the treaty specified that "the British Government whose Protectorate over the Sikkim State is hereby recognised, has direct and exclusive control over the internal administration and foreign relations of that State, and except through and with the permission of the British neither the ruler of the State nor any of its officers shall have any official relations of any kind, formal or informal, with any other country."

On December 5, 1950, the Government of Independent India signed a treaty with Sikkim which confirmed her as a protectorate of India, and while giving her internal autonomy, made India responsible for her defense and her territorial integrity and ceded to India the right to station troops, build strategic roads and communications, and take absolute control over Sikkim's external relations.

Peking has refused to accept Sikkim and Bhutan as protectorates of India, and has made clear her unwillingness to discuss with India the boundaries of these two kingdoms.

The Chinese claims are never inhibited by the span of time or historical changes. The Indian state of Assam, the North East Frontier Agency (which is separated from Tibet by the MacMahon Line, over which India and China fought in October 1962), and the Indian cities of Darjeeling and Kalimpong are all claimed by the Chinese—Assam because it was conquered from Burma by the British after the first Burmese War in 1828; the North East Frontier Agency because it is claimed as a part of Tibet; Darjeeling and Kalimpong because the former originally belonged to Sikkim and the latter to Bhutan.

There are other claims the Chinese make on vast tracts of Indian territory. But the point which needs emphasising is that those in India who propagate the idea of arriving at an agreement with China by condoning her aggression on the Aksai-Chin plateau in Ladakh or accepting her modification of the McMahon Line, deliberately play down the fact that China's dispute with India is not confined to two areas of disagreement. China's claims are numerous and preposterous. Those who propose a solution of Sino-India differences through a dialogue confined to their dispute over Ladakh and the North East Frontier Agency, confuse the real nature of the conflict between the two countries. Their viewpoint is no less macabre in context of China's known intentions toward India than was Panikkar's when he said "the only area where our interests overlapped was in Tibet." Well worth remembering in this context are Mao's dictums that "When actually eating, we do it a mouthful at a time," and that it is impossible "to swallow the entire feast in a single mouthful!"

An insight into the Chinese definition of an "entire feast" is provided by a book entitled *A Brief History of Modern China* by Liu Pei-Hua, published by the Yichung Book Company in March 1954. This book shows a map of "Chinese Territories Taken by the Imperialists in the Old Democratic Revolutionary Era (1840–1919)," territories now claimed by China as right-

For explanation of numbers, see the text. Heavy dashes show borders of China in 1840, before the Opium War. Heavy dash-dot line shows borders of China in 1919.

fully her own. The accompanying map has been drawn after this Chinese map; the original Chinese text for the map reads:

1. The Great North-West "was seized by Imperialist Russia under the Treaty of Chuguchak, 1864." It covers huge segments of the present-day Soviet Republics of Kazakhstan, Kirgizia and Tadzhikistan.

2. The Pamirs was "secretly divided between Britain and Russia in 1896."

3. Nepal "went under the British after 'Independence' in 1898."

4. Ch-Meng-Hsiung (present-day Sikkim) was "occupied by Britain in 1889."

5. Pu-tan (the whole of Bhutan) "went under Britain after 'Independence' in 1865."

6. Ah-sa-mi, which includes not only Assam but also the North East Frontier Agency and Nagaland, was "given to Britain by Burma in 1826."

7. Burma "became a part of British Empire in 1886."

8. The Andaman Islands "went under Britain."

9. Ma-la-chia (the whole of present-day Malaya) was "occupied by Britain in 1895."

10. Hsien-Lo (the whole of Thailand) was "declared 'Independent' under joint Anglo-French control in 1904."

11. Annam (covering present-day North and South Vietnam, Laos, and Cambodia) was "captured by the French in 1885."

12. Taiwan and P'enghu Islands were "relinquished to Japan in accordance with the Treaty of Shimonoseki, 1895."

13. Su-Lu Island was "occupied by the British."

14. The Region where the British crossed the Border and committed aggression.

15. Liu-Ch'iu (Ryukyu Islands), which went under Japan in 1879.

16. Ch'ao-hsien (present-day North and South Korea).

17 and 18. The Great Northeast, covering a huge area of the Soviet Far East, "was given to Russia under the Treaties of Aigun (1895) and Peking (1860)."

19. K'u-Ye (Sakkhalin), which is now part of the Soviet Union.[2]

[2] *Link*, (Delhi), November 11, 1962.

China's claims on Russian territory are something for Russia to worry about, just as it is for all those other countries whose territories China covets. What should concern India, however, is that in addition to her designs on Nepal, Bhutan, Sikkim, and Assam, China considers Burma her region too. While her other claims can be dismissed as absurd, China's gradual inroads into Burma are disquieting. Invidiously and imperceptibly, the Chinese have been infiltrating into Burma for over eight years, creating a dangerous and potentially explosive situation along India's eastern borders.

The platitudes and the vows of friendship made during Shastri's visit to Burma in December, 1965, cannot gloss over Burma's recent uncivilized behavior toward Indians settled there. More than 130,000 Indians have been turned out and their movable properties, shops, businesses, assets in banks, jewelry, automobiles, household goods and personal effects expropriated. More disturbing, and revealing, is the fact that within days of the India-Pakistan conflict in September, 1965, when even the Chinese ultimatum to India was still pending, the Burmese Government's English daily, *The Guardian,* ran letters in its columns which said, among other things, that

> Several peoples of Assam are more akin to the Burmese than to the Aryans and Dravidians. . . . Some of the peoples in Assam are just a continuation of what is called Chin, but may appropriately be termed Lushai. . . . Are not the Andamans in Burmese territorial waters? . . . The Chittagong hill districts of East Pakistan, the Mizo district and its adjoining islands in Assam, Manipur State, the Nagaland in India and Burma, a special division of the Chins, are all inhabited by a tribe of the same religion, customs and cultures as the Tibeto-Burmans who call themselves by several names as Mizo, Lushai, Naga . . . but they are known as the Lushai and Nagas in India and the Chins and Nagas in Burma. . . . The unnatural division of the Tibeto-Burmans of the Mongolian race was a result of British treachery.

This correspondence is interesting. First of all, there is no such thing as an independent or free press in Burma. The papers, like everything else in that country, belong to the state, and whatever appears in them must have the sanction of the Government. That publication of such provocative and insolent statements as the above should have been permitted, at so inappropriate a time is indicative of nothing else but a deliberate attempt on the part of the Government to bait and provoke India. It is inconceivable for Burma to want to do that unless it was done under pressure from China. And that underscores the fact that China is obviously in a position now in Burma to apply various kinds of pressures on her Government. It would be of little consequence if such letters were published in a free press, but when they are published in a tightly controlled, Government-owned newspaper, it is an altogether different matter.

On the other side of the coin is the intriguing fact that while "Burma's nationalisation laws have driven a large number of Indians to India, the Chinese, who were also equally affected by the same laws, have somehow managed to stick around under some excuse or the other. Who can assist them except the Chinese Embassy to stay put?" Burmese leaders say that "while India has generously agreed to take back the Indians desirous of returning to India, the Chinese have never made such an offer. Perhaps the Chinese Government wants its people to stay on so that their services can be utilised, if necessary, for subversion. The houses and flats vacated by Indians in the recent exodus have all been occupied by the Chinese and for the first time the Chinese have appeared in many areas in Rangoon, outside Chinatown."[3]

Reports from Burma suggest—understandably, not much is allowed to be reported out of the country—that more Chinese are being seen not only in parts of Rangoon, but increasingly throughout the country. Silently, without seeming to, the Chinese are stealthily infiltrating Burma. Their capacity to patiently wait out the period of inaction until action is required of them is infinite. It is being put to maximum use in Burma. Alongside it, a parallel infiltration by pro-Peking Burmese into all echelons of government is taking place. China's aims in Burma

[3] K. Rangaswami: "China's Insidious Hand against India," *The Hindu*, December 31, 1965.

are obvious: by controlling Burma physically or through a puppet regime, China can permanently surround India with hostile neighbors along her entire 6,140-mile-long frontier (India-China-Tibet: 2,640 miles; India-Pakistan: 2,700 miles; India-Burma: about 800 miles; total 6,140 miles).

It is difficult to understand why India "generously agrees to take back Indians," in the plight in which countries like Burma choose to send them out. They have every right to be where they are, and India should firmly support their right. By agreeing to their repatriation she not only becomes party to acts of expropriation which deprive them of what is theirs by dint of effort and application spread over two or three generations, but by repatriating them India leaves the field wide open for further consolidation by the Chinese. It doesn't do her image much good, either, to be pushed around all the time by any and every country.

The situation in Burma today is ideal for China, who knows how to exploit internal dissent and disorder to her own advantage. As to the extent of disorder which exists in Burma, General Ne Win described it recently: "The country has not known unity since Independence and it is divided politically, economically, socially and racially. The task of leading the country now is like having to lead an army in disarray and it is a very onerous one, requiring all of one's energy, thought and action for rebuilding the broken fabric of unity."

So far as India is concerned, if Ne Win is unable to control the pro-Peking elements within Burma, India's security along her eastern borders will be in serious jeopardy. That is something India can hardly be expected to stand by idly and watch.

The Coming Years

A school of thought in India feels that ideally the Mekong River should be the line dividing the Chinese and Indian spheres of influence—not an unreasonable objective to aim at. This thought must have been in Nehru's mind too when he visited Cambodia in 1954, since he referred to Cambodia then as a country on the cultural frontier between India and China. This objective could form the basis for new and more dynamic Indian policies in the Southeast Asian region in the second half of the sixties. But since China in the coming years is not likely to leave countries around India alone, it would be a good principle for India eventually to consider extending her interest to countries beyond the Mekong Delta and all the way to Outer Mongolia.

Till such time as the Mekong hypothesis becomes the basis for policy, India needs to take some hard decisions. Her hitherto passive role in Laos, for instance, could be replaced by active support for the neutralist government in its struggle against Pathet Lao inroads. Since China has for so long sustained and supported anti-Indian elements in countries on India's periphery, India should do everything to encourage anti-Peking elements in countries on China's periphery. By strengthening their hands, she could help them to arrest China's outward push.

India's firm stand in Laos could have a marked effect on Cambodia. Prince Sihanouk, whose uncertain moods are deprecated in the inner councils of New Delhi, has no particular reason to be impressed by India. He was India's friend at one point, and his changed attitude could conceivably stem from lack of confidence in India's ability to buttress the smaller states of Southeast Asia against the threat from expansionist China. Anyone else in Sihanouk's position would feel the same, perched precariously as he is with six million subjects on the borders of a China of 750 million.

Vietnam ought to loom as large in Indian calculations as it does in the world's. If the Viet Cong overrun South Vietnam, China's influence would extend all the way to the Gulf of Siam, and even if it didn't take Thailand in its crunch right away, China's outward push would come dangerously close to India. A section of opinion in India which is in a position to influence official policy holds the view that the confrontation between North and South Vietnam is not necessarily a confrontation between the United States and China. This kind of reasoning acts against India's interests because it sets store by a hypothesis in preference to hard realities. The Viet Cong is the subversive arm of the North Vietnam regime and it is being used by the North to subvert the South. To project the thesis that North Vietnamese activity in South Vietnam, through the agency of the Viet Cong, has nothing to do with Chinese aims, is wishful thinking. The North is making a naked bid for power, and its actions cloak China's special motives in that region. That fact must be squarely faced. Neither can India afford to take the risk of gambling on the long odds that once the two Vietnams are unified under the "nationalist" North Vietnamese regime, the reunited country will reassert its traditional hostility toward China. North Vietnam is too committed to China, has for too long been supported by arms, equipment, economic, and industrial aid from that country, and infiltrated and subverted for over a decade by cadres loyal to Peking. It is illogical to expect it to break away from China's orbit once it is reunified. If no sudden transformation is expected—and none should be—there is little reason for India to place her bets on a distant dream. In politics hard choices have to be made. Indian interests in that region require South Vietnam to retain its identity as an anti-Peking power. Since it cannot do that in the forseeable future without American help, continuous flow of that help to South Vietnam, military as well as economic, should be of comfort to India. For her to feel uneasy over American presence in Vietnam can only mean confused perspectives. Actual realities, not academicism, should influence India's policy toward Vietnam. And the reality is that South Vietnam, outside the domination of North Vietnam and of China, is a bird in hand, whereas a reunited Vietnam steering a course independent of China is a mythical bird in a very distant bush.

India's attitude toward China should, rationally, be influenced by no other criteria than her past experience of her neighbor; China's declared territorial objectives; indisputable evidence of the aggression, sedition, and subversion she is capable of; and recognition of the fact that submission to China's demands once, twice, or any number of times is no way out of the conflict of interest between the two.

India must also relentlessly bear in mind the fact

that Chinese capabilities in the paramilitary field—the entire spectrum of insurgency, of which guerilla warfare is but a part—are high, particularly in South-East Asia. With a relatively slight investment of resources, and at very little risk, it stands to receive a disproportionate return. China can easily exfiltrate selected young men and women for intensive political indoctrination and training as propagandists, organisers, terrorists, saboteurs and guerillas. These agents can then be brought back as nuclei for cells. Several such training centres are said to be in Yunan. These reports are probably correct; the procedure is a logical one, for South-East Asia provides a target area suitable in all respects for the application of Mao's theories of protracted insurgent war. One may suspect that when China's troops pulled out of the North East Frontier Area (NEFA) they took with them a number of candidates for this schooling and it should come as no surprise to the Indian Government if, in say 1967, it finds itself suddenly faced with this very threat in that region.[4]

An eruption in the North East Frontier Agency, an area in any case claimed in its entirety by China, is logical. But it would be equally logical to expect activities inspired, directed, and implemented by a schizoid China in any one of half a dozen other places. India must be prepared for them. Even more than that, her aim should be to retaliate on territory of her own choosing. An appropriate analogy would be that just as Indian strategists had planned the opening of a front against Pakistan in the Lahore sector in the event of Pakistani intransigence getting out of hand in Kashmir, similar strategy in respect of China requires to be meticulously drawn up too.

Because of China's aggressive expansionism and the consequent security requirements of India and Southeast Asia, defense should by definition, no longer mean defense of India alone but defense of Southeast Asia against a major, malevolent, and militant power.

---

[4] Samuel B. Griffith II: "Communist China's Capacity To Make War," *Foreign Affairs*, XLIII (January, 1965), p. 235.

7
Defense

Some lessons India chose to learn the hard way. Among them was this: that the boundaries of power have to extend well beyond a nation's frontiers if her national boundaries are to remain inviolate. Britain knew this. To defend her Indian empire she created through conquest or connivance spheres of influence in Afghanistan, Tibet, Burma, Malaya, and Singapore. Her aim was clear: to hold well beyond India's borders any threat to her security. As a reaction against Britain's methods, however, India refused to acknowledge even the validity of the principle. She was right in rejecting the use of force, but there was nothing to stop her from establishing a community of interests with other countries or discussing regional security with them.

Panikkar's observation is once more pertinent: "I had, even before I started for Peking, come to the conclusion that the British policy (which we were supposed to have inherited) of looking upon Tibet as an area in which we had special political interests, could not be maintained." India did have special political interests in Tibet, even though in 1950 she was not in a position to do much about them. There was no difference between Britain's interest in defending India prior to independence and India's interest in defending herself after independence. The concern of both was to secure the country against external threats. In repudiating Britain's policies India also repudiated the requirements of national security.

When she hastened to sign treaties with Nepal, Bhutan, and Sikkim, on the very same basis as Britain's treaties with them, she was revalidating a good precedent. But in neglecting to bring Southeast Asia within the orbit of her concern, India allowed herself to be sidetracked by her own confused ideologies.

As the nineteen-forties came to a close, it is doubtful if India read the writing on the wall: that Britain's pulling out left a power vacuum in Southeast Asia. Britain had no reason to explain the implications of this to India. Her aim was to continue to influence events, to shape them as if no vacuum existed, to maintain a balance of power between those dependent on her so that the trump card always remained in her hands. Whether she has succeeded in filling the vacuum by remote control, as it were, is an open question, but India certainly hasn't filled it.

Two factors in the main prevented India. One was an urge to play an esoteric role in international affairs. The other was the bogey of Pakistan as her main enemy. It became a national fixation and left her no time to frame more dynamic objectives. Between these two obsessive concerns the real danger was ignored: that of a great land power, China, relentelssly driving southward to fill Southeast Asia's power vacuum.

The partition of India, attended by some of the bloodiest and fiercest encounters in the history of man, has had a profound bearing on Asia politics. It is tragic that India accepted the false premise that Pakistan (a state created by Britain) was the major threat to her national security. She overlooked the fact that Britain, with shrewd political foresight, had used the fact of partition and the manner in which it took place to involve the two countries in a web of antagonisms, recriminations, and resentment so that a continuing state of hostility between them would become the main focus of their concern. As was to be expected, the outcome was that Pakistan, kept reasonably strong by Britain to balance any undue growth of power in India, continued to obsess India and prevent her from looking out toward Southeast Asia, her logical sphere of influence.

Now, as a consequence of the Indo-Pakistan conflict of September, 1965, a searching and serious analysis of the geopolitical demands of India's overall strategy is at last being made. The possibility of Sino-Pakistan collusion, India's increasing disenchantment with Britain, the gradual emergence of the defense services in India as a force likely to influence policy in the future, the prospects of China developing nuclear missiles and India producing her own nuclear bomb, are all likely to compel recognition of broader defense commitments. Surely these cannot be the defense of India or Southeast Asia against Pakistan! Their aim can only be defense of the whole region against China. This larger truth is now being perceived in India.

Regional Pacts

Subversion in Southeast Asian countries—part of the Chinese methodology for extending her hegemony over them—now aims also at directing the loyalty of their Communist Parties toward Peking. Since this subverts Russia's interests in the region, their struggle to create spheres of influence in Asia has given a new dimension to the dialogue of dissent between China and Russia. Apart from the polemic and the dialectic, the Chinese case is that Russia is not an Asian power. Even though it is India's policy to support the Soviet Union, an intensification of efforts is needed, to help Russia counter Chinese moves, since the Asian argument between the two Communist powers is only just beginning. The effects of their clash of interests in Asia "are difficult to estimate at this juncture, but they may be powerful, in that the Chinese are suggesting Asian solutions to Asian problems and affirming that the Soviet Union is not an Asian power."[1]

Since on China's prompting many Afro-Asian nations have

[1] Kennedy, p. 133.

refused to accept even Russia as an Asian power, it is easy to see how the United States' efforts to play a major political role in Asia are rendered absurd by China. Considering the climate of hostility generated against the United States's attempts to influence the politics of Asia, the discouraging outcome of her involvement with Pakistan, her expensive and complex commitments in Vietnam, and the mounting resentment at home of her Asian policies, it is doubtful if the United States will again commit herself to military support of any *one* country. Pakistan's *volte-face* in favor of China after receiving over $3 billion in military and economic aid from the United States has not been exactly encouraging. Even less so has America's much heavier commitment in Vietnam.

Equally disconcerting from her point of view is the patent fact that member-countries in military pacts like the Southeast Asia and Central Treaty Organizations would be unable to withstand an attack by China unless the United States committed her own troops. Against the background of Vietnam, America is bound to feel uneasy at such a prospect. The stockpiles of American arms in member countries have caused their neighbors to fear the imbalances created and have in effect split the Asian countries by proving divisive rather than cohesive.

India has to formulate a defense policy for the Southeast Asian region in the midst of these conflicting pulls. She cannot remain aloof while the United States, the Soviet Union, and China make major moves to secure their interests there. India ought to forget her "Afro" aspirations for a while and instead help find "Asian solutions to Asian problems." Afro-Arab countries will finally frame from their own experience a pattern of resistance to subversive Chinese methods. India's primary preoccupation must be her own security.

For many years nonalignment prevented India from appreciating that her national interests were closely involved in regional defense. It was a period during which any talk of collective security was branded as advocacy of furthering American, or Western, interests. The bigger the gathering of the so-called nonaligned—twenty-five countries at the Belgrade Conference in 1961 and forty-seven at the Cairo Conference in 1964—the more strident the chorus confusing the issue that the national interests of a country are paramount. Reaffirmation of nonaligned policies at such conferences did not mean that emerging countries were expected to slacken efforts to defend their territorial integrity. But for many years the nonaligned ideal did cause such a slack in India's defense efforts.

"Throughout the whole area of Southern Asia, China has major defensive concerns, expressed in the desire to see hostile powers withdrawn from any neighbouring territory from which Peking thinks that she can be threatened."[2] India's defense concern also requires active steps for not only removing hostile powers from her neighboring territory—by force if necessary—but also devising a framework for defense and mutual assistance in countries motivated by the will to resist Chinese subversion and expansionism. Military alliances have unfortunately been given a dubious meaning in India. The military is the instrument for implementing the national will. If the will of Indians is to defend their system of government, their national institutions, culture, and traditions from those who would destroy them, then "in the amoral world of power politics, the hollowness of reliance upon moral platitudes" is obvious. "India's limited military capability has been revealed, and the reluctance of her government to proffer assurance to India's weak neighbours—the arguments that India is too preoccupied with her own difficulties at present harm the prospects of an Indian leadership of the neutral states in mainland Southern Asia."[3]

Alone, India cannot stand militarily against China unless a new stimulus is introduced into her defense thinking. The first thing required is a substantial increase in the strength of her army. Then a change in her anti-Chinese defense posture, at present aimed against the northern borders. The Chinese threat through Burma has not been seriously considered so far, it seems.

[2] Ibid., p. 31.
[3] Ibid., p. 25.

Yet it is of vital concern, not only because India's border with Burma is very vulnerable but because its defense is a complex affair in view of a hostile East Pakistan pointing dangerously at India's precarious lines of communication leading to it through the narrow Bengal-Assam passage. Then again, the air defense of the crucial industrial belt of Bihar and West Bengal still depends largely on hopes of American air intervention. These are problems of urgency not only to India, but defense arrangements or alliances are important to all Asian countries with identical aims.

India could aim first for an alliance with Japan and Malaysia, later with Thailand, the Philippines, and possibly even Burma and Indonesia. There needn't be a very elaborate charter or manifesto to announce the inception of such an arrangement. A beginning could be made by: (1) holding staff talks to formulate common strategic aims; (2) chalking out regional appreciation of possible Chinese moves, both overt and covert; (3) instituting joint intelligence. From these could flow the logical moves dictated by discussion and appreciation of security problems.

With an army of 825,000, which equals the combined forces of Japan (180,000), Malaysia (19,000), Burma (100,000), Thailand (50,000), the Philippines (25,500), and Indonesia (350,000), India's contribution to a defense alliance would be considerable. The important thing is that the combined strength of all these forces would create a balance of power with China (army strength: 2,250,000). Even more important, any defense alliance resulting from an Asian resolve to resist Chinese inroads into their territories could expect to receive equipment and other support from the United States and the Soviet Union, which individual countries might not. It is in the national interests of these two countries to see such an alliance formed. Its members could in due course collaborate in manufacturing and producing their own equipment, just as India and the United Arab Republic are planning to manufacture jet aircraft jointly. Such an arrangement could form the basis for collaboration in the manufacture and production of military equipment, with the eventual aim of expanding it to other economic and industrial fields.

Japan has a dramatic role to play in the containment of China. In much the same way as Russia is increasing her trade with Japan,[4] with the aim of siphoning away business which Japan might otherwise transact with China, India could profit both by developing her trade with Japan and by weaning her away from any economic involvement with China which could later make it difficult for her to enter into an anti-Peking alliance. Japan's scientific, technological, and manufacturing sophistication make her the logical supplier of plant and equipment India requires. Her financial reserves, which spiraled during the economic miracle of the postwar years, can provide India with the financial loans she needs for some years to come.

Another advantage to be gained from collaboration with Japan is her experience of fighting the Chinese prior to the last war, and later, of fighting in every kind of Southeast Asian terrain. This could prove invaluable to India's defense forces. There is no reason why an arrangement for training in each other's defense establishments could not be worked out. Nor is there any reason for not upgrading the post of India's military attaché in Tokyo to a full-scale military mission for establishing a general staff liaison cell and common strategic planning. By any line of reasoning, Japan can play a very vital role in an Asian defense alliance and it would be wise of India to move decisively toward an understanding with her.

Parallel Efforts

Parallel to her efforts to establish defense pacts, India's obligations to her security require other steps, the foremost being a major effort to reduce her anti-Pakistan commitment to just a

---

[4] "Japan will build 100 ships for the Soviet Union during the next five years under a trade and payments agreement (signed in Moscow on January 21, 1965) . . . the total volume of trade in the next five years is expected to be over $2.5 billion both ways, a record in the trade history of the two countries. Japan will also supply the Soviet Union heavy industrial plants, machinery, chemicals and other industrial goods in exchange for mainly raw materials like lumber, oil and gas." *The Hindustan Times,* January 19, 1965.

holding role in Jammu and Kashmir, with a mechanized reserve in the Punjab. The bulk of India's infantry must be diverted to mountain-cum-jungle types of divisions for her northern and eastern borders and as possible Indian contributions to an Asian defense system, if one is established. But India cannot reduce her forces along her borders with Pakistan unless the two agree to a no-war treaty, and the United States and the Soviet Union agree to underwrite it. Pakistan's willingness to enter such a pact depends on her understanding with China, and the extent to which the United States and the Soviet Union are able to draw her away from Peking. Till such time, India, in planning the strength of her armed forces, can only go by the assumption that the commitment of her troops along Indo-Pakistan frontiers will remain on the present scale. New Delhi cannot hazard a reduction of troops in the Punjab or in Kashmir, especially since the supply lines to Indian troops facing the Chinese armies in the far off, critical areas of Ladakh would also be threatened. Surprise Pakistani attacks could sever these lines.

With major troop concentrations pinned down at the Pakistan and Tibet borders, the present-sized Indian army can function only as a defensive force. Unfortunately, military history does not record any battles fought successfully by purely defensive actions. According to Mao Tse-tung: "Active defence is also known as offensive defence, or defence through decisive engagements. Passive defence is actually a spurious kind of defence, and the only real defence is active defence, defence for the purpose of counter-attacking and taking the offensive."[5]

The chief of staff of China's National Liberation army, General Lo Jui-ching, explains Mao's theme in more graphic detail: "The strategy of active defense does not stop with driving the aggressor out of the country, but requires strategic pursuit to destroy the enemy at his starting point, to destroy him in his nest."[6]

[5] Lo Jui-ching, General: "China's Military Doctrine," Red Flag, May 10, 1965.
[6] Ibid.

For India to be able to take the offensive, should her strategy of containment call for it, her army would require its present strength of twenty divisions to be doubled if she is to operate on her own, or brought up to at least thirty divisions if she enters into an Asian military pact. There is every possibility of a situation arising in which India may be called upon to move into Tibet. The implications of China's formidable garrisoning there and of the major bases that are being established for use against India cannot be ignored.

China's undeclared use of force in Burma and the gradual subjugation of Burmese territory are bound to influence India's strategic concepts. "Burma's terrain is favourable to quiet insurgent organization and build-up; the northern and eastern parts of the country are remote and sparsely populated and can be supplied from China. Local take-overs in the north by puppets supported by 'Peoples Volunteers' would give the Chinese a number of bases for small-scale infiltration and attacks on Assam from the South. The area east of the Salween River is also particularly suitable."[7]

Indian leadership will have to be decisive about increasing the size of the armed forces when it becomes necessary, but no major military action against China can take place without the concert of other powers. It is not suggested that they come to India's help, but that an overall strategy be worked out with them. Such a strategy, for instance, could take the shape of a defensive-offensive move into western and central Tibet, a northern offensive through North Vietnam by United States-Saigon forces, a seaborne invasion of the Chinese mainland from Taiwan, a South Korean move across the Yalu, and a Russian-Mongolian-Japanese "containing" move in the north aimed at tying down large Chinese concentrations in the Peking-Manchurian region.

A good deal of squeamishness is shown in India not only toward making hard decisions, but even toward discussing them. There is no equivalent in India to London's Institute for Stra-

[7] Griffith, p. 235.

tegic Studies or the Rand Corporation in the United States. Politico-strategic problems, as extensions of national objectives, are seldom discussed with the verve and vigor a wide awake people are expected to show, thanks to the political attitudes of those who, by invidiously encouraging the belief that China will not aggress in South Asia, create suspicion and hostility toward defense pacts and even discussion of strategic matters. Meanwhile, ominous developments are taking place in China.

Nuclear Debate

On December 15, 1965, Robert S. McNamara, America's Secretary of Defense, told the North Atlantic Council in Paris that the Communist Chinese have exploded two nuclear devices and during the next two years may produce enough fissionable material to conduct a modest test program and to stockpile a small number of fission weapons; and that they appear to be making an intensive effort to develop a medium-range ballistic missile which could become operational by 1967. He said they could probably deploy several launchers by 1968 or 1969, and several dozens by 1976, since they have already begun an intercontinental ballistic missiles development program which could result in an initial deployment as early as 1975. Estimates were that their supply of fissionable material would support not only the ballistic missile program but also bombs for delivery by aircraft.

McNamara suggested that the Council should apply itself at its future meetings to discussing the military postures needed to prevent Chinese blackmail and the external support China's neighbors needed until their economic and political progress reduced their vulnerability and compelled China to modify its aggressive attitude.

Japanese experts forecast that China's first hydrogen bomb will be exploded in 1966. They say her missile program, under a former Massachussetts Institute of Technology professor, Chien Hsue-chen, is being developed at an accelerated pace. They predict that China will have 150 to 200 nuclear bombs by the end of 1967, and rockets with a range of 500 to 600 miles.

It is under the shadow of China's impending breakthrough as a nuclear power that the validity of the debate on whether or not India should develop nuclear capabilities of her own must be judged.

There are two sides to the debate. The first concerns India's security, to which all other considerations are subordinate. The second concerns India's obligations to the international community in its efforts to prevent proliferation of nuclear weapons. Although India has fulfilled her international obligations adequately in the last eighteen years, there can be no question of giving them precedence over the demands of her own security.

Do India's defense needs require nuclear capabilities? Views on this were hotly expressed soon after October 16, 1964, when China detonated her first nuclear explosion near the marshy salt basin of Lop Nor on the edge of Sinkiang's Takla Makan Desert. Controversy on whether or not India should make her own bomb is now fierce, especially since there are definite prospects of China developing a nuclear arsenal. The demand that India do the same is gathering great momentum in the country.

McNamara's December 15 statement underscores India's forebodings. If China will be in a position to threaten India's northern cities within two years, and "within, say, eight or ten years . . . will possess a missile with a range of 2,500 miles . . . it does not take much imagination to envisage a situation of diplomatic tension between India and China in the early nineteen-seventies, when a Chinese threat to destroy half-a-dozen crowded Indian cities might force some diplomatic humiliation on India that would be even more galling than the reverses of 1962. More than that, India's hopes of posing as the liberal alternative to China in Asia are jeopardized if she cannot prove that she is not only as technologically advanced but also as determined a nation."[8]

---

[8] Alistair Buchan: "Dilemma of India's Security," *The Listener* (May 13, 1965).

Even the more sober elements within India, though inclined to accept nuclear guarantees from major powers or an American nuclear umbrella, are skeptical about its value. One reason is that they "find it hard to believe . . . that their country could be regarded as a vital American interest, in the sense that western Europe is a vital American interest."[9]

Of relevance in this context is a statement made recently by John Kenneth Galbraith, the former United States ambassador to India: "It fell to me two years ago to be our executive when the dispute between China and India broke into open war. The policies which we concerted with the Indians and the British, and which combined support to the Indians with a *clear indication of our disinterest in promoting a war in those distant mountains,* passed through my hands."[1]

What happens in the event of a war in the distant Himalayas "promoted" by neither the United States nor India, but by the Chinese? A conflict, for instance, with limited objectives, such as a localized take-over attempt in North East Frontier Agency.

Even India's worst detractors cannot accuse her of promoting wars, but Chinese aggression in the Himalays and India's opening of a second or third front against the Chinese in Tibet might well be treated by the United States as Indian adventurism, thereby encouraging China to threaten India overtly with nuclear attacks. The United States and Britain frowned at India's opening of the Lahore front in the September, 1965, Indo-Pakistan conflict. What happens if they similarly disown the demands imposed on India by her military tactics, and leave her out on a limb with China? In September, 1965, when the threat of an outbreak of Sino-Indian hostilities in Sikkim was imminent, reports from Washington gave the impression that fighting confined to Sikkim would not be viewed as involving American interests. If America continues this attitude toward limited ag-

9 Ibid.
1 John Kenneth Galbraith: "Foreign Policy: The Stuck Whistle," *The American Review* (October, 1965).

gression, China is bound to be encouraged in her insiduous attempts at piecemeal territorial gains.

It is impossible for any nuclear guarantee to define clearly the the conditions which would make it operative, or the eventualities covered by it. There is also the credibility factor, crucial to nuclear balance in the world. "It is the expectation of American analysts that Chinese propaganda will invest [their] detonation with a false credibility in order to undermine Asian faith in the credibility of the American nuclear deterrent."[2]

The credibility in America's will to use the nuclear deterrent in the Asian setting is not very high as it is. And it is open to question whether the United States would retaliate in the event of China landing a nuclear rocket or two in India's "distant mountains." The considerations before the United States would be that in the event of her retaliating against China with even one strike, Russia would be compelled to retaliate against the United States in order to establish credibility in her deterrent. And Russian retaliation could well trigger a nuclear war.

Would the United States want to take the risk of triggering a nuclear war for a rocket or two dropped on some Indian emplacement in the "distant mountains"? China, on the other hand, could gain great credibility for her nuclear capability at India's expense.

There can be very little doubt that possession of a nuclear stockpile, even an extremely small one, could create much-needed confidence in India's capacity to demonstrate highly sophisticated scientific and technological skills. It can also create confidence in India's commitments to any defense alliance she may establish with Southeast Asian countries. It can ensure political stability within India—a strong Central Government with confidence in the country's nuclear capabilities could resist internal pressures to acquiesce to China's nuclear blackmailing. In the absence of India's own nuclear deterrent such pressures are inevitable from groups in India who can be expected to mobilize opinion favoring a conciliatory and submissive attitude toward China.

[2] Kennedy, p. 37.

The next question of course is: Has India the ability to become a nuclear power? William C. Foster, the director of the United States's Arms Control and Disarmament Agency, feels that "the Indian program for exploitation of the atom is almost certainly more impressive than that of China."[3] Alistair Buchan, director of London's Institute for Strategic Studies says that "there is no doubt about her technical capacity. For about fifteen years India has been devoting a high percentage of her limited scientific resources to nuclear research. . . . There is no reason to doubt Dr. Bhabha's claim that India could explode her first nuclear device within twelve months of deciding to do so. Figures have been canvassed in India suggesting that India could build up a stock of fifty 20-KT bombs for as little as £18,000,000." Buchan agrees with this estimate of cost but feels that ground-to-ground rockets and nuclear warheads with the "ability to threaten reprisal against the chief Chinese cities with thermonuclear weapons, would cost India something in the order of £1,800,000,000, or 100 times the figure that is given for a small stock of plutonium bombs . . . if India tried to achieve such a capability over a six-year period it would mean a 45 per cent increase in her current level of defence expenditure."[4]

So far as the cost of producing nuclear warheads is concerned, Buchan's estimate, equivalent to $5,073,900,000 would mean an additional expenditure of $845,600,000 a year if spread over a six-year period. This would without doubt be a burden on India's strained economic resources, but the precondition to any undertaking involving development of nuclear weapons is a revamping of India's economic policies. The boldness required of Indian leadership could be best shown by tailoring the Indian economy to meet the new demands made upon it and ridding it of superfluous state industrial undertakings. They could be turned over to the private sector on the basis of a formula which should not be too difficult to devise, while the state could concentrate its

[3] William C. Foster: "New Directions in Arms Control," *Foreign Affairs* (July, 1965).
[4] Buchan, "Dilemma."

resources on the nuclear program. The additional resources could be raised through a 10 to 15 per cent cut in Government expenditure, restraints on consumption, increased production, and ruthless scaling-down of Government investments in long-term capital-intensive projects. None of these would be very great sacrifices. They should be more acceptable than living under the constant threat of nuclear blackmail by China, or as "a nursling of the great powers."

It is conceivable that in much the same way as the North Atlantic Treaty Organization is provided with nuclear weapons by the United States, an Asian defense alliance could also secure nuclear weapons from her. But a defense alliance requires time to set up, and meanwhile disturbing reports of China's race toward nuclear self-sufficiency gives an edge and a sharpness to India's anxieties.

A very valid and interesting case was recently made out in favor of India producing nuclear weapons.

> I do not believe that the nuclear powers are acting in their best scientific traditions when they seek to impose nuclear impotence upon non-nuclear nations. . . . For any part of the world to assume the nuclear competence (including the bomb) is something which that part, and only that part, is morally competent to possess is an arrogance which can spread only fear and hate. I think it is axiomatic that a people which has indigenously developed the ability to bring off a nuclear explosion will deal with that power responsibly. . . . India can explode a bomb, and, contrary to popular impression, the cost would not importantly impair her economic development—not a fraction of the amount by which her progress is impaired by archaic administration. India needs a solid and continuing assurance that she can succeed by some standard other than those of her own anachronisms. To explode a bomb might provide that assurance and give a boost to Indian science. . . . She is as dependent upon science for the good life as is all the rest of the world.[5]

[5] Leland Hazard: "Strong Medicine for India," *The Atlantic* (December, 1965).

Any defense concept initiated by India for the Southeast Asian region presupposes a potent leadership as well as political stability and a willingness to demonstrate her usefulness as an ally with impressive programs of dynamic economic development at home. No alliance, understanding, or arrangement is possible if India's own foundations are shaky. India's allies will of necessity observe for themselves the dynamics, or lack of them, in India's economy. They will know how far she is able to help them in their development objectives, the extent of her ability to stand by them militarily, and the degree to which she is able to revitalize her political system and administration and prove that they are as efficient and dedicated as China's in pursuing their objectives.

Ultimately, the security of any country undoubtedly depends on its economic base. But that base cannot be developed unless those who would destroy it are deterred. To defend their development, nations and their leaders have to make harsh decisions. They have to have the stature and the strength to reject "isms" if national interests require it of them. Opposition to military and political alignments within a country, despite the dictates of national security, can be as dangerous as the designs of an enemy across its borders. The exertion of power has to be against the enemy, not against those who advocate a spirited stand against him.

8

Outlook on the Mid-Seventies

*I*TEM: On the evening of March 6, 1966, a vanguard of the Indian Army's relief column reached Aijal, headquarters of the remote and almost inaccessible Mizo Hills district of India's eastern state of Assam. The relief of Aijal ended for a time the brief revolt of the tribals led by the Mizo National Front.

ITEM: India's restless, frequently lawless, always angry city of Calcutta is neither inaccessible nor tribal, at least not in the same sense the Mizos are. On March 10 the Leftist Parties in Calcutta paralyzed life in that city of 6.5 million as a protest against the Government's policies and the arrests of their leaders. The strike was the most successful ever organized. Before the day was over rampaging mobs had set fire to trains, buses, and Government properties, looted shops, clashed repeatedly with police, and made a mockery of law, order, and civic and human decency and dignity.[1] The demonstrations were not confined to Calcutta but

---

1 Calculating the cost of the events in Calcutta on March 10, *The Statesman* (March 28, 1966) wrote that loss in terms of national income came to $4,439,000, the loss for the two subsequent days when life in the city remained seriously disturbed to $5,814,000, and the cost of property destroyed to about $3,488,000. The total loss added up to $13,740,000.

spread like wildfire through the crucial border state of West Bengal.

ITEM: On March 11, one day after the Calcutta demonstrations, violence erupted once again, this time a thousand miles away in the city of Amritsar in another sensitive border state, Punjab. The mobs there were led by the militant Hindu revivalist party, the Jana Sangh. The Sangh was infuriated at the Congress Party's decision to give the Sikhs the right to use their own script and language in the areas where they were in a majority. Within days the violence spread to other towns in the Punjab: Jullundar, Ludhiana, Pathankot, Ambala, and others. In the town of Panipat three veteran congressmen were burned alive.

ITEM: On March 14 the backlash of the Jana Sangh's Punjab agitation hit the capital of India and before the day was over shops in Delhi had been burned and looted, tear-gas shells fired at crazed mobs who overturned and set fire to vehicles, beat up innocent bystanders, and intimidated shopkeepers.

Crisis of Leadership

The events of those nine days in March were an explosive indictment of years of ineffective domestic leadership. They were proof, if any proof is required, of the fact that the biggest crisis in India today is the crisis of leadership.

Poor leadership is not confined to the Congress Party, which has been in power since independence, but is equally characteristic of most Opposition parties in India. Opposition excesses have often far exceeded the real or imaginary crimes of Government. On February 21, 1966, an Opposition member in the West Bengal Assembly walked up to the Finance Minister, snatched the budget papers from his hands, and tore them up. Less than a month later the deputy leader of the Jana Sangh group in the Madhya Pradesh Assembly threw shoes at the Speaker's head. On March 30 the Indian Parliament was adjourned abruptly for the first time in its history because of the unruly and indecorous behavior of some Opposition members. The disturbing thing is that these irresponsible acts, within the legislatures and outside of them, could eventually destroy the democratic institutions India has so assiduously built up since independence.

In the years since the Second World War student agitations, instigated by ruthless power groups, have brought down the governments of many countries. By inciting students to leave their schools, colleges and polytechnics, as was done in the opening months of 1966, Opposition parties in India showed poor judgment of the far-reaching consequences of such brash actions. The destruction of Government property too is inevitably followed by expenditure of Government money to replace it, money which has to be diverted from other more vital and constructive needs. If the aim of the Opposition in India is to create conditions in which Government sinks deeper into the quagmire, then little confidence can be placed in either its purposes or patriotism.

Because it has held uninterrupted power in India ever since independence, the Congress Party must in the final count be held responsible for a leadership which has lacked dynamism, which has permitted the questionable practices of its own members to set a pernicious example to others, which has made dreary platitudes a substitute for positive action, and which—because of its economic dogmas and their impact on the lives of the people —has driven the people to despair. Since the shaping and implementation of India's policies in the coming years will largely be directed by the Congress Party, as it is sure to be returned to power in the general elections in February, 1967, some of its compromises and the corruption of its values deserve a closer look.

For years the great debate in India centered around the question: "After Nehru, who?" When Nehru died the smooth transition of power proved that the anxiety underlying the debate had been unfounded. The democratic principle was vindicated. But the frenetic politicking behind the scenes showed that no principles were too valuable to sacrifice in the frantic bid for power. True, horse-trading goes on in every democratic country. Patronage is handed out and deals are made, but when these involve caste, language, religious, and regional loyalties, as they continue to do in India, a dangerously sinister and divisive element is introduced into the country's already taut political fabric.

Nehru's great strength was the absolute power he wielded in the Congress Party. The Chief Ministers and others in the states owed their political existence to him. But though Nehru held unquestioned power he was unable to exercise it to further the ideals to which he himself subscribed. It was in his time that the tragedy of redrawing the boundaries of India's states along linguistic lines was enacted. The lid on this Pandora's box is still to be shut. The precedent Nehru set—under pressure, no doubt—will prove even more damaging in time, till a determined leadership puts a stop to it. The demand for an independent Nagaland, and, more recently, the Mizo Hills agitation, the break-away demand for a Dravidistan in the south, the unseemly bickering between Maharashtra and Mysore over who should get Goa and Belgaum, the agitation by the projected state of Haryana for inclusion of large tracts of neighboring territories in it, are all symptoms of a wasting disease which a show of wisdom, firmness, and foresight in the early years could have helped to avoid.

Will India's present leadership be able to stop the rot which threatens the country's constitutional institutions and aspirations? The advantage Nehru's successors do not have—least of all his daughter, Indira Gandhi—is that while the Congress Party politicians were beholden to Nehru for the positions of power occupied by them, Shastri and now Mrs. Gandhi are beholden to Congress politicians for the Prime Minister's office. In electing Mrs. Gandhi to office, the Members of Parliament and the gray eminences behind them, the states's Chief Ministers, were left in little doubt of their new power as the king-makers. Increasingly, the regional political czars will now hold to ransom the progress of the country, and be more able to wilfully impose their regional whims over national needs. Unless this ruinous trend is reversed the emergence of India as a dynamic political force in Asia is impossible. If, on the other hand, the country's man power and material resources can be welded together by a strong Central Government with the sole and obsessive aim of getting the country's economic and social institutions off the ground, India can yet prove something to a world which is skeptical of her capacity to play a significant role in Asian affairs.

Indira Gandhi

Can Mrs. Indira Gandhi provide the leadership needed to pull the country out of the economic morass it is in, or to arrest the divisive forces before they destroy the federal character of the Indian Union? Does she have the toughness required to oppose China's aims along India's borders, or the resilience to reject the slogans of yesterday in the interests of today's and tomorrow's realities?

Among the ranking Congress politicians in India today Mrs. Gandhi does stand out as a person who has the makings of the kind of leader required. Her most important asset is that she is free of any communal or regional bias, a significant qualification since practically no other politician in India today is free of his own narrow provincial loyalties. During her term as Congress president in 1959 she did show, however, that expediency needn't necessarily be frowned upon in the quest for power. In that year she founded an electoral alliance with the Muslim League in Kerala with the aim of defeating the Communists at the polls, despite the fact that the Muslim League's rabidly communal politics had contributed their fair share to the partition of India and the resulting massacres. She justified her action by saying: "I do not believe the Muslim League is any more communal than anyone else in Kerala."[2] Ideals do get jettisoned in the heady pursuit of power, and compromises are made to get into positions of power. But compromises like the electoral alliance with the League have contributed considerably to the general cynicism with which the public views political doings in India.

[2] Welles Hangen: *After Nehru, Who?* (New York: Harcourt, Brace and World, Inc.; 1963), p. 175.

All the same there is no denying the fact that Indira Gandhi's personal loyalties are not focused on any narrow, sectarian considerations but on larger, national interests. The irony of it, however, is that though she herself does not subscribe to the petty provincialism of the majority in the Congress Party, she owes her ascension to the Prime Ministership to those who are provincial in their outlook. Two alternatives lie before her—either to conform to their thinking, or to assert herself and aim at drawing increasing support for her policies from the more progressive elements in the Party. The closing months of 1966 will provide a clearer picture of her political strategy. As the time approaches for the 1967 general elections, and the handing out of tickets to Congress candidates takes on a sharper edge, the power struggle between Indira Gandhi and the king-makers will inevitably begin.

The president of the Congress Party, K. Kamaraj, whose brittle use of his presidential authority ensured the elections of Shastri and Indira Gandhi to the Prime Ministership, will want his own hand-picked candidates returned to Parliament and the state legislatures. Only thus can he ensure continuity of his own power. Indira Gandhi, on the other hand, is neither by temperament nor training a person likely to play second fiddle to a party strong man. The dressing-down Kamaraj saw fit to administer to the Government at the Jaipur session of the Congress in February, 1966, could not have made Mrs. Gandhi very happy. It is therefore in the cards that she and her supporters within the Congress Party will make every effort to see their favored candidates get the tickets. Despite the fact that Kamaraj brought Indira Gandhi into power, a struggle between the two is possible.

At the same time Kamaraj's own position is not entirely unassailable, and even though he is the uncrowned king of Tamilnad (the Tamil-speaking areas of the south) a revolt within his ranks could weaken Kamaraj's position in his own home base. With Indira Gandhi's backing such a revolt could well be led by C. Subramaniam, the Union Food Minister. Kamaraj is also known to have strong feelings about the imposition of Hindi on the non-Hindi-speaking areas of the south, an attitude which in the event of a showdown could cost him the support of the equally fanatical language diehards of the north. Thus, from Kamaraj's point of view Indira Gandhi qualifies as the candidate least likely to embarrass the south. The possibility of the two reaching a durable understanding cannot therefore be discounted, since in the politics of India interdependence between the north and south is inescapable.

The twists and turns of politics often make possible the inconceivable. If Morarji Desai, a former finance minister and a self-professed moralist in his efforts to succeed Nehru, could form an alliance with Krishna Menon, a man he had implacably opposed in the past, then the possibility of other realignments in the Congress Party cannot be discounted. Nor, for that matter, the possibility of Mrs. Gandhi joining hands with Desai to oust Kamaraj!

Should Mrs. Gandhi come into power with a sizable following of her own after the elections, what sort of policies would she follow? She would first of all need to show the capacity and courage to correct the confused perspectives which plague the Indian economy and the wisdom to replace them with bold and dynamic concepts to cure the country's economic ills. Then too, strength of purpose is required of her to place the security of the country above the imaginary stigma Indians attach to defense-oriented alliances. Insofar as the Congress Party is concerned she will need to take punitive steps to rid the Party of those elements which over the years have made political corruption a credo of the Congress politician. And lastly, she will need dogged determination to complete reforms so that paralyzing administrative delays are eliminated to the advantage of the country's countless development schemes.

There is no doubt that some of the romanticism with which Nehru vested his Socialist ideas has rubbed off on his daughter. Whether she will see the problems which are laying waste the Indian economy through the nostalgia for that era, or will apply to them the hard-headed and realistic solutions which have proved successful elsewhere, is not as yet very clear. Her term in office has been too brief, and 1966 being a pre-election year her pronouncements so far have followed the safe party line. But the danger to her own political future as well as to the country lies in following lackluster policies whose sole aim is to play safe. Nothing, for instance, prevents Mrs. Gandhi from scrapping Government controls on sugar and cloth or from abolishing the food zones which have created evil and artificial barriers between the different Indian states. When Shastri took the initiative and decontrolled cement in India despite the fierce opposition of many congressmen, a bag of cement which had sold in the black market at twice the fixed price was within months selling at the list price. The only people who suffered from free sale of cement were the black-marketeers; yet even now many men in the ruling party are not reconciled to its decontrol. It proves that it is not the public but vested interests within and without the Congress Party which benefit most from artificially created scarcities. The procedures for licensing new industries could be simplified too, as could the existing tax structure.

None of these moves would adversely affect the fortunes of the Congress Party in the coming elections, and even if they did Mrs. Gandhi's decisive stand could prove that she places the interests of the country and the common man before those of the Party.

Despite tedious table-thumping oratory which extols the virtues of socialism day in and day out in India, the leadership at the top has so far failed to appreciate the simple truth that the first thing to do is to create wealth to get the wheels of industry and commerce humming, before coming to the problem of preventing its concentration. In trying to mop up wealth without creating it first, in putting the cart before the horse, Indian leaders have created a quaint and quixotic impression of themselves in India and abroad.

In a recent conversation with a Congress Member of Parliament I was told that talk of socialism is very important because it helps to balance the pressures exerted by big business! A cynical statement, at best. Apart from the fact that such talk is merely meant to balance big business and not make socialism an actual working reality, the important question is: why does the Government have to resort to subterfuge to deal with big business? If its demands are legitimate, Government should accede to them; if they are not, it should reject them. However, since the Congress Party is heavily subsidized by business groups and these have their own powerful lobbies within the Party, the need for double-talk on the part of Congress leaders becomes easier to understand.

In practice this double-talk works in favor of the business sector since it allows it to function in conditions of scarcities and monopolies. If there were no protected industries and there was fierce competition in all spheres of production, not only would the resulting prices favor the ordinary consumer but the profits accruing to the manufacturers would be more reasonable than at present. That would be a truly socialistic society—not one beset by shortages, controls, and runaway prices.

Mrs. Gandhi's pronouncements on China since she assumed office have been encouraging. In an interview with a visiting editor from the United Arab Republic in February, 1966, she said she had begun to sense the Chinese danger as far back as 1954. In another interview she said India was determined to resist the Chinese push along her borders. But she has also repeatedly emphasized that India is nonaligned: an ambiguous statement. Indians find it difficult to understand why Americans are not aligned with them in their attitude toward Pakistan. Americans find it equally baffling to be told that India is nonaligned, despite changing international alignments in the sixties. A close and careful study of the Chinese aims in Asia can leave little doubt of her intentions with regard to countries on her periphery. India must take the necessary measures to defend her national security; and if that means the setting up of an Asian defense system— something for which India must take the initiative—any squeamishness toward it can only be a sign of weakness. If the United States and even the Soviet Union are willing to aid such an Asian-sponsored alliance, member countries—including India—

should have no hesitation in discussing such aid. Bold and decisive action, not mere statements, is required.

Mrs. Gandhi will meet her match in the members of her own party when she tries to boot out the corrupt elements in their ranks or those who over the years have defeated government policies while outwardly paying lip service to them. They might well finish her political career, but then there is always the unique possibility in India that the direct support of the people for a popular Prime Minister could provide him or her with the backing needed to carry out measures frowned upon by elements within the Party.

If Mrs. Gandhi secures the active support of the civil servants for her programs, instead of just their passive acceptance, she ought to carry through many crash programs despite lack of enthusiasm of her own party members. I am not among those who make a fetish of condemning senior Indian civil servants in season and out. It is the administrative experience of the Indian Civil Service which has held this country together through its many vicissitudes since independence. The politicians, with their lack of experience and judgment, would long ago have made a mess of things but for the fact that men trained in the hard school of administering a vast country with perennial problems and fearsome contradictions were able to keep things going. That some of them were unable to rise to the new challenges before them or connived with the politicians to build their own bureaucratic empires does not change the fact that their experience proved a valuable asset to the country, which even now should harness their talents to take it through its dark and demanding period of travail.

Bureaucracy exists in every country, and it is seldom an exciting experience to deal with it whether in India or elsewhere. It is specially oppressive in India because it operates against a background of shortages and a staggering complex of controls. Since the system in India functions on the principle that it is good to suspect every man's motives, elaborate sanctions of a dozen ministers and departments are required to implement even a minor proposal, a practice which by now has assumed surrealistic overtones.

Six years ago Frank Moraes wrote in his book *India Today* that "The sense of undue regimentation, of unnecessary governmental intrusion not only in public spheres of commerce, industry and professional life, but also in the ordinary business of everyday life and living oppresses many in India . . . the excessive bureaucratisation of a country ruled by a new class comparatively unused to authority and unfamiliar with the business of government creates a sensation of the State as a Great Leviathan to whom the people are expected and encouraged to look for everything."[3]

Without doubt the reaction today of those accused of regimenting the country would be that the same sort of thing was said six years ago, and that despite the gloomy prophecies time had passed by. It may have passed by, but time has not left things untouched. The leisurely, almost aloofly paternalistic approach to the politics of India is no longer valid today. No matter how extensively the sociologists, economists, and political pundits examine and assess the minds and motivations of Indians and explain them away in rare terms, the fact remains that in this age of communications Indians are no longer unknowing of the good things in life that people in other countries have, nor are they likely to accept indefinitely being denied similar things by an ineffective leadership with its ineffectual policies. The pressures are building up, a fact which is yet to receive recognition from those who shape policies and those who defend them in Parliament and the press. Mrs. Gandhi would be doing a service to her own political career as well as to the country by recognizing the fact that these pressures do exist. If no shattering or calamitous event has so far taken place in India, it is entirely impermissible to assume that none will in the future. Time is not on the side of the ineffective. What needs to be realized is that the capabilities of India's present leadership will be increasingly

3 (New York: The Macmillan Co.; 1960), p. 238.

judged not on the basis of their personal attributes but the effectiveness of their leadership in its entirety.

In a country faced by an awesome array of problems—all requiring special solutions with a degree of urgency—mobilization of talents in the country ought to be an obligation of those in power. Yet the Government's refusal to draw on the talent available in the spheres of business, learning, the professions, and other disciplines, is inexcusable as well as indefensible. Years ago, when she was the Congress president, Mrs. Gandhi herself felt that some such induction was indicated. "I would like to see active people, non-party and from other parties, working together with Congress. . . . In this way not only would a much larger section of the people be actually involved in constructive work, but party pressures would be less able to obstruct people or programmes."[4] Now that she is in a position to give shape to this view, Mrs. Gandhi would do well to look beyond her Party for talents the country sorely needs.

The Indian Prime Minister could also usefully take a leaf out of the late President Kennedy's book. The brain trust Kennedy set up to advise him on America's domestic, economic, and foreign policy problems was a notable attempt to bring the thinking of the finest minds in America to bear on the country's problems. At the same time it was an attempt to bridge the gulf between the thinkers on the one hand and politicians and career men on the other. Unfortunately, in India the system operates on the assumption that there are no brains worth picking outside of the administration and the Congress Party. Parliament—though in theory, at least, it represents the people—in practice jealousy insists that only members of Parliament should give advice, and determinedly keeps others outside the precincts of policy-making. The result is that some of the most versatile and brilliant men in the country are excluded from deliberations which profoundly affect India's future, a practice which makes Britain's Establishment look open ended by comparison.

Here again only a uniquely confident leadership can break

[4] In an interview with *Link* magazine.

down the existing barriers. The fact that there is no mood of public participation in the affairs of the country and that national purposes do not generate excitement but only a sense of futility proves that those in power have done little to involve those people whose identification with national goals would have contributed to the quality of the Indian effort in every field.

The attempt here is not to review all the areas in which India requires new capabilities to pull her out of her present inertia. Only the more demanding challenges are mentioned in passing in order to show that the integrity and ability of the Indian leadership at the top can be judged only by the manner in which these problems are tackled. The dual Indian characteristic of providing an esoteric explanation for any and all kinds of bungling and accepting poor performance out of a sense of *tantric* charity is responsible for much of the mediocrity in the country. More taxing standards and a more critical approach to them are now needed.

Thus Mrs. Gandhi's capabilities, or those of any other Prime Minister who might assume office in 1967, will be judged only by the competence, the courage, and the conviction with which she or he tackles these problems.

The "Isms" in India

The lurking tragedy which threatens an otherwise triumphant Indian democracy is that democracy has itself become an end instead of a means for securing for the individual his fundamental human rights—a fair deal at the hands of the state, a good life. His rights are farcical if he has nothing to eat, yet staggering compromises continue to be made—not in the interests of the individual, but in the so-called interests of democracy. Casteism, regionalism, linguism, and other "-isms" are tolerated and in fact encouraged on the spurious plea that to stifle them would be undemocratic. Yet in daily life their practice works against the interests of millions of Indians. The ironic thing is that the compromises of the party in power are not imposed from the outside but always by those influential persons within it who have reached high office by trading on caste and communal loyalties rather than by abiding with the party's principles and ideals. The result is that the caste system—"the most brilliant, the most fantastic piece of social engineering which has ever been the product of human ingenuity . . . for the artificial creation of a superior race"[5]—is as strongly prevalent as before, acting as a drag on the country's emotional integration and progress. More serious than the problem of integration is the antidemocratic manner in which caste lobbies function in a democracy. In a large number of cases the qualification of candidates to electoral office is their caste and religion, which ensures them the support of their own groups. The Congress Party has over the years perpetuated this practice. Even in the case of a Muslim leader of a stature like Maulana Azad, a predominantly Muslim constituency was chosen for him in 1952 (the Gurgaon constituency in the Punjab, where the Meos are in a majority). At other places the Congress approached minority voters through religious and communal organizations. In Delhi in 1957 the decisive Muslim vote in the Delhi City constituency was secured through the Jamiat-ul-Ulema, a communal organization of the Muslims.

More than any other man in India, Nehru sensed the dimensions of the danger communalism posed to India's unity, but because the Congress Party was an amorphous mass by then, he was unable to influence its attitudes and actions along the lines of his own idealism. Far too many congressmen were opposed to his liberal thinking and they saw to it that his pronouncements rejecting communalism came nowhere near translation into practice. V. D. Savarkar, a militant Hindu nationalist, once claimed that hundreds of Hindu congressmen congratulated him for the stand taken by his party, the Hindu Mahasabha (which stands for the establishment of Hindu *raj* in India), on various issues on which he had opposed the Congress.

Communal rivalries in India have exploded into violence before and can do so again, since they are no less ignitable now

[5] Ashok Rudra: "Myth of Tolerance," *Seminar* (March, 1965), p. 24.

than they were in the past. The Hindu-Muslim riots which gripped the town of Jabalpur in the central Indian state of Madhya Pradesh in February, 1961, and the Hindu-Sikh conflict in Punjab in March, 1966, were indicative not so much of passions aroused in passing but of deep-seated, long-dormant resentments rooted in communal bias. If the outcome of the Indo-Pakistan fighting of September, 1965, had gone against India, it is conceivable that the fury of the majority community might have turned on the Muslim minority. Though fears like this are frequently left unstated, they need underscoring for two reasons. Firstly, because the hypnosis induced by self-assuring statements on communal harmony is not likely to lessen the communal danger. And secondly, because by emphasizing the risks of communal violence which could result under certain conditions, sane elements within India will realize the dangers Indian democracy faces at the hands of communalists in the country. It is necessary to bring home this realization abroad too, in order to gain for India sympathetic support for her special predicament.

In delineating the jagged edges of India's political and social institutions the aim is not merely to report the situation as it exists but to graphically project the staggering nature of the problems faced here and the encrustation of centuries which through relentless efforts has to be broken.

A point being currently debated in India is whether changes in the electoral system wouldn't be a good thing for the resolution of some of these problems in order to bring about a two-party system in the country. This would ensure a continuing check on the performance of the party in power, and provide a democratic alternative to it. Those who favor this change feel it would introduce new dynamics into the working of democracy in India. More specifically, the point made is that the fragmentation of the vote under the present electoral laws results in the Congress Party holding about three fourths of the seats in Parliament and two thirds in the state legislatures, despite the fact that it has never secured an absolute majority in any of the general elections. The reason for this is that the opposition vote is split between twenty-one political parties recognized by the election commissioner and about three times the number competing without official recognition. In addition a great many Independent candidates compete in each election and their number is many times more than the total seats contested by them. This absurd splintering of the polled votes results in a diffusion of what could be a majority vote, among a welter of diverse political parties and Independents.

One suggestion for rectifying this situation is to amend the electoral law to eliminate small parties and to restrict the election to only party candidates. Some European countries have adopted this practice in order to nudge smaller parties into merging with each other, thus preventing their proliferation and the consequent fragmentation of the vote. Another suggestion is for more exacting qualifications for candidates, along with a condition requiring a minimum number of supporters to endorse each application. For instance, in a constituency of two hundred villages a minimum of ten sponsors from each village could be stipulated, and simultaneously the initial deposit could be increased ten times, from perhaps $100 to $1,000. Democratic traditions would not suffer since even the poorest candidate could get his initial two thousand sponsors to contribute half a dollar each in case he was unable to raise the deposit himself. There is no denying the fact that a healthier party balance could result through elimination of spurious contests.

There are as many arguments against electoral changes. One view is that "the phenomena of a large body of independent candidates and of highly successful local parties and groups are precisely the features of a developing politic organising and building itself . . . at the same time keeping open various centres of protest and ventilation and various opportunities for criticism and debate."[6] This idea, though theoretically sound, has in practice succeeded in spawning no worth-while opposition to

[6] Rajni Kothari: "The Pattern of Dominance," *Seminar* (April, 1966), p. 45.

the Congress Party; it also skirts the problem of fragmentation of the vote.

In the final analysis, while some changes in the electoral system could help, ultimately the growing political restiveness in the country will provide its own checks and balances on the vagaries and whims of older politicians. The startlingly radical shifts in recent economic thinking in the Sovet Union as well as in the conduct of her foreign policy show that even where there is no opposition whatsoever, a hard-headed generation of political realists and technocrats can sense the winds of change and steer the ship of state accordingly. What an enlightened leadership in India could do is examine dispassionately and realistically the score card of its achievements and failures in the years since independence and then apply the necessary correctives.

Political old-timers still dominate the scene in India. To some extent this is understandable because of the part they played in the independence struggle. But nineteen years is reasonable time for anyone to get the desire for power out of his system. To take India into the modern age requires mobilization of those special talents, qualifications, and disciplines which others continuously draw upon in their own countries to keep abreast of the changing times. It is not the prejudices and dogmas of yesterday which will help India meet the exacting demands of today and tomorrow. The obligation of any forward-looking leadership is to realize the vital nature of this simple twentieth-century truth.

Areas of Opportunity

The bonds which need breaking to release India from the shackles of the past are undoubtedly many but it would be possible to show spectacular achievements by cutting just a few of them. The most important breakthrough has to be in the economic sphere. Other areas in which catalytic action could activate great changes are: control of population, scientific education, introduction of television, tough policing of political interference in the country's permanent administration, and a determined effort to pull India back from the isolationism she is being driven into by curbs on travel, education abroad, and so on.

The staggering nature of India's population problem can be realized from the fact that her present population of 485 million could conceivably reach a figure of 900 million by the end of this century at the present rate of growth, which adds 11 million to the total every year.

India's population has increased by 150 million since independence; today it is twice that of Africa and more than that of the entire American continent. India's annual population increase equals the entire population of Australia. Thus if significant gains are not soon registered in lowering the birth rate, India's real nightmare is yet to begin. Though great humanitarian gains have been logged through reducing the rate of infant mortality, eradicating disease, and increasing life expectancy from thirty-two to forty-seven years during the last fifteen years, the achievements of this sort have given a new dimension to the problem of overpopulation. No marked improvement in India's food problem or in the standard of living of her people is possible unless the frightening prospect of an exploding population is effectively countered.

Before analyzing the effectiveness of the Indian effort thus far some unique aspects of this problem which continue to test the preseverance and ingenuity of India's family planners need to be spelt out. Ashish Bose, of India's Institute of Economic Growth, has placed this problem in perspective with unusual perceptivity. Quoting Nehru ("I address large rural audiences and almost always I speak of family planning to them . . . their reactions are . . . of amusement whenever I refer to this matter, general laughter in the audience and a certain shyness . . ."), Bose comes to the main point when he says: "While historians like Arnold Toynbee and scientists like Julian Huxley warn us of the great threat to human existence brought about by the population explosion, demographers write whole books on the impact of population growth on per capita income in 1981 or 2001, planners emphasise the urgency of population control and family planners wax eloquent on the virtues of the small family pattern, India's rural millions in their ignorance view the problem with amusement, laughter and a certain shyness."[7]

The problem of influencing, educating, in fact, enthusing millions of people skeptical of a program which destroys time-honored prerogatives and questions established codes of social and personal conduct is not easy of solution. Nor can it be forgotten that not only in India but elsewhere in the world there are limits to which government may go in dictating a pattern for the personal lives of the people. Even during the British rule there was no such interference or imposition. Consequently, in independent India it is natural that barriers are put up by a baffled and often resentful people against those who would want them to give up their one last personal privilege and pleasure.

It is not as if there is any organized resistance to family planning in India. In a country as diverse as this there cannot be any unified opposition to it. But it is often very difficult to dislodge people from positions firmly founded on socio-economic logic. Here again, Bose's observations on the subject of the premium put on sons in India are of interest. "Many western writers think that the preference for sons is primarily a religious or social phenomenon. It is not. In fact it is deeply rooted in economic conditions. In a country where there is no comprehensive social security programme, no old age pension, no sickness allowance, no unemployment insurance, parents have to depend almost wholly on their sons in times of emergencies and particularly in old age. Daughters are married away and social custom does not favour taking of financial assistance from married daughters and sons-in-law. But it is in the fitness of things . . . either the parents stay in the house of one of the sons or get regular financial assistance from all the sons. . . . This is in fact a form of built-in social insurance. This attitude is absolutely rational from the point of view of the strategy of survival; persons who see in the marked preference for sons signs of primitive backwardness only display their profound ignorance of social

[7] Ashish Bose: "Population Control," *Seminar* (May, 1962), p. 11.

reality. And persons who dogmatically hold the view that the size of the family should be invariably limited to three children (irrespective of the sex composition of the children), may be good statisticians but are poor students of human arithmetic."[8] There are numerous other areas of resistance. Yet the encouraging thing is that because there is no organized opposition to family planning, some ground has been gained in the past few years. But despite the fact that India was the first country in the world to adopt population control as state policy, the problem is only now beginning to be faced on an extended national scale. Though finance is a major worry the fact still remains that in the Second Plan, out of $10,571,000 provided for family planning, only $6,342,000 were spent; in fact only 60 per cent of the budget was utilized. Yet, though the critical proportions of this problem have only in recent years been appreciated by the administration, the endless and infinitely trying nature of this work has taken its toll of time.

Basically the problem is one of organization and personnel. With over 80 per cent of Indians living in nearly 600,000 villages—and the birthrate is the highest in these villages—reaching them and working among them in a sustained and effective manner presents overwhelming personnel and organizational problems which in turn pose financial problems. Even if the organizational and financial hurdles were crossed, the number of doctors, nurses and trained social workers required would create a next to impossible situation. This aspect has to be considered against the background of overall shortages of medical personnel in India.

Overriding all this is the question of methods to be used. India has tried out a wide spectrum, ranging from Gandhi's method of self-restraint to the rhythm, foam tablets, and diaphragm and jelly methods. Each of them for one reason or another (some of the reasons being special to India) has proved unsuccessful. The planners now rest their hopes on a large-scale sterilization pro-

[8] Bose, p. 12–13.

gram and the use of the "loop" (intrauterine device), the newest and most promising discovery thus far. There has been animated debate on whether abortion should be legalized, and the very fact that this issue is being debated at all is remarkable in view of the tradition-bound conservatism which influences much of Indian thinking. On the face of it abortion seems impracticable because of the high outlays required for medical and surgical facilities which would have to be established all over the country, a project India is in no position to launch either physically or financially.

The target India's planners have before them is to reduce the birth rate from forty to twenty-five per thousand by the mid seventies and to halve it in the decade after that. The aim instead should be to halve the birth rate within a decade and then to determine the financial outlay required to realize this objective. The Planning Commission has budgeted $216,700,000 for family planning in the Fourth Plan. How this figure has been arrived at is not very clear, but since there can be no disputing the importance of allocating the highest priority to family planning, the Government should consider revising this figure upward with the aim of halving the birth rate within the seventies.

Within days of taking over the Prime Ministership Mrs. Gandhi has shown an able grasp of this problem by setting up a new department of family planning (within the Ministry of Health) with a senior administrator in charge. But unless extraordinary powers are given to this department (perhaps it should even be raised to the status of a ministry) the mere fact of setting it up is not likely to produce any spectacular results. The case for a constitutional amendment to make the family planning program a federal instead of a state function must also be examined.

Like food, family planning has been accepted as a national problem and given the highest priority. Yet, while the food ministers have come up for severe criticism for failures on the food front, no such resentment has been expressed against those who after twelve years of trying have been unable to reduce the birth rate at all. This easy attitude toward the most challenging problem facing India has to change if she is to pit herself realistically and purposefully against the problems of privation and poverty.

"India is far behind in general scientific achievement," observed a recent visitor from the United States. "She has had no Nobel Prize winner in physics since 1930, and none ever in chemistry or in medicine and psychology—a sad record. She can defend herself by eschewing science and relapsing into Indian spirituality but her scientists know better. She is as dependent upon science for the good life as is all the rest of the world." Yet, he went on to observe, "incongruously, non-scientific India has developed nuclear competence to produce the bomb and explode it."[9] The puzzling picture of a nation lagging behind in the scientific field, yet possessing areas of excellence to the extent of being able to master nuclear science, highlights once again the paradoxes of India's efforts.

Talk of India eschewing science and relapsing into Indian spirituality comes uncomfortably close to the truth because a very influential section of opinion within the ruling Congress Party articulates at every turn the view that India should rely more on its ancient systems of learning and knowledge and not be unduly enamoured of the advances made by the West. While retrograde thinking of this kind has not reversed the tide of progress, it does confuse issues and slow down the pace. (The priority given to Prohibition, at a colossal expense, at a time when technological and scientific education is starved for funds is another instance of the kind of thinking which seriously undermines India's efforts.) In a modern technological age in which a direct equation is possible between the country's scientific capabilities and the quality of the national output, it is possible to understand the glaring unevenness which characterizes the Indian effort. This unevenness not only affects national security—which in the present age requires of a country sophisticated scientific skills superior to others—but industry and economy and in fact the entire national

[9] Leland Hazard: "Strong Medicine for India," *The Atlantic* (December, 1965).

purpose are dependent on the nation's ability to mobilize its own talents.

The excellence of India's atomic energy establishment is by no means accidental. The exacting standards set there for the training of scientists result from a clear conception of the functions they are expected to perform. They are trained for specific roles and there is no ambiguity or speculative element to diffuse the purposes for which the training program is established.

The situation in the rest of India is exactly the reverse. To take one instance, while forecasts predict that there will be eight to nine thousand fewer engineers than are required at the end of the Fourth Plan, a great many of those who graduate will still be out of jobs! South India's *The Hindu* (August 28, 1965) attributes this to the fact that "the delay in their absorption stems from their lack of practical industrial experience. . . . Industries complain of shortage of technical personnel but what they mean is dearth of engineers with sufficient practical experience who can be put in charge straight away. Efforts to get industries to provide facilities for the practical training of the engineering students have not been very successful so far." Here is a situation in which there is no coordination between the training institutions, the pattern of education they provide, and the agencies which will eventually absorb the students from these institutions. In a sense a major part of the effort and outlay is wasted since neither the demands of industry nor those of scientific establishments are adequately met nor is an ever-expanding cadre of scientists with creative and inventive abilities built up.

A major breakthrough in the scientific and technological fields is needed, not impressive in statistical terms alone but one which is able to fulfill its prime purpose of giving a new thrust to the advancement of science and industry in India. New engineering colleges and polytechnics are beginning to proliferate, but their ability to create a technological revolution is in serious doubt. Until they can—and only a hard-driving educational revolution fired by a sense of great purpose can achieve this—India will be unable to take her place beside nations which have mastered the marvels of modern technology.

The fact that there is scarcely any television worth the name in India can be attributed to no other reason but that the extraordinary potential of this scientific marvel has never truly become explicit to the leadership in India. In an age of communications the advantages of dramatically communicating with every corner of a country as complex and diverse as India have been scarcely recognized. In a country in which the colossal problem of fourteen major and hundreds of minor languages is rendered even more difficult by the fact that over 80 per cent of the people are illiterate, television presents unique possibilities for bridging this seemingly unbridgeable communications gap between the Indian peoples.

Despite the fact that the Government of India is likely to accept the recommendations of a high-powered committee which has suggested the setting up over the next seven to ten years of a television network covering 113 towns and a quarter of a million villages, at a cost of $216,700,000, the nagging feeling exists that even if the project were initiated on the scale recommended its potential might never be realized if it acted as another department of the Government. There are reasons for these misgivings, one being the insistence on the part of Government and the Congress Party on maintaining an inflexible attitude toward arguments which favor private ownership of television. In an impassioned statement in Parliament, a Congress member expressed horror at the thought of having "outsiders" (meaning private enterprise in India!) controlling this important medium. But the outsiders would not be picked at random. They would be responsible institutions capable of putting up the necessary capital and able to meet Government's licensing requirements. Having three or four independent networks would presumably insure a higher caliber of broadcasts. In order to leapfrog over other means of education and communication and deal directly with the momentous problems of the day in a moving and dramatic manner through TV, Indian television would have to mobilize the country's creative minds to make the necessary impact on the people. But creative people seldom give their best in the stifling atmosphere of a stuffy Government department. Nor can their talents be ever paid for adequately if the buyer has a monopoly over them. The mediocrity of Government's All India Radio after three decades of broadcasting experience is as good an indication as any of television's future in India if it is treated as an adjunct to a Government ministry.

And yet, the possibilities TV presents are breathtaking.

Communalism, casteism, and linguism; the marvels of modern technology; the calamitous cost in human as well as material terms of violence born of ignorance and intolerance; the excitement, adventure, and rewards a developing economy can offer to those with aspirations and initiative; the true cost in human terms of unplanned families and an uncontrolled birth rate—these and a hundred other burning issues could be projected with ingenuity before India's millions. The allure of this new medium combined with excellence in programing could bring about an almost incalculable change in the outlook of the people.

Administrative delays in India have achieved a unique notoriety. The conclusions of any independent survey aimed at assessing in fiscal terms the national loss which results from these delays would be scandalous. No single factor has contributed more toward clogging the administrative machinery than political interference in the working of the administration.

A line of division between the political spheres and the permanent executive is basic to the efficient working of a democracy. But when a political party attempts to usurp the functions of the executive and to influence implementation, the results— as is evident in the Indian context—can be disastrous. A psychology of inaction flows from such interference. The executive will not act unless it is sure its decision will not tread on any political toes. It will not act against the interests of the political party in power. The damaging effects of this psychology are obvious in India. Ineffective or partisan implementation and loss of wide-based public confidence are clearly evident too.

The practice of political interference is glaringly evident at the level of district administration, which provides the basic structure for the entire administrative scaffolding in India. Since the votes come from the rural areas in the districts it is here that local politicians exert the greatest influence on the district administration. To justify this wholly incorrect practice, the comforting theory is advanced that administration in a democracy is everyone's business and that the executive which implements Government policies must be overseen. This is a fallacious argument. Administration is as much a science as any other specialized skill required to run a modern state. It calls for special talents, training, and wide experience, which cannot be provided by party hacks whose sole interest in any specific issue is an entirely limited and subjective one.

By making a mockery of the rules of business and paralyzing the administration through continuous interference, the efficiency of the Indian administration has been reduced to a disastrously low level. Not only has the executive's will to take independent decisions been sapped, but an elaborate framework of "channels" for routing all proposals has been devised in order to disperse the onus of decision-making among as many people as possible.

A fascinating study in contrasts is provided by the intensity of the current rethinking on this subject in countries like the Soviet Union, Yugoslavia, and others. In a recent article, "Freeing Economics from Politics in Yugoslavia" (*The Statesman*, April 6, 1966), the process of depoliticalization of Yugoslavia's economy was analyzed at length. President Tito's own views have favored freeing state enterprises from "various pressures from above"; to bring this about "party members found to be sabotaging implementation of the current economic reform may discover themselves to be outside the Party." The principle is the same: the state cannot function efficiently nor carry through national plans and objectives if specialized agencies are subject to continuous political pressures.

Delays are endemic to progress, and the extent to which India's development schemes suffer from harrowing administrative delays is well known both in India and abroad. For a new drive to be injected into the working of the agencies responsible for the implementation of India's plans, a brilliantly conceived program of reforms is necessary, along with the will on the part of the Prime Minister to ruthlessly implement it.

Whether the Indian leadership is willing to admit it or not, its policies are gradually taking the country into an isolationist phase in which curbs on travel and restrictions on students going abroad and on imports of books and periodicals into India are, among other things, shutting the outside world out for most Indians. Gradually and imperceptibly a *khadi* curtain is being drawn around India. Naturally, it is a curtain with a difference. Its purpose is to keep Indians within India and to isolate them from current trends abroad. The adverse consequences of the status quo which has resulted from this are already visible in many ways, but their unfortunate impact on the minds and thinking of Indians will be more evident in the coming years.

The introspection, the sense of false satisfaction, the lack of opportunity to measure its own standards with others, the shutting out of new horizons, will all in time affect the quality of contemporary Indian effort. Indians are being ill-equipped for the challenging role they will have to play opposite their counterparts in the more aggressive and advanced societies.

The reason given for these ever-increasing curbs is a shortage of foreign exchange. The official stand is that the country has no exchange to spare for travel, or for such nonessential purposes as liberal imports of newspapers, magazines, and books from abroad! And yet travel is possible for those of the New Class, or those able to satisfy the elaborate requirements of the sanctioning authorities. In the bewildering tangle of rules and regulations in which the average Indian's life is enmeshed, the long-term implications of this rule have been accepted without close examination by either the public or those who have framed it.

More than most other things, India needs the methodology, the scientific and technological know-how, the processes and the proficiencies of the West and of Japan, so that the special skills which have given those countries a lead in the world of today can help India as well. By denying Indians the opportunity to see, understand, and absorb this knowledge and these qualities the Indian leadership is selling short not only the present but also the next generation of Indians.

The confidence, the poise, and the sense of purpose which characterizes students who qualify in universities abroad in comparison to their counterparts in India indicates simultaneously the headway which has to be made by educational institutions here, as well as the advantages of giving those who can afford to go abroad the opportunity of doing so. Nor is any academician or business or professional man likely to be left untouched by the experience of observing and participating in his own special field of interest abroad.

The sum total of the experiences Indians are able to acquire abroad will be reflected in the quality and content of contemporary Indian effort. Unless the quality of such effort improves and India is able to master modern techniques, the flow of gold will always be out of India and not into it. In such circumstances the foreign exchange position will hardly ever improve!

The amount of exchange involved in permitting Indians free travel or allowing for liberal imports of books and periodicals or even specialized talents from abroad is a fraction of the exchange which is drained away each year by the more unethical practices of overinvoicing purchases of capital plant and equipment abroad, or through gold smuggling and such practices.

Since Mrs. Gandhi brings a modern outlook to her office she should ask for an objective study of this problem and should order removal of such curbs if she is convinced that the damage they do is far in excess of any likely savings in foreign exchange.

Conclusion

The second decade of India's independence is drawing to a close. In these twenty years phenomenal changes have taken place in this historic land. Where a few years ago the creaking of bullock cart wheels and the chirping of crickets were the only sounds heard, the clang of heavy industry now reverberates through the countryside. Where once fireflies flickered at night, the flames of India's oil refineries now burn brightly. From the aircraft plants of Bangalore, in the south, to the locomotive workshops at Chittaranjan, in West Bengal; from the Bhakra dam in the north to the Bhilai steel plant in central India there is evidence enough of a people on the move, of ceaseless nervous activity aimed at bridging the lag of centuries in decades.

But human beings, despite the grandeur of the dreams they dream and the visions they carry within them, are in the end subject to human frustrations which are the inescapable burden of human existence. It is sometimes forgotten that India is waging a fight on two great fronts: a fight against poverty and backwardness, which is the fate of a long-oppressed people, and another against attitudes and prejudices that are centuries old. The second, in the end result, is a more difficult fight. Unless it is won the other can never be fully won—a fact often overlooked by those who criticize India for her ways without realizing that such criticism is based on present-day standards evolved over a length of time.

Yet impatience cannot be wholly excluded from any assessment of India's achievements and failures. It stems from the realization that India is tantalizingly close to spectacular breakthroughs in the economic and social spheres and to emerging as a nation of significance in Asia. If dated and doctrinaire thinking is defeating India's great purposes, impatience with such thinking has to be expressed: what is more such thinking must be severely crticized. That such criticism is possible augurs well for India. It augurs well for Asia too.

Bibliography

Allan, J., Sir T. Wolseley Haig, H. H. Dodwell, R. R. Sethi: *The Cambridge Shorter History of India*. New Delhi: S. Chand and Co.; 1964.

Annual Register Office, Calcutta: *Indian Annual Register, 1946*. Vol. II, 1947.

Bansal, G. L.: "Industrial Development in India." *India 1958: Exhibition Souvenir*.

Bauer, P. T.: "Does Foreign Aid Really Help?" London: *Daily Telegraph*, August 2, 1965.

Bell, Sir Charles: *Tibet—Past and Present*. Oxford: The Clarendon Press; 1924.

Bhatia, B. M.: *Famines in India*. Bombay: Asia Publishing House; 1963.

Bose, Ashish: "Population Control." *Seminar*. New Delhi: May, 1962.

Buchan, Alistair: "Dilemma of India's Security." *The Listener*, May 13, 1965.

———— (ed.): *China And The Peace of Asia*. London: Chatto and Windus, Ltd. (for the Institute of Strategic Studies); 1965.

Campbell-Johnson, Allan: *Mission with Mountbatten*. London: Robert Hale Ltd.; 1952.

Chanda, Asok: *Federalism in India*. New York: The Macmillan Co.; 1956.

Clubb, O. Edmund: "China's Position in Asia." *Journal of International Affairs*, XVII, (1963), No. 2.

Coker, Francis W.: *Recent Political Thought*. Calcutta: The World Press Ltd.; n.d.

Cole, Allan B.: "Political Contrasts—China, India and Japan," *Journal of International Affairs*, XVII, (1963), No. 2.

Curl, Peter U. (ed.): *Documents on American Foreign Relations, 1954.* New York: Harper & Brothers; 1955.

Daily Telegraph. London: June 16, 1964.

Eastern Economist. New Delhi: Annual Number (1965).

The Eastern Economist Ltd., New Delhi: *India's Progress Since Independence—A Statistical Bird's-Eye View.* 1965.

The Economist: "Growth and Government" (editorial), March 20, 1960.

Eeklen, W. F. Van: *Indian Foreign Policy and the Border Dispute with China.* The Hague: Martinus Nijhoff; 1964.

The Famine Enquiry Commission Report on Bengal (1945).

Fischer, Margaret W., Leo E. Rose, Robert Huttenback: *Himalayan Battleground—Sino-Indian Rivalry in Ladakh.* London: Pall Mall Press, Ltd.; 1963.

Ford Foundation, the Agricultural Production Team: *Report on India's Food Crisis and Steps to Meet it.* Issued by the Government of India, the Ministry of Food and Agriculture and the Ministry of Community Development and Cooperation; April, 1959.

Foster, William C.: "New Directions in Arms Control." *Foreign Affairs,* July, 1965.

Gadgil, D. R.: *Planning and Economic Policy in India.* Bombay: Asia Publishing House; 1965.

Galbraith, John Kenneth: "Rival Economic Theories In India." *Foreign Affairs,* XXXVI (1957–8).

———: "Foreign Policy: The Stuck Whistle." *The American Review,* October, 1965.

The Government of India (Planning Commission): *First Five-Year Plan.* 1953.

———: *Second Five-Year Plan.* 1956.

———: *Third Five-Year Plan.* 1962.

———: *The Planning Process.* October, 1963.

———: *The Gazette of India Extraordinary.* New Delhi: April 6, 1948; No. 1 (3)–44 (13)/48.

———: (Ministry of Commerce and Industry): *India 1958: Exhibition Souvenir.*

————: (Ministry of Finance): *India—Pocket Book of Information; 1965.*

————: (Director General of Commercial Intelligence and Statistics): *Statistical Tables of British India.*

————: (Publications Division, Ministry of Information and Broadcasting): *China's Betrayal of India.* November, 1962.

————: (External Publicity Division of the Ministry of External Affairs): *China's Aggression in War and Peace* (letters of the Prime Minister of India). December 8, 1962.

————: *White Paper No. 8* (Notes, Memoranda, and Letters, an Exchange Between the Governments of India and China, October, 1962–January 1963).

————: *White Paper* on Jammu and Kashmir.

Griffith, Samuel B., II: "Communist China's Capacity to Make War." *Foreign Affairs,* XXXXIII (January, 1965), No. 2.

Hangen, Welles: *After Nehru, Who?* London: Rupert Hart Davis; 1963.

Hanson, A. H.: "The Crisis of Indian Planning." *Political Quarterly,* XXXIV (1963).

Harrison, Selig: *The Most Dangerous Decades.* Princeton, N.J.: Princeton University Press; 1960.

Hazard, Leland: "Strong Medicine for India." *The Atlantic,* December 1965.

The Hindu: "Performance of Public Enterprise," February 27, 1965.

————: December 3, 1952.

————: August 28, 1965.

Hopper, W. David: "The Mainsprings of Agricultural Growth." Memorial lecture for the eighteenth annual conference of the Indian Society of Agricultural Statistics, January 28–30, 1965.

The Indian Express, September 18, 1965.

Indian Famine Commission of 1880 (a report).

Jain, Girilal: *Panchsheela and After.* Bombay: Asia Publishing House; 1960.

Jui-ching, General Lo: "China's Military Doctrine." *Red Flag,* May 10, 1965.

Karunakaran, K. P. (ed).: *Outside The Contest.* New Delhi: People's Publishing House; 1963.

Kashin, A.: "Nepal: Chinese Stepping Stone to India—II." *The Indian Express,* September 8, 1965.

Kennedy, D. E.: *The Security of Southern Asia*. London: Chatto and Windus, Ltd. (for the Institute of Strategic Studies); 1965.

Khanna, K. B.: "Reorganising the Western Alliance." *The Times of India*, November 27, 1965.

Kothari, Rajni: "The Pattern of Dominance." *Seminar*, April, 1966.

Majumdar, R. C.: *History of the Freedom Movement in India*. Calcutta: Firma K. L. Mukhopadhyay; Vol. I, 1962; Vol. II, 1963.

Malenbaum, Wilfred: *Prospects for Indian Development*. London: George Allen & Unwin, Ltd.; 1962.

Mao Tse-tung: *Chinese Revolution and the Communist Party of China*. Bombay: People's Publishing House Ltd.; 1959.

Menon, K. P. S.: *The Flying Troika: A Political Diary of India's Ambassador to Russia, 1952–61*. London: Oxford University Press; 1963.

——: "India's Relations with the Soviet Union." *International Studies*, V (July–October, 1963), Nos. 1–2.

Menon, V. P.: *The Transfer of Power in India*. Bombay: Orient Longmans Private Ltd.; 1957.

Moraes, Frank: "The Hundred Days." *The Indian Express*, August 23, 1965.

——: *India Today*. New York: The Macmillan Co.; 1960.

Morley, James W.: "Japan's Position in Asia." *Journal of International Affairs*, XVII (1963), No. 2.

Mosley, Leonard: *The Last Days of the British Raj*. New York: Harcourt, Brace and World, Inc.; 1961.

Mulgaokar, S.: "National Affairs: The High Road to Progress." *The Hindustan Times*, August 11, 1965.

Munshi, K. M., *Gujarata and Its Literature*. Bombay: Longmans Green and Co.; 1935.

National Development Council: *Fourth Five-Year Plan, Resources, Outlays and Programmes*. New Delhi: September 1965.

Palkhivala, N. A.: *The Highest Taxed Nation*. Bombay: P. B. Manaktala and Sons Private Ltd.; 1965.

Pannikar, K. M.: *In Two Chinas*. London: George Allen & Unwin, Ltd.; 1955.

Patterson, George N.: *Peking Versus Delhi*. London: Faber and Faber; 1963.

Patterson, William D.: "A View From India." *Saturday Review*, October 30, 1965.

Prasad, Rajendra: *Autobiography*. Bombay: Asia Publishing House; 1957.

Rajan, M. S.: *India in World Affairs, 1954–56*. Bombay: Asia Publishing House; 1964.

Randhawa, M. S.; "The Role of Science and Technology in Indian Agriculture" (a research paper, for the symposium held under the auspices of the Indian Parliamentary Scientific Committee on the Role of Science and Irrigation in Agricultural Production, Parliament House, New Delhi, September 17, 1963).

Rangaswami, K.: "China's Insidious Hand Against India." *The Hindu*, December 31, 1965.

Rawlinson, H. G.: *India, A Short Cultural History*. London: The Cresset Press; 1954.

Ray, Hemen: "The Policy of Russia Towards Sino-Indian Conflict." *The Political Quarterly*, January–March, 1965.

Reserve Bank of India: *Report of Currency and Finance for the Year 1963–64*. Bombay: 1964.

Rudra, Ashok: "Myth of Tolerance." *Seminar*, March, 1965.

Singh, S. Nihal: "New Delhi Must Think Anew on South-East Asia." *The Statesman*, August 24, 1965.

The Statesman: December 7, 1965; March 28, 1966; April 6, 1966.

Tata, J. R. D.: "J.R.D. Tata Calls for Urgent Re-Thinking on Planning" (an address to the Central Advisory Council of Industries, New Delhi). *Economic Times*, August 3, 1965.

Taylor, Carl C., Douglas Ensminger, Helen W. Johnson, and Jean Joyce: *Indian's Roots of Democracy*. Bombay: Orient Longmans Ltd.; 1965.

Thimayya, General K. S.: "Chinese Aggression and After." *International Studies*, V (July–October, 1963), Nos. 1–2.

Time, The Weekly News Magazine: December 3, 1965; December 10, 1965.

Trumbull, Robert: *As I See India*: New York: William Sloane Associates; 1956.

United States Government: *Congressional Record, Proceedings and Debates of the 84th Congress, 2nd Session*. CII (June 27, 1956), No. 107.

Varma, S. P.: *Struggle for the Himalayas*: New Delhi: University Publishers; 1965.

Venkatasubbiah, H.: *Indian Economy Since Independence*. Bombay: Asia Publishing House; 1961.

Verghese, B. G.: "The National Scene: No Rebates for Caution." *The Times of India*, July 22, 1965.

Ward, Barbara: *The Plan Under Pressure*. Bombay: Asia Publishing House; 1963.

William, L. F. Rushbrook, C. B. E.: "The New Phase In India—Pakistan Relations." *Asian Review*, July, 1960.

Young India, April 14, 1920.

Zagoria, Donald S.: "A World in Mao Tse-tung's Image." The Washington *Post*, September 19, 1965.

Index

A Note About the Author

PATWANT SINGH was born in 1925 in New Delhi, India, and was educated there. At seventeen he decided to make a fortune for himself in his father's construction firm—which at least took him to all parts of India on high-priority projects during and after the war. In 1953 in Bombay he started his first magazine, *Indian Builder; The Pharmaceutist* (1955) and *Design* (1957) followed rapidly; all three are flourishing. Mr. Singh edits *Design* himself, concentrating on the problems of urban living, architecture, the visual and performing arts, and graphic and industrial design. Articles by him have also appeared in New York (in such publications as *Forum, Craft Horizons,* and others), Canada (in *The Ottawa Citizen*), and elsewhere. He has achieved international recognition as a lecturer, being invited to West Germany in 1960; Melbourne, Australia, in 1965; and to the United States in 1961, 1963, and 1964, under the sponsorship of the State Department, the International Design Conference, and the World Congress of Craftsmen, respectively. His interest gradually turned to politics and government because of their overwhelming importance to the arts and a country's creative life in general. India became the inevitable subject of his first book, since it is the scene of events that are likely to help shape the international situation for decades to come. Mr. Singh lives in New Delhi.

A Note on the Type

The text of this book was set on the Linotype in Fairfield, a type face designed by the distinguished American artist and engraver, Rudolph Ruzicka. This type displays the sober and sane qualities of a master craftsman whose talent has long been dedicated to clarity. Rudolph Ruzicka was born in Bohemia in 1883 and came to America in 1894. He has designed and illustrated many books and has created a considerable list of individual prints in a variety of techniques.

This book was composed by Hallmark Typographers, Inc., N.Y., and printed and bound by The Haddon Craftsmen, Inc., Scranton, Pa.